AF699033

LEXECONICS: THE INTERACTION OF LAW AND ECONOMICS

SOCIAL DIMENSIONS OF ECONOMICS

A series of books
sponsored by
the Department of Economics,
The City College of the
City University of New York

Volume 2

K
487.63
L49
LAW LIBRARY
GOLDEN GATE UNIVERSITY

LEXECONICS: THE INTERACTION OF LAW AND ECONOMICS

GERALD SIRKIN

EDITOR

Martinus Nijhoff Publishing
Boston/The Hague/London

Distributors for North America:

Martinus Nijhoff Publishing
Kluwer Boston, Inc.
190 Old Derby Street
Hingham, Massachusetts 02043, U.S.A.

Distributors outside North America:

Kluwer Academic Publishers Group
Distribution Centre
P.O. Box 322
3300 AH Dordrecht, The Netherlands

Library of Congress Cataloging in Publication Data

Main entry under title:

Lexeconics, the interaction of law and economics

(Social dimensions of economics; v. 2)
Papers presented at the sixth annual conference of the Economics Department of the City College of the City University of New York, held May 11, 1978.
Bibliography: p.
1. Law — Economic aspects — Congresses. I. Sirkin, Gerald 1920 — II. New York (City). City College. Dept. of Economics. III. Title. IV. Series
K487.E3L49 340'.11 80-23437
ISBN 0-89838-053-7

Copyright © 1981 by Martinus Nijhoff Publishing

No part of this book may be reproduced in any form by print, photoprint, microfilm, or any other means without written permission from the publisher.

Printed in the United States of America

Preface

On May 11, 1978, the Economics Department of the City College of the City University of New York held its sixth annual conference. Seven papers, each with a comment, were delivered and are published in this volume.

This publication has been made possible by income from the Henry Schwager Fund.

Gerald Sirkin

The City College of the City University of New York.

Contents

Introduction

GERALD SIRKIN *

The great growth of government economic regulation during the past forty years has stimulated a concomitant growth in the study of the interaction of law and economics. As a field of study, it is still so young that it remains undefined and unmapped. In fact this field of study is as yet unnamed. To repair the latter deficiency I propose the name *lexeconics*. A definition of lexeconics will be more difficult to provide.

Must we labor to define the term? The temptation is strong to apply Viner's convenient formula and say, "Lexeconics is what lexeconists do." But there is a useful purpose to be served by attempting to draw at least a rough map of the area to be covered by lexeconics. Without a map, lexeconists will not only be likely to wander into territory already occupied by other explorers, but they will be prone to investigate familiar ground instead of investigating important areas concerning which they should be conscious.

The familiar territory of lexeconists has been the analysis of particular laws. Economic analysis has been used to investigate the consequences of specific laws, to predict the consequences of laws. and to contribute to the formulation of laws. The leading textbook in the field,[1] intended for law students, shows how virtually all categories of law can be analyzed in terms of "economic efficiency."

---

* Professor of Economics, The City College of the City University of New York.

Law schools have another interest in economics. Economic analysis can be used to affect the outcome of litigation:

> That judges are concerned with more than just the precedents is often revealed in the inquiries and comments they make during the course of the proceedings. It happens that after spending weeks or months studying the legal arguments, lawyers arrive in court only to find that much of their preparation has been for naught. The judges seem as or more concerned with the impact of a ruling than with the legal distinctions. The final opinion, however, is not likely to reveal any of these "extra-legal" considerations.
>
> Sometimes when existing precedents are overruled, or matters of wide significance decided, judges will buttress their legal conclusions with materials from the social sciences. Only then does the public become aware of a procedure that may be more the rule than the exception in judicial decision-making. If pragmatism is inherent in the process, it behooves the future advocate or jurist to prepare accordingly. One means to that end is an appreciation of economic analysis with its concern for costs and consequences. Its use might determine the outcome of litigation.[2]

The bland manner in which Siegan accepts judicial "pragmatism," that is, the displacement of the rule of law by the rule of judges' preferences for particular outcomes, should alert us to the fact that lexeconics has been neglecting a major part of its domain. Indeed, the bland manner in which most of the nation has been accepting the shift of the judiciary from applying existing law to creating law and administering government programs should long ago have warned us of this neglect.

We need not so much economic analysis of individual laws as analysis of the revelation between economics and the *legal system.* The evolution of the American legal system from the rule of law toward the rule of men, — a development of increasing concern — is a subject to which a number of disciplines, but especially economics, should contribute. The special contribution of economics rests partly on the circumstance that most of the changing shape of our legal system originated in the growth of economic regulation and therefore that the nature of the economic system and the nature of the legal system are interrelated. Even more important, economics, as the science of choice or decision making, brings powerful analytical tools to the investigation of a decision-making system like the law and its interaction with other decision-making systems like the market, legislation, and government administation.

I do not mean to imply that the neglect of the interaction of economics and the legal system has been absolute: It has been relative to the amount of attention that has been devoted to the economics of specific laws. Substantial work on the legal system has been done by economists. Hayek has written on the interaction of the economic system and the legal system *(The Road to Serfdom,*[3] *The Constitution of Liberty*[4]*)* and has analyzed law as a decision-making system *(Law, Legislation and Liberty*[5]*).* Buchanan's *The Limits of Liberty*[6] applies economic method to the fundamental problems of legal systems. Some other important works could be cited.

Nevertheless, the lexeconic effort has been made predominantly in the economics of laws, an effort that may actually be, as Buchanan has warned, detrimental to the legal system:

> If lawyers, and law schools, seek to introduce more economic theory into their training in order to become more informed potential legislators and advisors to legislators, my support remains unqualified and enthusiastic. If, however, they seek to become and to train potential jurists who are instructed to have no qualms about legislating for us all, the pragmatic improvements that result might forestall rather than hasten the changes in jurisprudential attitudes that are essential for a return to operative constitutional democracy.[7]

If good economics is not to produce bad law, the "old" lexeconics — the economics of laws and legal cases —must be combined with the "new" lexeconics — the application of economic analysis to legal systems.

The agenda of the new lexeconics includes a number of topics the investigation of which has barely begun. Industry studies — for example, studies that treat the court system as an industry and analyze production functions, cost functions, returns to investment, and the other elements of productive efficiency — constitute a promising field of analysis. The crime industry and its relation to the legal system can also be elucidated by the standard methods of economic analysis.

The utility function of judges is an important subject for investigation. Although economists specializing in public choice have dealt with the utility functions of politicians and bureaucrats, they have paid relatively little attention to the utility functions of judges. The independence of the judiciary from the electorate and from elected representatives leaves judges more freedom to satisfy their utility functions than that exercised by either politicians or bureaucrats.

The subject awaiting analysis by lexeconists (and others), which seems to me first in urgency and difficulty, is the encroachment of the judiciary on the functions of the legislature.

> It seems self-evident to me that the judge should not change the basic law because, in such behavior, he would be explicitly abandoning his role of jurist for that of legislator. He would be "making law," and regardless of the criteria which guide his decisions, his action is unbounded by the complex pull and haul of representation among separate interests, the very center of democratic process. In saying that the jurist should enforce existing law rather than enact new legislation, I am, of course, aware of the absence of any firm dividing line between these in any empirical or descriptive sense. I also recognize that the hierarchical structure of the American court system promotes rather than retards judicial intrusion into legislative process. My emphasis is on the desirability of keeping the two conceptually distinct, despite the practical difficulties that may be confronted.[8]

Lawyers have not succeeded in, and probably have despaired of, drawing a "firm dividing line" between judging and legislating or in "keeping the two conceptually distinct."[9] Perhaps the concepts and empirical methods of economics can help.

These and other "big questions," as well as specific analyses of proliferating regulations, are waiting for lexeconic treatment. The studies in this volume, representing a cross section of various kinds of lexeconics, contribute toward reducing the great backlog of work before us.

NOTES

1. Richard A. Posner, *Economic Analysis of Law* (Boston: Little, Brown & Co., 1977), 2nd. ed.

2. Bernard H. Siegan, ed., *The Interaction of Economics and Law* (Lexington, Massachusetts: Lexington Books, 1977), p. viii.

3. Chicago: University of Chicago Press, 1944.

4. Chicago: University of Chicago Press, 1960.

5. Chicago: University of Chicago Press, 1973, vol. 1; 1976, vol. 2.

6. Chicago; University of Chicago Press, 1975.

7. James M. Buchanan, "Good Economics — Bad Law,"*Virginia Law Review* (1974), vol. 60, p. 491.

8. James M. Buchanan, *Ibid.,* pp. 490-491.

9. "Some will contend our form of government is in peril when the court substitutes its judgment for the legislature's, and any influences leading to that result should be discouraged. The question presented has long troubled judges and commentators and does not lend itself to ready solution. Regardless of the answer — and it is not my purpose to give one in these pages — it is doubtful that change will occur. The practices that I have described are so common and accepted and have prevailed for so long that only flagrant abuses provoke any serious complaints in the legislatures. Self-restraint can limit these judicial proclivities, but experience suggests that this quality is not a dominant characteristic of judges, nor should it be when protected rights are at stake. Moreover, courts have to engage in legislating when they change the rules or prior interpretations of them to make the law current and relevant." Bernard H. Siegan, *op. cit.,* p. viii.

California Water Law and Its Economic Effects on Southern California

DAVID L. SHAPIRO *

Many economic studies have examined the economic effects of water law. These studies tend to cover much of the same ground and to arrive at rather parallel conclusions. It would serve little purpose therefore to tread that same ground here and to present another detailed examination of California water law and its economic effects. This paper eschews such an effort and confines itself to summarizing other studies that describe the salient features of California water law.[1] Those studies generally attribute at least part of the blame for observed inefficiencies in water use to water law and its rigidities. This paper takes an entirely different tack in that it attempts to explain why existing water law is unequal to the task of directing water to its most valuable uses.It concludes that water law, as someone said about Christianity, is a wonderful system; what a pity that is has never been used! It concludes further that the reason that water law is not used to resolve water disputes is found in extra-legal considerations. The reasons for the inability of water law to resolve disputes can be analyzed most conveniently by the method of analysis developed in the contemporary theory of the economics of bureaucracy, or in the closely aligned field known as public choice. This analysis dispenses with some of the conventional assumptions of traditional economic theory with respect to public decision makers, leading to some rather different and

* U. S. Department of Energy. This paper was completed some time before the author became associated with the Department of Energy. The Department is not responsible for nor does it endorse the views or analysis presented in this paper.

surprising results. Before applying this theory to the present situation, this paper outlines some of the precepts of that theory as well as some of its applications. After doing so, it applies the theory to water law in southern California. It concludes that various bureaucratic machinations in California have, in effect, given that area a reprieve from the very unwise commitment to enter into the Feather River project and that the efficiency of water use in that area can be improved by escaping that commitment.

THE SALIENT FEATURES OF CALIFORNIA WATER LAW

Most studies of the economic effects of water law in the western United States emphasize obstacles to the transferability of property rights that are inherent in that law. Although transferability remains a hypothetical possibility, the probabilities of such transfers taking place are virtually negligible. This *de facto* lack of transferability leads to many allocative anomalies, as has been documented in economic literature. It is not surprising that anomalies have arisen, because any time that the power of sale is inhibited (*alienated,* in legal jargon), resources will not be transferred to their most valuable uses.[2]

This lack of transferability stems in part at least from some of the physical characteristics of water. For one thing, water from a flowing stream cannot be partitioned and access denied to nonowners or even divided among joint owners. This leads to inevitable confusion and conflicts of rights among competing claimants to a given supply of water. Confusion and conflict pose very serious problems for the courts or commissions adjudicating those rights. Particularly troublesome have been the problems associated with spillover effects, the adverse (or possibly favorable) effects that one party's use inflicts on some other user of the water. For example, pollution by an upstream user will inflict a spillover effect on a downstream user.[3]

Even at common law the courts have been very reluctant to come to grips with the difficult problems involved. An examination of the so-called *riparian doctrine* well illustrates this point. This doctrine evolved in Great Britain and was adopted in the eastern United States. Both of these regions are "humid" regions, which means that rainfall can be relied upon to furnish water throughout the year. In such regions the principal water problems involve rights to flowing streams.[4] For this reason the common law courts concerned themselves with the rights of riparian owners, that is, the owners of land adjoining a flowing stream. However, the courts chose to take the easy way out of resolving the rather difficult problem of defining the extent of the owners' property rights.

Several plots usually adjoin a flowing stream. The plots have different dimensions, both in area and in front footage. Moreover, they are usually used for different purposes or may yield different rates of production if used for the same purpose, as for example, farming. The plots may also use alternative sources of water supply. In short, the economic value of the water to different plots may vary considerably. Also different owners might have acquired their plots at different times, paid different prices for them, and so on. Therefore, landowners might have used varying amounts of water over time periods of varying length. No attempts have been made by the courts to take these or any similar considerations into account in determining the rights of competing riparian owners. Instead, the courts have made the sweeping judgment that all riparian owners have full rights to all of the water in streams subject only to the rights of others. Such a determination ignored the necessity of coming to grips with any of the problems enumerated above. This determination also had the effect of precluding virtually all transfers of water rights by riparian owners because of the nebulous nature of these rights. It is not surprising that economists have almost universally condemned the riparian doctrine as perpetrating economic inefficiencies in water use.

The exigencies of western water conditions led to the development of still another legal doctrine that was grounded a bit more in economic common sense. This doctrine was the so-called *appropriative doctrine* that allowed a landlocked landowner to divert water from a stream if that water could be put to "beneficial use." It appears to have evolved in California during the great Gold Rush when large amounts of water were required for the placer mining of gold. As the state continued to develop, the doctrine was invoked by agricultural users, and its use in the mining industry declined. (Later appropriative rights were claimed by public agencies, both federal and state, on behalf of consumers, agricultural as well as municipal.) As time wore on, municipal uses of water became the subject of appropriations. Involved in the appropriative process was a system of registration and priorities. The appropriation had to be registered with an administrative agency so that priorities could be established. But more significant than any of the procedures involved in the process was the assertion by administrative agencies that they have the right to rule on prospective transfers of rights and to prohibit them if they deemed them inappropriate.

The appropriative doctrine appears to have furnished the basis for economically sensible transfers of property rights in water. However, such transfers have not occurred because of the interpretations of the administrative agencies and of the courts. The basis of the appropriative right rests on the necessity of putting the water to beneficial use. However, if the appropriator applies to transfer his or her right to the water, the application is tantamount to conceding that the water is not being put to beneficial use. This procedure leads to a situation in which the attempt to transfer the right to the water may result in the loss of the water right.

And so the appropriate doctrine, under court and administrative interpretation, has led to the same lack of transferability as did the riparian doctrine. For all intents and purposes, water rights are nontransferable in California. The economic effects on this lack of transferability have been well documented. In brief, water has remained in uneconomic uses even when economically beneficial transfers have been possible. Even worse, the existing system of law has been unequal to the task of resolving disputes over water rights. The recommendations that have been made to resolve the problem have generally revolved around suggested changes in existing water law. These studies focus on the law as the cause of the misallocation observed in the case of water. All of these studies agree implicitly that changes in the law will help to correct these misallocations. What these studies have not considered is the degree to which the impotence of the law is a function of other forces in society. In particular, the state of the law can be attributed largely to bureaucratic machinations that have characterized the allocation of water in recent years. This being the case, an examination of the forces leading to the present state of the law should begin by analyzing the activities of bureaucrats. The author of this paper proposes to do this by examining the motivations and objectives of those planning water projects as well as the motivations and goals of those charged with adjudicating competing and conflicting rights to water. It is hoped that the analysis will explain the configuration of water rights and the state of water law.

THE ECONOMICS OF BUREAUCRACY

The economics of bureaucracy, as indicated above, involves nothing more than applying the precepts of price theory to bureaucratic situations. Before doing this, however, it may be advisable to define what is meant by a bureaucrat. As the term denotes, bureaucrats are those who direct the activities of governmental agencies. The term is defined in the dictionary as "An official of a bureau, especially one pursuing a narrow and arbitrary routine. . ." Of course, it is also desirable to define bureaucracy. The dictionary gives several definitions of the term. The definition that accords with the use of the term in this paper is the one that reads, "Government officials, collectively." (2)

In other words, bureaucrats are government officials charged with directing the activities of governmental agencies. They could include the appointed directors of agencies such as, for example, the Secretary of the Interior or they could include the career public servants as exemplified by the Commissioner of Reclamation who directs the day-to-day operations of that bureau.[5] Rather than employing this term throughout this discussion, we will use the more neutral term *agency managers.* This use parallels the practice of referring to those who direct private firms as firm managers. Although agency **manager** is a loose term (as is firm manager), the thought conveyed is that the term refers to those who actually direct the operations of an enterprise.

The first problem faced in analyzing agency activities is to identify the basic motivations of agency officials with regard to agency activities. Economists usually assume that in the private sector firm, managers are primarily concerned with pursuing profits, which consist, of course, of the difference between gross revenues and costs. (The economist terms this concern the assumption of profit maximization.) If agency officials were to act analogously, they would attempt to maximize the difference between gross benefits and costs.[6] Such a maximization would ensure that resources are being used well, in the sense that maximum benefits are being achieved for given costs. (This conception accords with the economist's notion of economic efficiency.) It should also be pointed out that such a maximization is the legal mission of many public agencies, including the goals of almost all of the water agencies.

Apart from the legal injunction, the officials have very little motivation to pursue economic efficiency, for there is precious little gain that will accrue to agency officials from such a course of action. The financial rewards of agency managers do not depend in any significant way on producing an excess of benefits over costs. Their salaries, promotional possibilities, and perquisites of office are not highly correlated with the efficiency of their agencies (as defined above). Inasmuch as the legal missions of all agencies involve the pursuit of economic efficiency, a question arises concerning whether anything in the system compels compliance with the agency's legal mission. The writer of this report has argued elsewhere that the enforcement mechanisms that exist are generally impotent to compel compliance. (5), (13) (These mechanisms include the organization of disaffected taxpaying groups, the investigation and censure by governmental agencies, such as the General Accounting Office, and the activity of public agencies competing for funds in the legislature.) In view of this impotence, the agency managers are relatively free to pursue goals that may well conflict with economic efficiency.

INVESTMENT DECISIONS BY AGENCY MANAGERS

The purported goal of any investment decision is to receive some return over the amount invested. It is reasonable to assume that the investor will seek the highest return, taking into account the amount of risk that is to be incurred.[7]

Ignoring the problem of uncertainty for the moment, the private manager, whose income is highly correlated with the profits of the enterprise, is indeed motivated to find the most profitable investment available for a given degree of risk. If the investment succeeds, the manager can appropriate part of the gain that is realized. The motivation of managers to seek the most profitable investments helps to ensure that resources will flow to their most valuable uses. This situation differs markedly in the case of agency managers, for they are not motivated to seek investments that offer the greatest returns because they cannot appropriate any significant portion of net benefits. In general, public agencies have no profit sharing, and there is no feasible way to measure the performance of an agency by using the yardstick of net benefits. There are several reasons that explain the failure to develop standards for judging performances. First, there is nothing akin to a profit and loss statement for a public agency. Although several agencies are enjoined to develop benefit-cost studies, rarely, if ever, is a determination of the economic effects of a given project or sets of projects undertaken after construction. The situation is analogous to that of a private manager who is judged on the profit that he or she estimates will accrue from a project. Moreover, without any accounting of net benefits, it is difficult, if not impossible, for either (1) outside managers to compete for agency jobs on the basis of improving the net benefits rendered by the agency, or (2) managers of other agencies to compete for funds in legislature in the basis of superior performance. In short, nothing within the system appears to furnish a reckoning of economic efficiency, let alone the compulsion to pursue it. Still the lack of standards for judging a performance does not forclose the possibility that officials may pursue net benefits, because that is their legal mission. It should therefore yield at least the intangible reward of a job well done. Indeed, they would probably do so if other goals and motivations did not intervene. The goals of increasing agency size probably offer much more in the way of rewards to agency managers and that that goal is consequently pursued.

INCREASED AGENCY SIZE AS A MANAGERIAL GOAL

A very important variable to any manager (public or private) is the size of his enterprise. An owner will prefer a larger enterprise to a smaller one only if it is more profitable. When the connection between profits and managerial income becomes tenuous, a manager may be more than willing to trade off size for profitability. Unless a manager shares in the profits of an enterprise, the incremental size of an organization tends to offer incremental returns. These returns can be both of the pecuniary and nonpecuniary variety. Managers of larger enterprises, be they public or private, generally receive larger financial compensation than do their counterparts in smaller organizations. Certainly the officials of the Metropolitan Water District receive higher salaries than those paid to officials of lesser water agencies. Another example was given by a colleague, Timothy Hogan, who pointed out that the salaries of hospital administrators (in nonprofit hospitals) generally bear some regular relationship to the number of beds in the hospital.

There tends to be greater prestige or status accorded within a profession (or trade) if one is the manager of a larger organisation than if one is the manager of a smaller one. The prestige and standing are not as ephemeral as they may first appear to be. A manager (or other employee) having greater prestige or greater standing can generally increase his wealth as a result. This opportunity to increase wealth can be realized in at least two ways. One way is to parlay this standing into a higher paid job with another employer. Alternatively a manager can use the threat of leaving his or her employment in order to increase his or her salary at his or her employment. For example, the highest officials of the Los Angeles Department of Water and Power and the Metropolitan Water District are generally engineers, and these positions are thought to be highly prestigious within the engineering profession.

It follows that managers in general are strongly motivated to increase the size and the prestige of their agencies so that their own standings and prestige will thereby be enhanced. It follows that managers in all enterprises are strongly motivated to increase the size of their enterprises. In the private sector rather severe punishments can result from expansions that turn out to be unwise. The bankruptcy annals are filled with examples of firms that expanded unwisely, at least as judged by subsequent events. Even if a private firm continues in business, an ill-advised investment can be very costly to an individual manager. One suspects that managers were in trouble at Ford Motor Company after the unfortunate episode with the Edsel.[8] However, as judged by results, the situation appears to be far different in the public sector . Inefficient use of resources does not appear to be followed by the loss of stewardship over these resources. The history of water resource development in general and of Southern California water development in particular is replete with examples of Edsel-like investment decisions. Yet the agency managers who made these mistakes continue in their direction of the agencies and continue to make unwise decisions.[9]

We will explore the reasons for the differing situations in the public and private sectors. Until we do so in the following section, we accept the proposition that public managers possess rather extensive latitude in indulging their expansionary proclivities. We explore the manner in which expansion is accomplished along with its implications for economic efficiency. In order to do this, it is necessary to take into account the role of organized presssure groups.[10]

PRESSURE GROUP SUPPORT AND AGENCY SIZE

With strong motivation to increase agency size, managers are led to make common cause with interested pressure groups within the electorate. The basis for this coalition is, of course, the appropriation processes in the legislature, whereby the funding of projects or the expansion of agency activities takes place. Naturally, there is intense rivalry among agencies for these funds. Legislators must arbitrate between claims in appropriating funds. Other things being equal, legislators tend to approve projects that benefit their constituencies. This approval invokes the familiar notions of logrolling and pork barrel legislation, suggesting that projects tailored to the constituencies of influential legislators have a far better chance of funding than do those that are not so directed. The way to influence legislators is to design projects that will garner widespread support among their continuencies. If groups of voters are persuaded that a particular agency activity will benefit them, they will be inclined to work with that agency in its quest for funds. This activity translates itself into an investment in agency support manifested by the formation of voters into organized pressure groups. Letter writing and judicious donations are examples of activities undertaken to influence legislators. The legislators may respond by promoting the project or agency in question. If this collaboration is successful, agency plans are brought to fruition, and agency is thereby expanded.

It should be emphasized that all parties to these transactions may well be acting in good faith, that is, agency managers believe that they are designing very useful projects, and pressure group members believe that such projects are in the "public good."

Agencies are supposed to consider the costs of projects as well as their benefits. However, it is also the case that the legislature is likely to adopt a projects to the extent that the net private benefits to pressure group members are maximized. To the extent that benefits outweigh the costs of pressure group members, they are likely to invest in lobbying support for a project.[11] This proposition places great pressure on agency managers. Projects that please constituent pressure group members must be found if appropriations are to be made to increase agency size. If available, projects that are good in the sense that social benefits exceed social costs may stand very little chance of being funded. This poses difficulties for the agency manager, for his survival dictates that projects be found that can be funded. If "good" projects can be found, so much the better. If, however, good projects cannot be found, managers may select the best projects that can be funded. Unhappily, these projects may well be ones the net social benefits of which may fail to exceed net social costs. This failure may not be apparent to one who views benefits with rose-colored glasses. In such a situation, there is a strong tendency to engage in advocacy, that is, the practice of making the strongest possible case in favor of the project's potential benefits. A more neutral, or indeed a more critical, examination could easily lead to a rejection of the project. When this optimistic view of benefits is combined with a conservative view of costs, an otherwise unfavorable benefit-cost ratio can be converted in to a very favorable one.

It follows from this analysis that managers may be prone to advocate projects that yield benefits to constituent pressure group members whether these projects actually benefit the public at large. Such advocacy implies, however, that nonpressure group members, in the aggregate, may suffer on account of the project in question or more generally, on account of agency expansion. That is, the benefits of the project may fail to equal the project costs, and consequently the taxpaying public is in effect paying more than the value of goods or services that are rendered for its benefit. (An economist would say that public investment may well have a negative rate of return; that is, that the overall costs of the project exceed benefits.) Even if this is not the case and benefits exceed costs, it is entirely possible that benefits are conferred on one group of taxpayers, whereas the costs are imposed on an entirely different group. In these two situations there exists economic incentive for the afflicted taxpayers to band together to oppose the projects that are inimical to their interests. The problem here is that the costs of organizing opposition to a particular project may well exceed the benefits that can flow from such an action. The benefits would be comprised of some fairly modest reductions in the individual taxes of the opposers. Although the reduction in taxation would be formidable in the aggregate, the amounts accruing to any one individual would tend to be negligible. Well-financed organizations such as *Nadar's Raiders* and *Common Cause* may have the wherewithal to oppose undesired public projects, but opposition is generally too expensive for ordinary groups of taxpayers to organize. As noted earlier, there may be forces within the government that may serve to limit the expansionary activities of the agencies. There are units within the government that are charged with monitoring the activities of public agencies with regard to economic efficiency. Two such units, for example, are the General Accounting Office and the Office of Management and Budget (OMB). The latter agency, in particular, has probably made incremental improvements in tne efficiency of public projects. However, the final decisions regarding public investments are made in the legislature where the symbiosis betweeen legislators and pressure group members determines the funding of projects.

EMPIRICAL EVIDENCE OF PLANNER PREFERENCE

The water resource field is rich in examples of the working of this process. Two examples may be cited to illustrate the point. Both the Central Valley Project and the Feather River Project (both of which are in California) have been found to be of questionable merit as far as economic efficiency is concerned. The benefit-cost ratios of both projects are probably below unity. The history of both projects, however, clearly shows the interactions between interested pressure groups and the agencies in question (the Bureau of Reclamation in the case of the Central Valley project and the California Department of Water Resources in the case of the Feather River project).[12] Rather detailed descriptions of these interactions are contained in the literature cited. It is dubious that these projects would have come into being without these interactions. The rates of return on both projects are probably negative. Another example of a continual drive for agency expansion is the Metropolitan Water District of southern California (MWD). This agency has continuously entered into commitments, including desalinization projects, despite the dubious economic merits of these enterprises.

PUBLIC ADJUDICATION DECISIONS

The foregoing section has summarized the economics of bureaucracy as applied to public investment decisions. This discussion may seem peripheral to the critical theme of this chapter, which relates to the legal framework of the water industry in southern California. The law of water rights in California, at least as it stands today, is shaped and formed by the interaction of two sets of bureaucratic decisions. One set is that comprised of investment decisions. The other set, to be discussed in this section, is that comprised of adjudicating decisions. Water rights, like any other set of rights, are subject to conflict when they are asserted by competing claimants. Before attempting to integrate these two sets of rights, we shall examine adjudicating decisions.

PUBLIC ADJUDICATING DECISIONS

The application of bureaucratic economics to public adjudicating decisions poses far greater complexities than do public investment decisions. Indeed, very little analysis has been pursued, let alone attempted, in this field.[13]

Let us consider first the decision-making progress used by one who is called on to adjust conflicting property rights. Let us say that we have two parties whose property rights are incompatible. For example, there are two parties *A* and *B*, each of whom asserts the exclusive right to a resource valued at $1.00. The defeated right then becomes completely worthless, for the exercise of one right negates the competing one. We speculate that the elements involved in the decision are:

1. Fairness
2. The good of society
3. The self-interest of the adjudicator.

This list can be rephrased in conventional economic terms:

1. Equity
2. Efficiency (in the sense that society in the aggregate gains a store of resources)

3. Utility maximization (for the adjudicator).

We shall explore the correspondence between the two lists.

1. Fairness - Equity

Any individual who is forced to make a decision involving a conflicting rights will always, we argue, attempt to preserve his or her self-image of being fair and equitable. In making such a decision no one would ever say or would even want to admit to himself or herself that an unfair decision was made. A teacher giving a grade and a parent arbitrating between two children will always argue that they are doing what is *fair.* Fairness as the basis of decision making poses formidable problems for analysis because its meaning can vary rather markedly for individuals.[14] Moreover, the definition of fairness can change significantly over time. For example, in 1898, the Supreme Court of the United States held that separate but equal facilities for whites and blacks were fair. In 1954, however, separate but equal was thought to be inherently unfair by the successor court. It would be tempting to argue that there are certain basic standards that most people accept, that decisions can be explicated on this basis, and that the Court was in error the first time around. However, this type of argument can be demolished. For example, a good case of an acceptable standard of fairness would be the fulfillment of a contract voluntarily entered into by an individual. Yet during the Great Depression, the courts saw fit to abrogate or at least modify contractual obligations in order to protect poor people.

All that can be said is that fairness is a "wild card" and that prudence dictates that no effort be made to incorporate it into the analysis. However, analysis, we think, can be based on the two remaining factors in the decision-making process.

2. Economic Efficiency.

The second factor is more susceptible to analytical treatment than is the first. This factor may be termed the *good of society,* but we argue that this condition roughly accords with the notion of economic efficiency. When a decision is made involving the alternative use of resources, the decision, other things equal, will generally tend to direct resources to their most highly valued uses. For example, in a condemnation proceeding the courts will try to ensure that the award reflects the true opportunity cost of the land taken, thereby ensuring the efficient use of resources. In regulatory actions the arguments revolve around the appropriate rate of return on investment, and in those cases the goal of economic efficiency becomes rather explicit. We should hasten to add, however, that the discussions and arguments are not phrased in terms of economic efficiency nor in terms that are in any way related to the language of the economist. Nonetheless, we submit that what is generally construed to be for the good of society by the courts amounts to the economist's notion of efficiency.

3. Self-Interest.

The last category, self-interest, translates easily into the familiar economic notion of utility maximization; that is, officials will render adjudications that serve their self-interests. (This statement is not so cynical as it sounds, for self-interest can consist of equity — the good of society in addition to explicit personal gain.) Keeping these ideas in mind, we shall examine various bureaucratic theories of the adjudicatory process.

BUREAUCRATIC THEORIES OF THE ADJUDICATORY PROCESS

1. The simplest of all possible bureaucratic theories of adjudication can be called a theory of corruption. This theory simply holds that the adjudicator sells himself to the highest bidder. According to this theory, cases are decided on unadulterated self-interest, which implies that "justice can be purchased for a price." Although some and perhaps many adjudicators are corrupt and dishonest, this explanation would hardly serve as a general one, particularly in the United States. Although it would be hazardous to venture that all

corruption is exposed, it does seem safe to say that the amount that is exposed gives some idea of the total extent of actual corruption. The relatively small amount that is exposed in adjudicating decisions tends to discredit this theory.

2. The next (and most widely accepted) theory is based on the self-interest and personal gain of the adjudicator but restricts itself to noncorrupt behavior. In other words, nothing is done that is illegal. The central premise of this theory is that every decision is weighed (and weighted) in terms of the personal benefits and personal costs accruing to the adjudicator. Some of the subtheories falling in this category are listed below.

a. *The regulated regulating the regulator.* This theory is commonly associated with George Stigler, its best known expositor. The argument, however, appears to be essentially an empirical one based on results that are thought to confirm the hypothesis. Cited are the activities of such agencies as the Interstate Commerce Commission and the Civil Aeronautics Board that appear rather clearly to be directed toward the cartelization of the industries in question. This kind of regulation is manifested by edicts limiting competition and setting rates roughly in accord with those desired by industry members.

This argument does not explicate why the regulator is in fact captured by the regulated. Presumably, the rewards flowing to the regulators from following this course of action are greater than those that would accrue to them from pursuing a policy of serving the interests of the intended beneficiaries of the regulation.

b. *The minimum squak theory.* This argument is associated with George Hilton, who argues that adjudicators attempt to maximize their personal fortunes both during their tenure as adjudicators and after the end of such tenure. (10) Such maximization, it is argued, is accomplished by pacifying individuals who assert conflicting property rights. Hilton described how the Interstate Commerce Commission ensures monopoly rents for the regulated firms while simultaneously dissipating a portion of those rents in order to provide uneconomic services to consumer groups.

Hilton's argument suggests that regulatory behavior is not too far removed from corruption in the sense that adjudicators may be very interested in pursuing future employment opportunities in the regulated industries. In this pursuit of financial gain, adjudicators weigh their decisions accordingly. They can capitalize on their decisions by subsequent employment in the benefited industry at the termination of their relatively short regulatory commission terms.

This seemingly plausible explanation is not all that persuasive under scrutiny. It could, of course, be the case that an explicit agreement is entered into between the regulated and the adjudicators before decisions are made. (This explanation revolves around the corruption hypothesis that was rejected for lack of generality.) We question, however, whether in general firms would prefer to hire adjudicators who have proved themselves to be subservient in their decisions. We speculate that the reverse may be closer to the truth of the matter. To illustrate this point by analogy, let us say that an accused criminal is seeking legal counsel. Would he seek a former prosecutor who was bought by defendants or would the accused seek a former prosecutor who had always been favorably disposed to defendants? We think that the reverse would hold true, that is, that it would be far more prudent for the accused criminal to employ the best and the most severe former prosecutor that could be found. Such a counsel would presumably be most familiar with the ways of prosecutors and would be the most adept at countering their ploys. Why would regulators act in different ways? A former regulator who was anti-firm may be far more desirable than one who favored the firm being regulated. The tough former regulator could be adept at coping with his former associates on the commission. A hard-liner may be better able to deal effectively with succesor hard-liners on the commission.[15] These considerations, diminish the persuasiveness of the hypothesis that regulators favor their future employers.

These various explanations all have merit. But they not only appear to lack generality as theories, they exhibit inconsistencies. If regulators are captured by industry, why do they dissipate monopoly rents? It is argued that they do this to ensure survival in office. But if prospects of future employment are sufficiently great, why should survival concern them? These theories would suggest that regulation and licensing in different jurisdictions would exhibit rather consistent patterns, for there would be no reason to expect New York State regulators to differ from their counterparts in California. And yet there do appear to be different regulatory patterns in different jurisdictions.

3. Another attempt to explain regulatory adjudicating decisions employs a utility maximizing model. The utility functions are specified (at least in general form), and the regulator is then described as maximizing this function. The marginal utilities are equalized in the traditional fashion of economics, and the resultant algebraic statements are presented as an explanation of regulatory behavior. In other words, the decisions made by regulators are the ones that bring them the greatest welfare or satisfaction. (11)

We are, of course, impressed by this ambitious attempt to generalize existing models. Two comments are in order, however. First, the model specified is implicit in existing models and adds nothing new of substance. The capture of the regulator by the industry and the minimum squawk ideas are based implicitly on utility maximizing considerations by the regulators.

Second, and more important, this utility maximizing model shares the characteristic with other models of being virtually irrefutable and therefore amounts to a tautological statement. What kinds of evidence could be adduced that would refute the basic hypothesis? The model suggests on after the fact explanation of anything that happens and therefore is not very useful as a predictive device. For example, if the regulator favors the industry, that action can be taken as evidence that he is maximizing his utility; if he favors consumer groups, he does the same thing, and so on.[16]

We come to the conclusion that despite the validity of the arguments made, they offer incomplete explanations and may even be inconsistent. An alternative explanation is offered in an attempt to correct these defects.

A HYPOTHESIS ABOUT ADJUDICATORS' BEHAVIOR

We do not attempt to make any general explanation of adjudicatory behavior that would encompass the courts. Instead, we restrict our attention to administrative agencies whose primary functions are to administer economic matters.[17]

In brief, this hypothesis is comprised of two elements: First, the agency in question is assigned a goal by thc law. This goal can be assigned by the authorizing statute and modified by the subsequent construction of that statute. However, the goal may develop, the agency is assigned a rather specific purpose. Such purpose may be explicit in the authorizing statute or may emerge out of subsequent cases. More specifically, the adjudicators will interpret the economic purposes of the agencies, and these interpretations will either be accepted or rejected by the courts in the judicial review process. (It is always the case that administrative decisions can be appealed to the courts.) Second: the adjudicators internalize the goals of the agencies, and these internalizations then color all of their decisions. Here we return to the point that a legal theory can be found to justify virtually any decision. It follows that adjudicators discover and employ those legal theories that help to fulfill the goal of their agencies. Then — and here is the crux of the argument — the adjudicators purposefully attempt to resolve all doubts and all questions in order to fulfill those goals. Seemingly tortured or strained interpretations will be justified on the basis that the broad purposes of the agencies have been furthered. Every decision is weighed carefully in terms of the implementation of agency goals.

It is possible, of course, that there can be a conflict between the goals of the agency and the self-interest of the adjudicator. However, we think that this circumstance is relatively unlikely. We argue that these interests will usually coincide. In general, the fortunes of officials are highly correlated with the fortunes of the agency. The agency's fortunes, after all, will generally be enhanced by serving the constituencies that brought the legislation into being. In some sense, the goals of the agency can be traced to the pressure groups that brought the authorizing legislation into being by lobbying for and formulating the legislation. Furthermore, pressure groups may help in effecting changes in the goals of the agency by promoting amendments to the original legislation.[18]

As political alignments change over time, however, the goals of agencies will also change, and these changes will be communicated to adjudicators who will their behavior accordingly.

Adjudicators act in the fashion postulated because such actions are consonant with their own self-interests or, stated differently, with utility maximization. They will act as the pressure groups involved in the legislation expect them to act and want them to act. Adjudicators wil be considered fair, independent, honest, and so on. They will be favorably considered for reappointment, or (to turn the Hiltonian argument on its head), they will be desirable employees in regulated industries as they were competent (if tough) adjudicators. They will have gained personal fulfillment for jobs well done and can therefore "live with their consciences." On the other hand, adjudicators who can "be bought off" by regulated industries may have dimmer rather than brighter futures.[19]

In sum, adjudicators know the goals of their agencies, internalize them, and adjudicate accordingly. Why then have economists been disturbed to the extent of generating voluminous literature on the subject? This literature concerns itself with the observed inefficiencies of resource use that is associated with regulation. However, economic efficiency is an ephemeral, if not an irrelevant, criterion by which to judge regulators or other adjudicators in the economic area. For example, the activities of licensing commissions and regulatory agencies are commonly cited as evidence that adjudicators help to promote suboptimal uses of resources. It will be recalled that adjudicators attempt to make decisions that promote the general welfare. Here then we can focus on the conflict between the economist and the adjudicator. The economist tends to equate general welfare with economic efficiency; that is, with the requirement that resources be directed to their most highly valued uses. The adjudicator, on the other hand, tends to equate the general welfare with carrying out the goals of his agency. To him, this is an efficient use of resources. After all, legislation is supposed to reflect the general welfare as expressed through the political process. Moreover, the courts are entrusted with the responsibility of preserving the general welfare. When the legislature and the courts communicate their interpretations of general welfare to the agencies, what other expression is required? Are the scribblings of academic economists, phrased as they are in terms of optimality conditions, bliss points, social welfare functions, and so on, to be given greater credence? The thrust of this argument is that economic efficiency, as understood by the economist, is *not* the true goal of the adjudicator and that there is precious little reason why one should expect it to be.

For these reasons we think that much adjudicatory behavior can be predicted by applying the internalization of goals model. We shall examine some examples of the process.

1. Licensing Agencies.

The easiest of all possible cases to examine are those that involve agencies that license members of occupations or professions. In these cases agency goals and the individual goals of adjudicators are indistinguishable. The goal of the agency is, in fact, to cartelize the occupation. This goal may be accomplished by enforcing "standards" that are designed to prevent "destructive competition." Whatever the putative goal, the methodology of achievement is to prevent the entry of new competitors. This goal is pursued zealously by the adjudicators, for example, licensing boards. They believe in good faith that the restriction of entry will accomplish the goal sought, which is, most assuredly, the case. An excellent example is the medical profession whose policy of restrictive entry has indeed accomplished the goal of improving standards. If entry is restricted, the obvious criterion for admitting members is the quality of prospective entrants, and so a policy of restriction will improve the overall quality of practitioners. Of course, it will also result in a much smaller supply of medical services and a higher income for licensed practitioners. Restricting entry to a profession leaves open the question of whether society is better off by having fewer services of a better quality or whether it is better off by having more services of poorer quality.

2. Regulatory Agencies.

The situation here is a bit more complex, but identifying goals can assist in the explication of behavior. A regulatory agency has two rather antagonistic goals. One goal is to ensure a "fair rate of return" to the regulated industry, and the other is to protect consumers. It is extremely difficult to translate these goals into conventional economic terms. A fair rate of return can be translated (loosely, of course) as the opportunity costs of resources employed by the industry in question. Such a determination involves evaluating the uses of resources elsewhere as well as making some allowance for risk. This rate can not be estimated by looking at one aggregate rate in the economy, for example, the "prime rate." Agency officials do in fact attempt to make such determinations, heavily influenced, of course, by evidence adduced in support of industry positions.

Regulatory agencies also attempt to internalize the other principal goal of regulation, that is, the protection of consumers. Protection tends to be negative, that is, regulators avoid doing what would be considered unfair to consumers rather than weighing the costs and the benefits of other actions. Regulators therefore feel justified in rendering benefits to consumers if the benefits are exceeded by the costs of provision. They may therefore sacrifice efficiency in order to do what is "right". However, they may feel obliged to assure the regulated firms of a "fair rate of return." These two goals can be reconciled by furnishing uneconomic services to consumers and then allowing sufficient monopoly profits to ensure a fair rate of return. In this fashion opposing pressure groups are pacified, industry pressure groups have revenues at least equal to opportunity costs, and consumers are given a "fair amount" of services even if these services cost more than the price that was paid for them. Thus the goals of the agency are fulfilled in the manner intended. The creation of monopoly profits, part of — but not all of — that are dissipated by supplying uneconomic services to consumers, satisfies all parties provided that the monopoly profits created for industries equal or exceed their fair rate of return. This conception of a fair rate of return differs from the economists' notion of efficiency, but no matter; regulatory agencies can be said to be carrying out their missions.

The hypothesis supported by the examples suggests that by identifying the goals of agencies or legislation, one should be able to predict the behavior of adjudicators regardless of the jurisdiction in which they operate.

THE LAW, BUREAUCRACY, AND WATER DISPUTES

The Supposed Failure of Water Law

The literature described earlier asserts repeatedly that water law in California fails to ensure that water is directed to its most valuable uses. This assertion is true because of the inability to effect transfers under interpretations of existing law. If the law were changed, it is argued, transfers could be facilitated and water would be transferred from less valuable to more valuable uses. Thus it is made to appear that law has an organic life of its own and that it is responsible for the allocative anomalies observed in water use. The chain of causation goes in the opposite direction in that the state of the law is shaped by other forces at work in California. In particular, the bureacratic expansion of water planning agencies has significantly contributed to the formation and the evolution of the law in recent years.

The law is not an organic entity but rather is formed and shaped by other forces in the society. Some of the writers who discuss water law and its allocative effects miss the point, laying the blame at the door of water law. Before attacking these problems, the role of the law in resolving economic disputes will be examined.

In every economic dispute the adjudicator resolves a set of property rights as a result of his decision. In the past economists were inclined to ask whether the set of rights involved improved or worsened the use of resources. More recently they have attached less significance to the question of whether resource use is improved. Instead, they ask whether the rights involved are vested with sufficient particularity, that is, after adjudication can the parties involved, as well as the world at large, be certain who in fact possesses the rights? This question is important because once the rights in question are fixed, the individuals involved can enter into the market and exchange them. In other words, the original vesting of rights is less important than the knowledge that rights can or cannot be exchanged freely. If they can be exchanged freely, ordinary market processes will guarantee that they will be acquired by those who value them most highly.[20] (19)

It follows from this argument that the law can inhibit the efficient use of resources in two ways. One way is by assigning rights in a manner that renders the subsequent transfer of resources too costly to effect. The other — and the manner that is germane to this discussion — is to fix rights with insufficient particularity. The ownership of rights is left in doubt or in limbo. In such a case, the adjudicator's decision will tend to paralyze subsequent change. It is manifestly impossible to exchange rights if the extent of the rights is uncertain. The buyer in such a situation may well be purchasing a lawsuit in addition to the property rights in question. This failure to define and specify rights will have the effect of leaving undisturbed any given configuration of resource ownership. Any opportunity to engage in mutually beneficial exchange will remain unexploited. Unless the law accomplishes its task of assigning rights with particularity, allocative anomalies are bound to result because of the foreclosure of exchange opportunities.

One last point is of special importance, that is, the existence and the extent of financial costs that are required to effect legal settlements. The legal resolution of rights can involve both considerable financial outlays as well as the passage of considerable periods of time. Until matters involved are resolved, the parties cannot identify the extent of their rights. Moreover, an element of uncertainty is inherent in any legal proceeding. A long costly legal enterprise may be undertaken only to culminate in defeat. (This consideration accounts for the widespread prevalence of compromise and settlement in legal actions, particularly on "the courthouse steps.") The costliness of legal actions can account in large measure for the failure to determine rights. This point is especially relevant to the consideration of water law that follows.

WATER RIGHTS PROBLEMS BRING WATER PROJECTS, WATER RIGHTS PROBLEMS, WATER PROJECTS . . .

The failure to resolve water rights problems in California can be attributed in large measure to the costliness of effecting settlements. The resolution of water rights problems requires the identification and the determination of the merits of a bewildering array of "spillover effects." The appropriative right by definition is based on the reasonable use of the water. As noted earlier, the right cannot be transferred unless there is interference with the reasonable use of others. These broad propositions coupled with the physical nature of water supply tend to pose very difficut problems in defining and specifying rights.[21]

Moreover, the problems created by attempted transfers are even more formidable. The complex chain of interdependencies outlined above is disturbed, and new complexities arise that tend to freeze existing patterns of water rights despite the changing economic forces that would otherwise dictate the transfer of rights. However, necessity does not dictate that the law resolve the rather difficult problems that arise out of changing economic circumstance. Resolving these problems has never been necessary, for new water supplies have always been available. It is impossible to tell what water law would have done, but it is out guess that the law would have been equal to the challenge.

Why then has law not been invoked? This question can be answered by citing the fact than an alternative supply of water could be obtained at less cost than the cost involved in resolving a controversy about water rights. When rights are in conflict and/or economically sensible transfers are desired, an alternative to problem solution is to have a governmental unit develop an alternative supply of water. The existence of additional supplies has made the resolution of rights controversies unnecessary and has allowed all claimants to satisfy their demands (read *needs*) at existing prices. This alternative was particularly attractive when public agencies did not use a market pricing mechanism in the sale of water but used prices that would ensure that water would be taken by users.[22] Prices bear virtually no relationship to the incremental costs of supplying water. The underpriced water then serves to resolve water rights problems.

These new supplies should resolve problems, and equilibrium should result. However, the determination of water rights is not quite that simple. The problem of defining and specifying water rights is no less troublesome for the agencies involved than it is for private individuals or private firms. The agencies do not wish to incur the costs (including finances and time) that would be required to solidify water rights.

As many economists have observed, water projects are undertaken in order to secure water rights. Compounding the problem is the fact that agencies seek to enlist a maximum of lobbying support (in order to enhance the possibilities of obtaining funding, as noted earlier). This effort makes it desirable for the agency to assert claims to as much water as possible in order to enlist the widest constituency that can be garnered in support of the project. In the process of building a concensus, rights of an exceedingly tenuous nature are asserted, and little or no effort is made to perfect those claims. This statement does not suggest that officials are dishonest in any way or that they attempt to engage in illegal activity. Rather, they tend to take the most optimistic view and construe any rights controversy accordingly. Simply put, they may accept on faith that the claimants possess the rights that they assert.

This failure to settle rights before projects are built results in rather severe controversies after they are completed. When those controversies cannot be resolved, the cycle begins anew, and the expedient of building more projects is resorted to in order to resolve the controversies created by older projects. Thus bureaucratic imperialism leads to projects to resolve existing water rights controversies; new projects in turn create new controversies, which in turn lead to new projects, and so forth.

We should reiterate the role of adjudicating agencies. At every stage in the proceeding an adjudicating agency must be involved in order to make a rights determination. The goals of the adjudicating agencies must be considered. Determinations tend to be made, as argued earlier, to accord with the goals of the adjudicating agency. The internalized goals of adjudicators do not necessarily coincide with the goals of the constructing agencies. The outcomes of the adjudication process may well be adverse to the positions espoused by the investing agencies, and so water rights problems are recreated. Moreover, the goals of the adjudicating agencies are altered when new directives are received from legislators. These directives, of course, reflect changes in the strength and in the position of pressure groups. It is vital to understand that rights never get resolved throughout this process, and so allocative anomalies endure.

THE CALIFORNIA EXPERIENCE

We will sketch the experience in California. A convenient place to start is the Shasta Dam in northern California. This dam was the first segment of the poliferating Central Valley project (CVP) of the Bureau of Reclamation. The impetus for this project arose out of the "crisis" in the Kaweah River system in the San Jaoquin Valley.[23]

Although the state of California had originally planned to build the CVP, the federal government undertook to do so in consequence of the Great Depression. The justification for the project was stabilizing income, and so both economic and legal justifications were considered unnecessary. No benefit-cost study preceded the construction of the project, and no attempt was made to settle the rights problem involved in obtaining water. Because of the physical characteristics of the project, the disregard of water rights problems created severe difficulty after the project was constructed.[24]

Problems arose from using the natural channel of the Sacramento River as a conduit of the water from the point of impoundment to the Sacramento–San Joaquin Delta some 200 odd miles to the south. Under riparian doctrine, however, the landowners whose land bordered the river asserted claims to the incremental water created by the project and diverted large amounts of it. These diversions diminished the amount of water that was available for delivery to the intended recipients south of the delta. Part, if not all, of the deficiency was made up by pumping additional water out of the delta in order to satisfy Bureau contracts.[25]

There is much to suggest that Bureau contracts south of the delta were satisfied out of delta water rather than out of water impounded at Shasta. (7) For this reason water rights problems multiplied. In fact, a protracted controversy over the rights to Sacramento water ensued. The Bureau believed that landowners were diverting more water than the amount to which they had valid rights. The Bureau was prepared to fight by petitioning the courts to obtain a determination of the rights involved. The water rights section of the Bureau made extensive title searches and accumulated a vast amount of documentation to support the Bureau's claims. It appeared that the rights to the water would be firmly established after litigation. However, the characteristic avoidance of water rights confrontations exhibited itself once more. Each time the Bureau headed for court, political forces intervened. A potent pressure group formed in the Sacramento River Valley and enlisted the powerful support of representative (later Senator) Clair Engel.[26]

The Department of the Interior undertook to prevent the adjudication, which was favorable to the diverters. Its decision was far more favorable than any court would reasonably have been expected to make. (The decision was dictated directly by Secretary of the Interior, Stewart Udall.) The determination of rights was based on fulfilling some goals of the agency rather than on an objective determination of the extent of the rights involved. (This determination could not have been done unless new water supplies were forthcoming in order to satisfy the competing claimants.) The controversy resembled a situation in which two parties to a lawsuit dispute the sum that one party owes to the other. Instead of resolving the problem, someone else adds sufficient money to the pot to satisfy both parties. In effect this is what happened here. The "shortage" created by the Sacramento diversions provoked the approval of still another project, the Trinity River addition to the CVP.[27] This shortage was used by others who desired the project for their own purposes, including the pressure group in the Western part of the Sacramento Valley that had received authorization for a project but had no water source. The most powerful promoter, however, was Clair Engel who wanted inexpensive electric power for the city of Sacramento. The Trinity addition offered a sufficient increment of water so that the rights problem did not have to be resolved, and newly appointed Secretary Udall made the political adjudication in 1961.[28]

The problems of water rights in northern California appear to have been solved. Seemingly, these problems have little relevance to southern California, which is the subject of this study. But southern California is involved because of the troublesome fact that the water flowing from the region north of the delta must pass through the delta to reach the southern part of the state. This is accomplished by a series of natural and artificial channels through the delta. Unfortunately the transmission of the water involves a commingling of project water with delta water. This commingling causes problem for projects that deliver water from north of the delta to the south of it. Leaving this problem for the moment, we shall consider water rights problems in southern California.

The city of Los Angeles is thought to have a continuing water problem. The fresh water naturally flowing into the coastal basin that constitutes Los Angeles and its environs can only support a minuscule population and so the importation of water continues to be necessary to promote the kind of growth that a large population requires.[29] Water rights problems have dogged Los Angeles every time that city officials have to import water into the basin. The first attempt resulted in the famous Owens River controversy.[30] When the Hoover Dam was planned, the city decided to contract for its water despite the fact that it had a sufficient supply of water, at least in the economic sense, from the Owens Valley area. The inexpensive power that would be generated by the Hoover Dam project was desired (and of great economic value to the city), and so Los Angeles agreed to take the water.[31]

In order to accomplish the objectives set forth in the contract, a new bureau was created — the Metropolitan Water District (MVD). (This entity was to have a great impact on water resource development in Southern California and incidentally on its water rights problems.) This bureacratic entity is a powerful one indeed. The powers of the agency are sufficiently broad to allow it to incur a loss on its sales to consumers. These losses can than be recouped by taxing property owners in the district without reference to the amount of water consumed. Through this mechanism, some taxpaying units pay a part of the cost of water consumed by other individuals in the district.[32]

Obviously, this procedure tends to waste resources, for consumers of water are not paying the actual costs involved. Consequently, they tend to use more water than they would if they were paying the true cost. (Economists argue that the best use of resources is achieved when each individual pays the incremental cost of delivering resources to him.) Otherwise, they argue, the resources should be used elsewhere, where consumers are taxed to pay for them, or not at all. The question of whether resources are used efficiently is less important to the discussion than is the use of cross-subsidization to effect the expansion of the agency's activities.

The decision to import Colorado River water was fraught with difficulty. In the first place, the rights to Colorado River water (the water impounded and delivered by means of the

Hoover project) were far from defined. This lack of definiton was confirmed by the famous *Arizona v. California* decision in which the United States Supreme Court subtracted a significant amount of water rights from the amount claimed by California and gave them to Arizona.(26) However, before this determination, the MWD made costly investments to import water from Colorado despite the shakiness of its rights.

Without resolving the legal and economic problems involved, the agency embarked on another investment venture the participation in the extremely large Feather River project (FRP) of the state of California. The decision to participate in this project seems to be inexplicable. But before discussing this decision, let us digress for a moment and describe some of the salient features of the project.

This project represents the first undertaking in the state's water plan (SWP), which is a grandiose venture to capture all of the "surplus" waters of the state and put them to beneficial use. The specific project consists of damming up the waters of the Feather River, which is a tributary of the Sacremento River. (The impoundment takes place not too far from the city of Sacramento.) After impoundment, those waters are released into the natural channel of the Sacramento River (as is the case in the Trinity River project), from which they flow to the troubled delta. The water is then sent south by means of an aqueduct to the formidable Tehachapi Mountains and then pumped over the mountains into the Los Angeles basin and to other points south. The project is an exceedingly costly undertaking. The water that it yields costs much more than other water available to the MWD. Nonetheless, the agency joined with other agencies in the southern Central Valley that did not have low-cost alternative sources of water. With the endorsement of the MWD and the political support that it was able to garner in southern California, the project was approved narrowly in a referendum held in 1960.[33]

At this juncture water rights problems that had been swept

under the rug, as well as unanticipated problems, began to prove nettlesome.

For one thing, *Arizona v. California* deprived California of rights to large supplies of water after facilities to transport that water from the Colorado River to Los Angeles and been constructed. Along the route of these facilities, however, a great deal of water was being delivered, under entitlements superior to those of Los Angeles, primarily to agricultural users in the Coachella area. The costs of transporting that water, if the rights could somehow be acquired, would be negligible because of the reduced capacity mandated by the decision. Second, the Feather River project ran into severe water rights problems. The project had been planned in the customary fashion. It involved contracting to deliver much more water than could be claimed under existing rights or even under authorized facilities. Unfortunately for the plan, the concern for ecology created a new set of problems for both the Bureau and its CVP and the state and its SWP. The state legislature passed an Environmental Protection Act and pursuant to this act, the state adjudicating agency, — the State Water Resources Control Board — rendered its controversial Decision D 1379. (25) This decision set salinity standards in the delta that had the effect of decreasing the amount of water that federal and state agencies could deliver to their users.[34]

This decision is an example of the internalization of goals hypothesis advanced earlier. The Environmental Protection Act established a new set of goals for the adjudicating agency. Despite the strenuous objections of the Bureau of Reclamation, the State Water Resources Control Board evidently resolved all doubts in favor of ecological considerations.

Furthermore, for almost the first time in the recent history of water rights controversies in California, it may prove to be very difficult to obtain new water supplies. Two planning decisions have served to exacerbate rather than diminish the problem. One was the refusal of the Bureau of Reclamation to build a peripheral canal around the delta that would have served to obviate the problems attendant on the commingling of the waters. The Bureau's refusal may mean that delta problems are likely to persist.[35]

The other planning decision of consequence was the decision of the California state legistlature to place a moratorium on implementing the Eel River project in northwestern California. This project was to be a major source of water for the SWP even though it would have been an extremely costly undertaking.

This enactment also had the effect of diminishing the supplies of water available to the state water plan and to southern California. In fact, it is possible to estimate when the state will be unable to meet its contractual commitments. Figure 1 illustrates the status of water rights in California.[36]

This chart was constructed by applying Decision D 1379 to the project water yield shown in Figures 39 and 40 of pages 160 and 161 of the Department of Water Resources Bulletin 160-70. As can be seen from the chart, the state will run out of water rights in the year 1983 and will not be able to honor its contractual commitments after that time. If the state cuts back its deliveries to accord with its diminished rights, the Bureau could continue to honor its commitments for the Central Valley project until the year 2006. However, if the state water plan and the Central Valley project somehow honor their commitments jointly, the two projects will exhaust their rights in 1990. Once more a water crisis will be imminent, albeit in a decade or two, and the failure to resolve water rights controversies will presumably lead once more to demands for the additional development of water resources.

Let us examine the impact that this problem could have on southern California. At first it would appear that the water rights problem poses a serious problem for that region. Paradoxically, this rights problem may prove to be a blessing

FIGURE 1

SACRAMENTO RIVER BASIN
AND DELTA - No Peripheral Canal

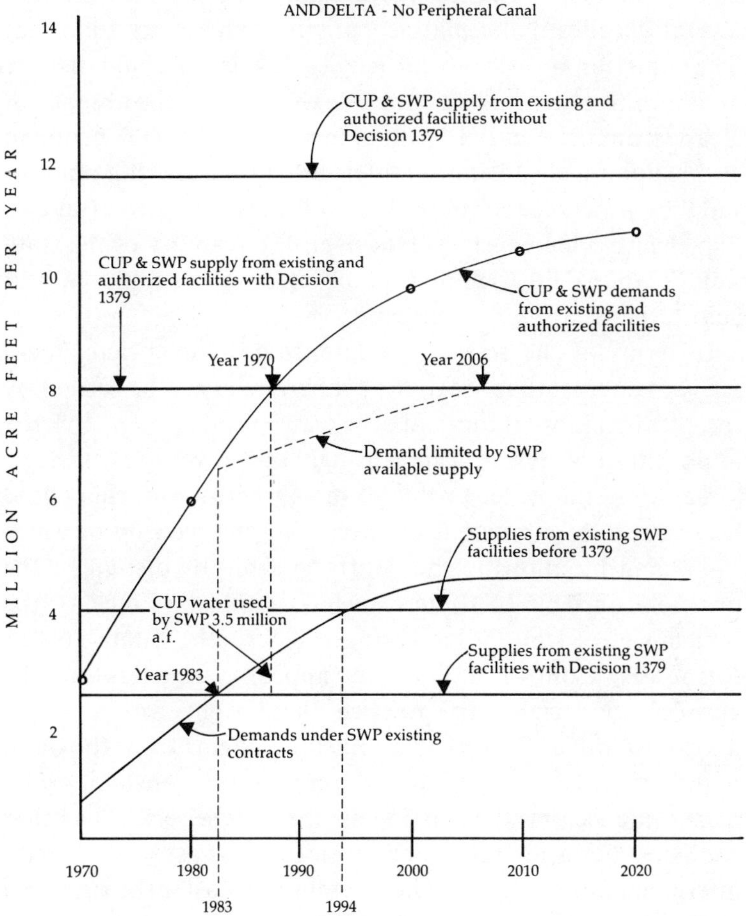

Source: Water Rights, Bureau of Reclamation.

in disguise for southern California. To understand this point, we refer to the Hirshleifer, DeHaven, and Milliman study (6). They argue that the Metropolitan Water District was pressured to enter into the state water plan, and they suggest that the water so obtained will be largely unsalable for the next several decades if the planned pricing policies are followed. (The reduction of price to sufficiently low levels could dispose of all of the water.) They conclude that " . . . in the absence of escape from the Feather River commitment, MWD's problem at this point is disposing of water rather than seeking out new supplies, however economical." (6) If they are correct (and we find their evidence very persuasive), the inability of the state water plan to deliver all of its contracted water supplies would help rather than injure the area.[37]

In terms of the frame of reference developed here, these analysts suggest that the rights controversies can be settled by the ordinary workings of the law rather than by the importation of new and increasingly costly supplies.[38]

Certainly the water problems of southern California could be lessened or eliminated by increasing the security of water rights and by allowing the courts to arbitrate disputes. One principal obstacle to some transfers should be noted — the reluctance of the adjudicating agency, the State Water Resources Control Board, to approve transfers of the appropriative right. In practice these rights prove to be nontransferable. Part of this reluctance stems from the basic nature of the right that renders any attempt to transfer it *prima facie* evidence that the existing use is not beneficial. The other problem pertainig to such transfers is associated with internalizations of goals. The attempt to transfer the right will be taken as evidence, it is feared by prospective transferers, that such waters are surplus waters. (1) A statute states that the property rights to all surplus waters are vested in the state and should be allocated in accordance with the state water plan. Any attempt to transfer water rights would have the effect of transferring title to the water to the state. The goal of the adjudicating agency that was transmitted to it by statute is that all transfers of water rights must be consistent with the purposes of the SWP. The holders of rights in California construe that stipulation to mean that any attempt to transfer a right will result in the loss of that right. (1)

CONCLUSION

This study leads to a rather melancholy conclusion with respect to rights problems. If past practices are followed (and we have every reason to believe that they will be), water rights controversies will be resolved in the traditional fashion; that is, controversies will be settled by importing new and increasingly costly supplies rather than by the resolving rights. The source of new supplies may be the Pacific Northwest, the desalinization of ocean waters, or other sources that cannot be identified now. (Hirshleifer and Milliman make the satirical suggestion that water should be imported from the moon if any is discovered there.) If such sources are tapped, the importation of supplies from these sources may very well lead to unforeseen rights controversies and to cries for new sources once more.

It is not that we recommend that new projects never be built. Instead, we recommend that public planners verify that existing supplies are being directed to their most valuable uses before importing new supplies into southern California. The economic use of water we think, will only be accomplished by strengthening property rights in water in California.[39]

This study suggests that the transfer of water rights in southern California is not a promising avenue for solving water problems. A transfer that may prove feasible is the one suggested by Hirshleifer and Milliman whereby the Metropolitan Water District purchases entitlements to Colorado River water from agricultural users.[40]

Although we have made no legal study of this matter, our impression is that the purchase of such rights could take place without running afoul of the Water Resources Control Board, for it would be a transfer from some beneficiaries of a federal project to other beneficiaries. However, almost any other transfer in California would presumably become ensnared in the thicket of difficulties outlined in this study. Indeed, with the increasing strictures on water supplies, the pressure on the adjudicating agency to safeguard the state water plan will, if anything, increase.

NOTES

1. Excellent summaries of the salient features can be found in (6) and (4).
2. A simple example may illustrate this point. If I have an item of value that could be sold for $100, I will not continue to own the item unless it yields a return to me in excess of $100. (This, of course, assumes that individuals attempt to gain maximum satisfaction out of resources and also that they have information about sale and purchase opportunities.) Otherwise, I will sell the item to someone who does value it at that price. If sale is forbidden, the resource will stay in the hands of an owner that values that resource less than prospective purchasers.
3. The report of the National Water Commission details the problems of water transferability flowing from the physical characteristics of water.(1)
4. For a comprehensive treatment of Western water law, the reader is referred to the several works of Wells Hutchins. (12) Closed systems such as lakes may have some intermingling effects, but these effects tend to be less severe than those involved in flowing streams.
5. Some of the works that analyze bureaucracy are (14), (15), and (16).
6. Benefits are roughly analogous to revenues but differ in that benefits include some items of values that are not reflected in revenues. For example, the flood control features of a water project may confer benefits even if it is not possible to change for them and thereby to produce revenues.
7. The problem of risk and uncertainty is very complex. For a review of the literature in this regard, see Hirshleifer and Shapiro. (3)
8. As Hirshleifer and Millman put it, stewardship over resources is lost in the private sector when used inefficiently. (4)
9. As Hirshleifer and Milliman complain, certainly they (the water officials) should not make the same mistakes, especially after having had previous mistakes pointed out by many economists. (4)
10. Louis De Alessi's article also relates to this point. (18)

11. A formal statement of this proposition, along with empirical support, is contained in (5).

12. For elaboration and corroboration of these points, the reader is referred to the following writings: (6) and (7).

13. One recent attempt in this direction has been made by Warren Samuels. (8).

14. An anecdote may illustrate the point. A state legislator in conversation once argued that a railroad must pay an equitable amount of taxation. When challenged about the meaning of the word *equitable,* he argued that equitable was what the legislature deemed to be equitable.

15. A rather minor consideration would be the benefits flowing from hiring a "tough" regulator from the commission.

16. The Russell-Shelton paper does make the valid point that the regulator in general, is not, guilty of corruption. They point out, quite rightly, that the miasma of the law can provide, a legal case for the particular result desired by the adjudicator. We agree, and our theory employs the same reasoning.

17. It is true that all adjudications, including those of the courts, could be constructed as having economic functions. However, we concentrate on adjudications the economic effects of which are direct. A criminal court, for example, has economic functions but not in the same sense as the Interstate Commerce Commission or the Civil Aeronautics Board.

18. It is tempting to think of the adjudicator as balancing the interests of competing groups in terms of their political clout. However, the balance of political clout could be an ever changing thing, that is, the balance of political power may be continually changing. The adjudicator in such a situation would be hard pressed to determine the preponderent force. It seems that information about the goals of the agency is easier to get.

19. This is to suggest that "honesty may be the best policy" in that competence may be a more highly valued commodity then is corruptibility.

20. Of course, the decision of the court will have distributive consequences, that is, the party awarded the rights will enjoy an increase in wealth, whereas the opposite will be true of the losing party. When the dust settles, however, the party who values the resources more highly will possess them.

21. The NWC report effectively details the problems involved in the specification of rights and in the attempted transffer of right. (1).

22. For example, in the Sacramento Canals Division of the Central Valley project, the Bureau of Reclamation reduced its price from \$3.50 to \$2.75 when sufficient water contracts could not be executed with agricultural users. (5), (20). The Metropolitan Water District has also been very generous to the San Diego Water Authority. That entity has in effect paid a much lower price for water than has Los Angeles. (4) Once again, the most reasonable explanation for this generosity is the desire of the MWD to expand the scope of its activities.

23. The paper of Mason Gaffney contains an explanation this "crisis". (21).

24. A more complete description of the legal problems associated with the project can be found in an article by Shapiro. (22).
25. There is an unlimited amount of water in the delta. The delta is formed by the confluence of rivers flowing north and south and then out from the delta through a series of bays into the Pacific Ocean. Consequently, no depletion of water results from the pumping of delta water. What does occur is that the inflow of additional water from the ocean increases to replace the water pumped out. The net result is the saline content of the water process (this process is called saline intrusion). This increased salinity in turn interferes with the consumptionn of the water in the delta.
26. This redoubtable figure for many years chaired the House Committee on the Interior and Insular Affairs, the committee that reports on reclamation legislation.
27. Several works of Shapiro discuss various aspects of this project, including its history, economic merit, and the bureaucratic forces that prompted it. (5), (20), and (22).
28. It should be added that the Trinity project is of exceedingly dubious economic merit. At almost all discount rates, it appears to exhibit costs in excess of benefits, and at reasonable rates (6 percent or above), the excess of costs over benefits becomes impressive.
29. This is not to suggest that all of the water that was imported was necessary for that growth, because a great deal less would have sufficed. The works of Milliman and Hirshleifer, DeHaven, and Milliman contain a wealth of factual material on this point as well as on many others made in this section. (4), (6) (24).
30. The controversy arose when the city built an aqueduct from a valley in the Sierra Nevada in order to transport water from the valley. The legitimacy of the city's rights to that water was questioned by the residents of that valley, and the ensuing controversy eventually reached such proportions that actual violence occurred. A detailed description of this controversy, as interesting as it may be, is not germane to this study. What is germane, however, is the fact that the controversy prompted a reluctance to pursue the resolution of rights throughout the state so that such acrimonious controversies would be avoided. In fact, the Owens River controversy is often described as the "rape" of the Owens Valley.
31. The works of Milliman are the primary data sources for this section. (24).
32. This allows the differential amounts that are paid for water by Los Angeles and San Diego that were referred to earlier.
33. Details and economic criticisms can be found in (6) and (7).
34. The board calculated inflows and outflows and on that basis decided how much water could be diverted from the delta. The point has been disputed by the federal government, and a lawsuit is in progress. With no pun intended, it is a murky area, and as we understand it, the Bureau contends that the adjudicating board is requiring it to furnish its own water in order to

maintain the requisite standards in the delta. Whatever the reality of the situation, the net effect is to diminish the net amount of water that can be delivered by both the Bureau and the state.

35. A very interesting question that has never been resolved is whether states have jurisdiction over the water rights to federal projects. The federal government has more or less submitted to state jurisdiction although never conceding the legal necessity of so doing. In the present controversy there may be some attempt to settle this open question. See (6) in this regard.

36. This figure, as well as much additional information, has been supplied to us by Mr. G. L. Renoud of the office of the Bureau of Reclamation in Sacramento. Mr. Renoud has been responsible for water rights activities in the Bureau office for some years and is an veritable treasure trove of information in this regard. We are deeply indebted to him for the unstinting assistance and cooperation. (We do not implicate him in this study, however.)

37. These writers also argue that the prices of existing supplies of water should be set at more economically sensible levels and that waste waters be considered for nonconsumptive uses. (6).

38. These authors advocate a series of legal reforms designed to strengthen rights in water so that market transfers can be effected and dispute adjudicated in a normal fashion. (6, p.364).

39. Evidence that water rights are not transferable in California can be gained by examing the reported decisions of the State Water Resources Control Board. Investigators of the National Water Commission examined the reported decisions from about 1960–1970 and found no transfers of the appropriative rights reported. (1) We have examined decisioins beyond that point to the present and also found no evidence of such transfers.

40. It will be recalled that *Arizona* v. *California* had the effect of giving Los Angeles unused capacity for the delivery of Colorado River water. Water purchased from agricultural users could therefore be transported at very low cost.

REFERENCES

1. C. Meyers and R. Posner. *Toward an Improved Market in Water Resources.* Washington: National Water Commission, 1971.

2. *Webster's New Collegiate Dictionary.* Springfield, Mass., 1959.

3. J. Hirshleifer and D. Shapiro. "Treatment of Risk and Uncertainty." *The Analysis and Evaluation of Public Expenditures: The PBS System.* vol. 1, Joint Economic Committee, U.S. Congress, 1965, pp.505–530. Reprinted in *Public Expenditures andPolicy Analysis,* R. Haveman and J. Margolis, eds. Chicago: Markham Publishing Co., 1970, pp.291–313.

4. J. Hirshleifer and J. Millman. "Urban Water Supply — A Second Look." *American Economic Review* (57) May 1967.

5. D. Shapiro. "Can Public Investment Have a Positive Rate on Return?" *Journal of Political Economy* (81) March–April 1973, pp.401–413.

6. J. Hirshleifer, J. DeHaven, and J. Milliman. *Water Supply Economics, Technology and Policy.* Chicago: University of Chicago Press, 1960.

7. J. Bain, R. Caves, and J. Margolis. *Northern California's Water Industry.* Baltimore: the Johns Hopkins Press, 1966.

8. W. Samuels. "Public Utilities and the Theory of Power." *Perspectives in Public Regulation.* M. Russell, ed. Carbondale, Illinois: Southern Illinois University Press, 1973.

9. G. Stigler. "The Theory of Economic Regulation." *The Bell Journal of Economics and Management Science.* Spring 1971, pp.3–21.

10. G. Hilton. "The Basic Behavior of Regulatory Commission." *American Economic Review* (62) May 1972, pp.47–54.

11. M. Russell and R. Shelton, "A Model of Regulatory Behavior." *(Unpublished manuscript, 1973).*

12. W. Hutchins. Water Rights Laws in the Nineteen Western States. Washington: United States Department of Agriculture, 1971.

13. D. Shapiro. "Pressure Groups and Public Investment Decisions: A Note." *Public Choice.* Spring 1971, pp.103–108.

14. A. Downs. *An Economic Theory of Democracy.* New York: Harper & Brothers, 1957.

15. ———, *Inside Bureaucracy.* Boston: Little, Brown and Company, 1967.

16. W. Niskanen. "Non-Market Decision Making: The Peculiar Economics of Bureaucracy." *American Economic Review* (58) May 1968, 293–305.

17. ———. *Bureaucracy and Representative Government.* Chicago: Aldine-Atherton, 1971.

18. L. DeAlessi. "Some Implications of Property Rights Structures within the Government." *American Economic Review* (59) March 1969, pp.13–24.

19. D. Shapiro. "A Note on Rent and the Coase Theorem." *Journal of Economic Theory* (7) January 1974. pp.125–128.

20. ———. "Statistical Appraisal of the Economic Efficiency of the Trinity River Division of the Central Valley Project of the United States Bureau of Reclamation." (Unpublished Ph. D. dissertation) University of California, Berkeley, 1966.

21. M. Gaffney. "Diseconomies Inherent in Western Water Laws: A California Case Study." ("Water and Range Resources and Economic Development of the West," Report no. 9), Proceedings of Western Agricultural Economic Research Council, Tucson, Arizona, January 23, 1961, 55–81.

22. D. Shapiro. "The Sacramento Diverters Controversy: A study in the Legal Adjustment of Externalities." *Water Resources Bulletin* (7) December 1971, 1267–72.

23. ."Water Rights and Wrongs." *The Annals of Regional Science.* December 1969, pp.139–147.

24. J. Milliman. "Economic Problems of the Metropolitan Water District of Southern California." *Proceedings of the 32nd Annual Conference of the Western Economic Association, 1957*. Salt Lake City, 1958, pp. 42–45.

25. *Decision 1379, Delta Water Rights Decision* Sacramento, California: State Water Resources Control Board, 1971.

26. *Arizona v. California*. 373 U.S. 546, 10 L. Ed. 2nd. 542, 83 Supreme Court 1468. Rehearing Denied 375 U.S. 892, II L. Ed. 2nd 122, 84 Supreme Court 144, 1963.

Comments on "California Law and Its Economic Effects on Southern California"

HAROLD M. HOCHMAN*

Dr. Shapiro's paper implies that the reasons why California law is ineffective in resolving water disputes are much more general than the specific points at issue. Proper incentives, he argues, are as essential as high-quality cost-benefit analyses to efficient public choice. But because bureaucratic incentives and Pareto efficiency are inconsistent, managers who have private stakes in outcomes cannot be trusted to make unbiased decisions.

Shapiro identifies two kinds of water rights — riparian and appropriative. Both are ill defined — his examples underscore the problems implicit in defining rights. Riparian owners have rights subject to the rights of others. That this statement is vague seems indisputable. Appropriative rights to divert water in order to put it to good use are quite limited because they are nontransferable, the courts having interpreted the sale of the property to which the water is diverted as an admission that it is not well-used. As Niskanen and Tullock suggest it is easier to initiate a new water project, even one that is uneconomic in cost-benefit terms, than to resolve disputes over existing

*Professor of Economics, Baruch College and the Graduate Center of the City University of New York.

rights. The result is the overbuilding or the overdevelopment of water projects.

For the student of law and economics, there are at least two ways in which the Shapiro argument is instructive. The first is that incentives, not transactions costs, are the primary impediments to the efficient allocation of water rights. Thus, in dealing with the allocation of water, we cannot proceed as if it were a straightforward Coasian problem. The second is that the parties to water rights decisions are not engaged in a constant-sum game, in which the decisions involve distributional problems. On the contrary, the primary participants have the bureaucratic power necessary to redirect rewards to themselves — in a manner that is difficult to discern because property rights are inherently ill-defined when the problem of bureaucratic incentives is added to the Coasian question.

Where, then, does Shapiro falter in his argument? He does, I believe, in prescribing solutions to these problems. Shapiro argues that efficient resource allocation requires defined rights and stringent limitations on the initiation of new projects. In effect, however, this prescription is tautological, because it amounts to saying that eliminating a disease requires a cure but (to continue my metaphor) does not specify the medication, the dosage, and the location of the pharmacy at which the prescription can be filled. In other words, it gives no clue about whether communities ought to turn to legislative or judicial procedures to resolve water rights issues or indeed whether either the legislature or the judiciary has the power to deal with them. But because it makes one thing clear — that self-interested bureaucrats, however well-intentioned, are not the proper arbiters of water rights — the argument is instructive. Because the process of resolving water rights involves countervailing interest groups, the demand for a clear definition of riparian and appropriative rights and the conditions under which they can be transferred to private parties or governments promises no guarantee of fulfillment.

A number of examples from areas that are more familiar to me shed some light on the problems inherent in the inadequate specification of water rights: A simple example is that environmentalists, in a situation that is the mirror image of the one discussed by Shapiro, appear to have been able to appropriate significant rights that had long been considered well-defined. A second example is zoning, in particular the anti-growth or no-growth movement that has dominated land-use planning in many places in recent years. A third example is rent control. When I arrived in New York in 1975, I believed that rent control was a dead issue because it had been legislated out of existence and was in effect a matter of "grandfathering." However dead rent control may appear to be, it is very much alive. Rent stabilization and a number of similar forms of intervention in the operation of housing markets amount to much the same thing. If push came to shove, and tenants were to feel a significant pinch as a consequence of rising rents in a free housing market, I have no doubt that the New York City Council would respond by clamping down on landlords, who are outnumbered by tenants. In other words, even if rights appear to be well specified, they may be subject to change because special interest groups can bring pressure to bear on public choice. To return to the water rights case, there is no assurance, even if such rights were specified, that they would be enforced once political pressure to build new water projects developed a head of steam.

Is there, then, a solution? That there is no panacea is obvious. But three points can be made. The first is that we should go back to Niskanen and examine the various palliatives for bureaucracy that he suggests. The second is that we should think about requiring referendum voting on projects that involve large investments of public funds, specifying say, as least a two-thirds majority for approval. The third relates to referenda on limiting taxes and expenditures such as California's Proposition One, which was defeated in 1974, but resuscitated in altered form in the Jarvis-Gann Amendment. Despite the defeat of the orginal initiative (an idea to which I was not nearly as sympathetic then as I seem to have become) similar referenda are now under consideration in many states, precisely because the public has become quite concerned with the kinds of problems that Shapiro describes. Referenda on tax limitation propose setting limits on the ability of bureau managers to pursue their private interests and, therefore, modify incentives that prevent the community from achieving an efficient system of water rights.

ERISA
and the Prudent Man Rule: Avoiding Perverse Results

ROGER D. BLAIR *

I. INTRODUCTION

A decade of intensive study and congressional hearings on private pension plans culminated in the Employee Retirement Income Security Act (ERISA) of 1974.[1] Signed into law on Labor Day 1974, ERISA was designed ostensibly to cope with the numerous shortcomings of unregulated private pension plans.[2] Although many aspects of ERISA have been controversial, the basic goal of retirement income security is not disputed.[3] Most employers have been disabused of any lingering notion that a pension is gratuitous or akin to a gold watch for long and faithful service to the firm. A pension is more properly recognized as deferred compensation that would otherwise have been reflected in current compensation or in current fringe benefits. One consequence of deferred compensation is that the employee must rely upon his (or her) employer to establish and maintain a fund that will be sufficient to provide retirement income. Congressional hearings, however, provided documented examples of workers who lost their anticipated pensions benefits for a variety of

*Professor of Economics, University of Florida.

reasons.[4] Specifically, Congress found that private pension plans were failing to honor their commitments because of the following deficiencies: (a) inadequate vesting provisions, (b) inadequate disclosure of information to participants, (c) inadequate funding to satisfy accrued benefit payments, (d) premature plan termination with inadequate protection of the vested interests of plan participants, and (e) inadequate fiduciary responsibility requirements.[5]

The provisions of ERISA were meant to ensure that private pension plans would be solvent when the time came for paying retirement benefits. To this end, ERISA attempted to deal with the deficiencies noted above by direct regulation. As a result, private pension plans face a massive reporting burden,[6] which falls disproportionately on small pension plans and threatens their survival. The mandatory vesting and funding provisions have imposed significant costs on the sponsors. No doubt, this has done much to remove the "something for nothing" illusion that Treynor (1977) discussed. The Pension Benefit Guaranty Corporation (PBGC) established by ERISA provides insurance for employee benefits in the event that the employer cannot honor his commitments. Interestingly, PBGC has been criticized for being inadequate by Herbert (1976) and for creating a moral hazard by Treynor (1977). Each of these general provisions deserves extensive — albeit separate —treatment. In this paper I shall focus on the remaining major provision of ERISA: the fiduciary responsibility rules.

In the next section I shall examine briefly the four general standards of conduct that ERISA requires of a pension plan's fiduciaries. Among these standards is a federal prudent man rule, which I shall analyze extensively. The prudent man rule of trust investment was developed at common law by the judiciary. In the wake of modern portfolio theory, the common law rule has received extensive criticism in recent review literature.[7] ERISA, however, provides a federal prudent man standard of behavior that appears to be somewhat different from that of the common law. These apparent differences will be examined below. Because the judiciary will be fleshing out federal standards of prudence, it should be admonished not to repeat the errors made in developing the prudent man rule of common law. It will be shown that improper standards may *reduce* the security of retirement benefits — a decidedly perverse result for legislation designed to enhance security.

FIDUCIARY STANDARDS OF CONDUCT UNDER ERISA

Before the enactment of ERISA, there were numerous instances of fiduciary abuses. For example, there were occasions when pension funds were invested in high-risk ventures with insufficient security.[8] In addition, there were cases when pension fund assets were used to meet the operating expenses of the employer.[9] Previous legislation, for example, the Welfare and Pension Plan Disclosure Act, did not provide for the enforcement of fiduciary obligations. Although criminal behavior was subject to the usual criminal sanctions, these were cumbersome to employ because of procedural problems and the high standard of proof demanded in criminal cases. In any event, criminal sanctions must rely on their deterrent effect because they involve no remedial provisions, that is, they cannot restore any of the lost assets.

The most important sanction was left to the discretion of the Internal Revenue Service (IRS). As a result of fiduciary improprieties, including engaging in prohibited transactions, IRS could disqualify a pensions plan from tax exempt status. This sanction hardly protects the interests of the plan's participants, for they would be the chief victims. ERISA sought to correct this situation by prescribing federal standards that would impact directly on the fiduciary.

ERISA, Section 3(21), defines a fiduciary as anyone who exercises discretion in the management of assets, renders investment advice for a fee, or possesses discretionary authority with respect to plan administration. Consequently, a very broad group of individuals is subject to ERISA's four general standards of fiduciary conduct:[10]

1. A fiduciary must act in the interest of a pension fund's participants and beneficiaries and for the exclusive purposes of (a) providing benefits to the fund's participants and their beneficiaries and (b) defraying reasonable administrative costs.

2. A fiduciary must act "with the care, skill, prudence, and diligence under the circumstances then prevailing that a prudent man acting in a like capacity and familiar with such matters would use in the conduct of an enterprise of a like character and with like aims."

3. A fiduciary must diversify the pension plan's investments to minimize the risk of large losses.

4. A fiduciary must comply with the pension plan's documents provided that these provisions are not inconsistent with the provisions of ERISA.

We are mainly interested in the second fiduciary standard: that of the federal prudent man. The ERISA standard applies to all aspects of fiduciary responsibility in the management and the operation of a pension fund, including, of course, portfolio management. By imposing the requirement that a fiduciary's conduct be that of a prudent man "familiar with such matters," ERISA appears to impose a prudent "expert" rule. Although this provision may reduce the number of people willing to be trustees,[11] such an outcome is not necessarily undesirable: "one who cannot exercise the care and skill of an ordinary, able businessman should not be handling pension funds."[12]

There are important differences between a trust fund and a pension fund. These distinctions demand somewhat different standards of prudence. But the fact remains that the statutory standards for prudent behavior lack the specificity that can only emerge from cases decided under ERISA. As a result, one should expect rather conservative behavior as trustees guard against the infamy of being involved in a test case. In addition, Section 409 of ERISA provides that any fiduciary who breaches any of his responsibilities or duties is liable personally for restoring any losses to the pension fund that result from his breach.[13] In this connection we should note that a breach need not be intentional. Personal liability may result from errors in judgment if there is an *ex post* determination of imprudence.

The only frame of reference for guiding fiduciary behavior is the prudent man rule of trust investment that emerged at common law. It may provide a benchmark for the development of the federal rule, for it is not unreasonable to suppose that the courts may rely upon common law standards in determining imprudent investments. Thus we shall turn to a brief examination of the prudent man rule at common law.

III. THE PRUDENT MAN RULE AT COMMON LAW

The investment behavior of trustees has tended to be conservative in the name of prudence. But conservation was not the intention at the birth of the prudent man. In the early 1800s there was a dirth of extremely safe investment opportunities.[14] As a result, there was a need for a rule of reason approach to trustee responsibilities. In 1830 such a rule was formulated in *Harvard College* v. *Amory,* which provides the classic statement of the prudent man rule:[15]

> All that can be required of a trustee, is that he shall conduct himself faithfully and exercise sound discretion. He is to observe how men of prudence, discretion and intelligence manage their own affairs, not in regard to speculation, but in regard to the permanent disposition of their funds, considering the probable income, as well as the probable safety of the capital to be invested.

This bold investment rule was narrowed by subsequent interpretation. As the economy of the United States matured and conserving trust principal became a more realistic goal, the tide began to turn toward a more conservative attitude. The New York court dramatically retreated from its discretionary rule in *King* v. *Talbot*[16] when it held that a prudent man would not purchase for a trust portfolio any share of stock in contrast to bonds or other obligations having specified yields and fixed maturities. This decision reflected the notion that fixed income securities are risk free. In nominal terms there may be no risk, but this notion is not true in real terms. By 1900 there were only a few states that continued to follow the Massachusetts prudent man rule. Instead, a majority of the states adopted the New York attitude that certain assets should be specifically excluded. Thus, there developed in these states legal lists that specified which classes of investments were eligible for trust portfolios. Designed to protect trust beneficiaries from inexperienced or ignorant trustees, the legal lists were dominated by government and municipal bonds but occasionally included other bonds and notes that could be selected according to prescribed formulas. This approach was not long lived in most states. For a variety of reasons, state after state retreated from the legal list approach until now there are only ten that follow it.[17]

Protection of the Beneficiaries.

Legal lists are comforting to the trustee in one sense. Uncertainty is reduced. If a trustee purchases an unauthorized security for inclusion in a trust portfolio, he assumes the burden of guaranteeing the investment against depreciation. Thus, trustees know that to protect themselves against personal liability they must eschew unauthorized securities. In contrast, the prudent man rule requires an exercise of judgment. Whether the trustee's judgment reflected the proper degree of prudence is to some extent a matter of opinion. With respect to the possible personal liability of the trustees for mistakes in judgment, the court in *Harvard College* v. *Amory* concluded in its final paragraph:

> Trustees are justly and uniformly considered favorably . . . they should not be held to make good, losses in the depreciation of stocks or the failure of the capital itself, which they held in trust, provided they conduct themselves honestly and discreetly and carefully . . . in the discharge of their trusts.

Somewhat later, however, after a more conservative attitude had set in, Justice Baines in *Hines* v. *Ayotte* offered a rule of caution:[18] "The motto 'safety first' applies no more strongly than in the investment of trust funds."

Of course, there is usually no question about the trustee's prudence if the portfolio performs well. But whether it does or not, the trustee may be subject to a surcharge suit. Although modern portfolio theory emphasizes the relationship between the risk of an individual asset and the risk of the entire portfolio, the prudent man rule focuses on the risk of capital loss associated with *each* security. The trustee is forced to adopt this narrow focus because investment losses may not be offset against investment gains.[19] Thus, a trust fund manager who increases the value of the trust principal while providing an ample return for the income recipients may find himself personally liable for the poor performance of a single security in the portfolio. This sad state of affairs results from the combination of two trust principles:

1. A trustee is liable for any losses incurred as a result of improper investments,
2. A trustee is not permitted to receive personal profits from the trust.

Because any offset of capital depreciation by capital gain would reduce the personal liability of the trustee, such an offset is interpreted as personal profit to the trustee and is forbidden. This illogical prohibition has led to several undesirable consequences, among which are the following:

1. Trustees are compelled to investigate the prospects of each security even though the search costs typically exceed the benefits in an efficient market.[20]
2. There is a fairly large body of empirical evidence that

confirms that actively managed portfolios rarely outperform passively managed portfolios.[21] Nonetheless, continuous review of the portfolio is in order if the trustee is to avoid personal liability.

3. Finally, there is an incentive for the trustee to hold an underdiversified portfolio, exposing the trust to a large amount of uncompensated risk. For purposes of diversification, the most desirable asset is one that correlates negatively with the rest of the portfolio.[22] When this is the case, the safety of the portfolio as a whole is enhanced. At the same time the investor is assured that when some of his assets do well, others will do poorly. The requirement of assuming personal liability for the poor performers, however, will dissuade the trustee from employing the methods of modern portfolio theory to the detriment of the trust beneficiaries. To the extent that low-risk, low-return securities are strongly positively correlated, very little risk reduction is achieved by holding a wide variety of securities.

Improper Investments.

As a general proposition, trust law draws a distinction between *speculative* securities and investment securities. Speculative securities have been deemed improper investments for a trustee because such securities have a relatively greater risk of capital loss than do those considered to be investment securities. Since the courts have stated that trust assets are not to be diverted to speculative investment, such securities have normally been excluded from consideration. But speculative securities can reduce the risk of an entire portfolio if their covariance with the rest of the portfolio is appropriate. Various kinds of investments have been found improper by the judiciary:[23]

1. securities in new and untried enterprises,

2. shares in a speculative corporation,
3. bonds selling at a large discount because of uncertainty of payment at maturity,
4. purchase of safe securities on margin, and
5. selling a security short.

A trustee who engages in any improper investment is asking for trouble in any surcharge suit. An improper investment is *prima facie* evidence that the investment was imprudent when made.

PORTFOLIO ANALYSIS OF THE PRUDENT MAN RULE

The prudent man rule has produced some effects that can be analyzed in a general portfolio model. If any asset portfolio can be characterized by its expected return, μ, and the standard deviation of its return, σ, then each portfolio can be identified by a point in mean-standard deviation space. We are particularly interested in the subset of portfolios that can be designated *efficient*. A portfolio is said to be efficient when no other portfolio with an equal expected return has a smaller standard deviation. The locus of all efficient portfolios forms the efficiency frontier *EF* in Figure 2. This is an envelope curve that separates unattainable portfolios from attainable but inefficient portfolios.[24]

Various judicial interpretations of the prudent man rule have resulted in restrictions on asset choices. If these restrictions are binding, this misguided effort at reducing the chance of a capital loss shifts the efficiency frontier from EF to E′F′ in Figure 1. To the extent that variance is associated with the riskiness of a portfolio, one can see that the main result of asset restrictions is to increase the risk that must be borne for any specified return. But there may be an obviously unintended result: The probability of capital loss may actually increase.

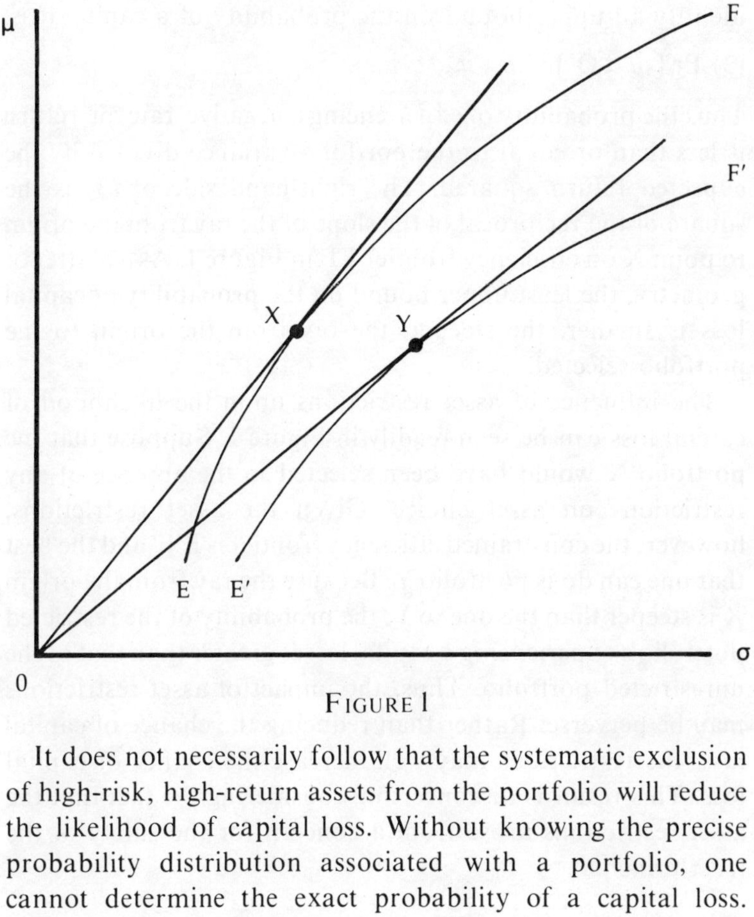

FIGURE 1

It does not necessarily follow that the systematic exclusion of high-risk, high-return assets from the portfolio will reduce the likelihood of capital loss. Without knowing the precise probability distribution associated with a portfolio, one cannot determine the exact probability of a capital loss. Approximations can be obtained, however, by using the Chebyshev Inequality, which states that[25]

(1) $\Pr[\,|(\mu-\bar{\mu})| > k\sigma\,] \leq 1/k^2$

or

(2) $\Pr[\,\mu < (\bar{\mu}-k\sigma)\,] \leq 1/k^2$

If we are concerned with negative returns, that is, capital losses, then we are interested in the case in which $\bar{\mu}-k\sigma = 0$, which means that $k=\bar{\mu}/\sigma$. Thus by substitution into (2), we can identify an upper bound on the probability of a capital loss:

$$(3)\ \Pr[\ \mu < 0\ ] \leq \sigma^2/\bar{\mu}^2$$

Thus the probability of experiencing a negative rate of return is less than or equal to the portfolio variance divided by the expected return squared. The right-hand side of (3) is the square of the reciprocal of the slope of the ray from the origin to point X on efficiency frontier EF in Figure 1. As a matter of geometry, the least upper bound on the probability of capital loss is smaller, the steeper, the ray from the origin to the portfolio selected.

The influence of asset restrictions upon the likelihood of capital loss can be seen readily in Figure 1. Suppose that the portfolio X would have been selected in the absence of any restrictions on asset choice. Given the asset restrictions, however, the constrained efficiency frontier is E′F′ and the best that one can do is portfolio Y. Because the ray from the origin X is steeper than the one to Y, the probability of the restricted portfolio's experiencing a capital loss is greater than that of the unrestricted portfolio. Thus, the impact of asset restrictions may be perverse: Rather than reducing the chance of capital loss, the restrictions may well increase the chance of capital loss. This result is disconcerting considering the fact that the asset restrictions arose from a concern for the safety of the trust principal.

V. THE PRUDENT MAN RULE UNDER ERISA

Most analysts have concluded that the common law standard of prudence is not appropriate for ERISA. Inasmuch as we have seen that the common law standard is not appropriate for trust purposes, this conclusion should not be surprising. But these commentators have emphasized the marked difference between the size, scope, and purpose of a personal trust and those of a pension fund.[26] In a personal trust there is a conflict between income beneficiaries and the remainder men that does not effect a pension fund.[27] Moreover, unlike most personal trusts, private pension funds experience a regular influx of contributions. This influx relieves the trustee of some liquidity pressure but compels him to make frequent investment decisions. The favorable tax treatment afforded pension plans also relieves the trustee of tax planning. Finally, it has been recognized that ERISA's standard of prudence should be flexible enough to cover pension plans of diverse size, complexity, and purpose. Because it would be neither desirable nor necessary to apply a single rigid rule, the peculiar facts of each case should determine the appropriate standard of prudence. It has been emphasized by Hutchinson (1975) that the courts ought to interpret the federal prudent man rule in light of the special nature and purpose of employee benefit plans.

The enactment of ERISA created an air of uncertainty regarding the acceptable behavior of pension fund fiduciaries. Although it is true subsequent lawsuits will flesh out the statutory standards, one should expect each fiduciary to avoid becoming a test case. It comes as no surprise to discover the following attitude: "We're all looking at unlimited liability, and one big question is how to protect ourselves."[28] There has been some concern that pension fund investment activity would become very conservative. In fact some observers predicted "a major shift back toward the fixed-income investments that predominated in pension fund portfolios in the 1950s."[29] There is some evidence that the movement toward conservatism may be underway. For example, in surveys conducted by the International Foundation of Employee Benefit Plans it was found that 64 percent of those surveyed in 1976 said that ERISA had made them more conservative. In the 1977 survey the number rose to 83 percent.

Similarly, Nancy Ross reports that "The most serious unintended result of the prudent man rule has been to make trustees unwilling to invest in other than blue-chip stocks, thus depriving smaller, newer, riskier enterprises of venture capital."[30] It appears that pension fund investment managers are doing "voluntarily" what the common law requires of trustees, namely, restricting assets. The perverse results of this restriction were described in the last section. This potential asset restriction has not gone unnoticed, Blakinger (1975) indicated that Congress had considered legislation that would exempt some one percent of a pension fund's assets from the prudent man rule. The ostensible aim of this legislation was to encourage investments in new or expanding firms that would have difficulty in attracting capital. Thus there was some recognition that such securities would be deemed imprudent investments for a pension fund.

VI. OPTIMAL BEHAVIOR OF ERISA'S PRUDENT MAN

The absence of lawsuits charging pensions fund portfolio managers with imprudent investments has the unfortunate consequence of leaving fiduciaries in a state of uncertainty. There is, however, a positive aspect to the absence of court decisions: Erroneous or misguided standards of prudence do not have the weight of judicial authority. Thus, there is still an opportunity to develop reasonable standards of prudence based on the language of ERISA and sound principles of portfolio analysis. From the language of ERISA's prudent man rule, one may conclude that a portfolio manager should be a prudent expert who must not only put forth his best efforts to avoid liability but should exercise sound judgment consistent with the character and aims of pension funds. Based upon this very broad set of instructions, one can prescribe some guiding principles that will not generate perverse results.

First, it should be clear from the discussion above that no assets should be excluded as being unsuitable on *a priori* grounds. A portfolio manager should be responsible for the portfolio as a whole and not for individual assets.[31] If an asset proves unsuitable for inclusion in the portfolio, that will surface in the derivation of the efficiency frontier.[32] The suitability of an asset cannot be determined without an examination of the asset's risk and return and its relationship to the portfolio as a whole. Whenever asset restrictions are binding constraints, the efficiency frontier is shifted down, as in Figures. But any legitimate objective can be accomplished at lower cost by other forms of regulation. Thus, asset restrictions should not be permitted, and prudent experts should select among efficiency portfolios.

Much of the current discussion of extreme conservatism in trust investment suggests that voluntary restriction affects asset selection. The ostensible purpose of this behavior is to guard against personal liability for the poor performance of individual assets. Our criteria suggest that such behavior ought to be subject to legal action. An expert portfolio manager who voluntarily excludes certain assets without regard to the impact upon the portfolio as a whole shifts the efficient frontier from EF to E′F′ in Figure 2. If some portfolio A is selected on E′F′, the prudent expert has exposed the pension fund to risk associated with the slope of the ray from the origin to A. But the expected return is only μ_A. For the same risk exposure the portfolio manager could have had portfolio B on EF, which has an expected return of μ_B. This conservative attitude should expose the fiduciary to personal liability of $\mu_B - \mu_A$ times the size of the portfolio. In effect, fiduciaries would be forced to exercise their expertise rather than adopt an imprudent, "safe" investment strategy.

Ultraconservatism aside, a prudent expert is still confronted with an important selection problem. The risk-return configuration varies along the efficient frontier, and,

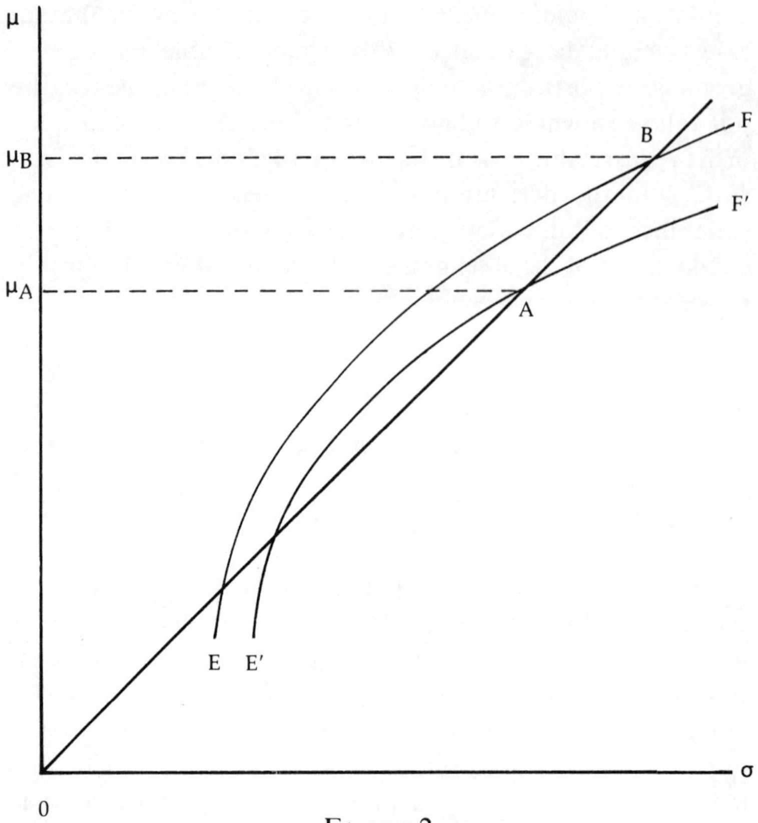

FIGURE 2

therefore, the portfolio manager must select some risk exposure that strikes him as optimal. This selection is not a trivial responsibility. Most people do not like risk but will accept nearly any risk if the expected return is considered great enough. In a defined contribution pension plan, each employee has his own account. The employer contributes on behalf of the employee according to some formula. The employee's retirement benefits then depend on the fund's performance.[33] Because attitudes toward risk vary among individuals, the portfolio manager has to perform a difficult balancing act. ERISA, however, contains provisions that will permit an individual to dictate the investment behavior of his share in the pension fund.[34] One procedure that could be followed is for the portfolio manager to select the safest, efficient portfolio. This would be portfolio X in Figure 1. Those employees who desire a more aggressive investment strategy must take the initiative by moving their shares into a higher risk-return posture. The additional costs incurred as a result of opting out of the safer portfolio will have to be borne by those responsible. For those employees who want a safer portfolio, we can only offer our sympathy; it does not exist.

In a defined benefit pension plan, the amount of the employee's pension benefit does not depend on fund performance. The employer's contribution must be sufficient to enable the fund to meet its obligations as they are due. Clearly, the employer bears all of the investment risk.[35] Favorable portfolio performance confers benefits on the employer. But ERISA demands that pension plans be managed for the exclusive benefit of their participants and beneficiaries. This statutory requirement should not result in extreme conservatism because it would have the effect of increasing the cost to the employer of providing any given benefit. This increase, of course, would reduce the size of the fixed benefit to which the employer will agree. It could also result in employers moving away from defined benefit to defined contribution plans. At a minimum, a portfolio manager ought to be able to select a portfolio such as X in Figure 1.

In selecting a portfolio the fiduciary should recognize the prospect of inflation because a portfolio of so-called low-risk, low-return assets may produce a negative *real* rate of return during an inflationary period. Restrictions on asset selection — whether imposed judicially or heeded voluntarily — increase the likelihood of this event by expanding artificially the demand for these assets. Considerations of inflation can be introduced into the analysis by restricting the efficient set to those portfolios (if any) that project an expected return in excess of the inflation rate. In effect the origin is shifted. If we let $\hat{\mu}$ denote the expected inflation rate in Figure 3, then all

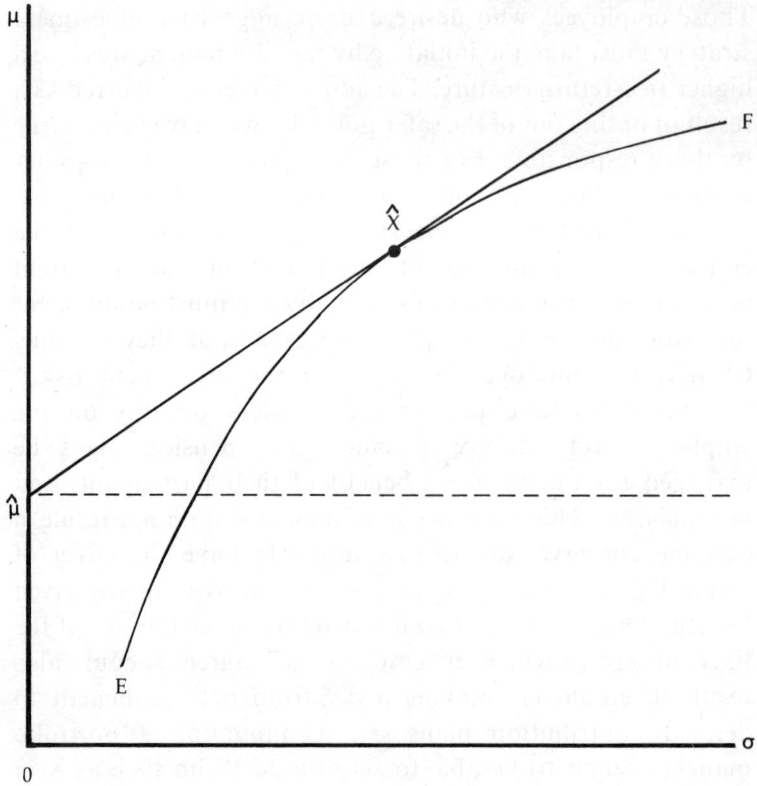

FIGURE 3

efficient portfolios with expected rates of return below $\hat{\mu}$ can be disregarded. Again, we can determine the portfolio with the least upper bound on the probability of experiencing a rate of return below $\hat{\mu}$ This portfolio can be designated X. A portfolio to the left of X on EF is riskier than X and has a lower expected return. Such portfolios are obviously imprudent. Portfolios to the right of X are somewhat riskier but hold the promise of greater return. These portfolios cannot be condemned as imprudent on an *a priori* basis.

In summary, modern portfolio theory can provide some guiding principles for the optimal investment behavior of ERISA's prudent man. Hard and fast rules cannot be laid down: Managing investments in a dynamic world requires flexibility guided by sound principles. If ERISA's language demands that a prudent expert be employed to manage the pension plan's portfolio, it may not be wise to do more by way of investment regulation.

VII. SUMMARY AND CONCLUDING REMARKS

Hutchinson (1976) raised an important question, namely, will the interpretation of ERISA advance two fundamental goals of public policy: "(1) ensuring the continued growth and economic stability of private pension and welfare plans, and (2) protecting the massive asset base which provides fringe benefit and retirement security to millions of workers and their families?" A complete answer to this question requires consideration of all aspects of ERISA, a task beyond the scope of this paper. The interpretation of the prudent man rule, however, impacts on both of these public policy goals. If private pension plans are to grow and prosper, they cannot be saddled with counterproductive investment rules. The old-fashioned prudent man of trust law may tend to reduce the portfolio return and reduce the security of the portfolio simultaneously. The prudent expert of ERISA must be guided by the principles of modern portfolio theory. If the pension plan is unable to cope with inflationary pressures, the pension fund will not be secure. Thus, the investment regulation must provide for the consideration of inflation risk.

Many of ERISA's provisions have dramatically increased administrative costs.[36] The requirement of a prudent expert no doubt adds to administrative costs. Given other restrictions, however, this requirement may be redundant inasmuch as firms have incentives to employ experts. In any event, the total impact on small pension plans may be devastating. As thousands of small plans terminate each year, one must be concerned with the extent to which those terminations can be attributed to ERISA. To the extent that there are significant scale economies in administering a pension fund under the ERISA requirements, the single employer plans may have to be replaced by multi-employer plans. If this does not create other problems, then the result may be sanguine. If, however, the former beneficiaries of terminated pension plans are left without the prospect of retirement income, an important public policy goal will not have been advanced.

NOTES

*This paper was written during the 1977-78 academic year while the author was serving as visiting scholar at the Center for the Study of American Business, Washington University. Financial support of preparation was received in the early stages from the Public Policy Research Center, University of Florida. Although the views expressed are strictly those of the author, my colleagues, Lee Benham and Murray Weidenbaum, provided constructive criticism of an earlier version. They cannot be blamed for what follows. My debt to Arnold A. Heggestad for previous collaboration is obvious.

1. Act of September 2, 1974, Public Law No. 93-406, 88 Stat. 829. Codification is scattered in various sections of 29 U.S.C.

2. In discussing the generality of these problems, one commentator remarked, "The first shaky premise was that there was a broad national problem to be dealt with. In fact, the instances of broken pension promises were not all that numerous, although sometimes tragic." The author concludes that, "As so often happens, a relatively narrow problem led government, into broad and, as it turned out, highly complex legislation," Editorial, "Pension Fund Problems," *Wall Street Journal,* February 13, 1976, p.8.

3. The *Wall Street Journal* did point out, however, that "Another premise in the 1974 Act was that government can reduce risk [of future payment] by edict." *Ibid.*

4. These hearings also revealed instances of inadequate pension plan

administration, misused and abused plan assets, criminal behavior, and violations of fundamental fiduciary obligations. See Hutchinson (1976) for some discussion of the impetus for regulation. Other developments are discussed by Chadwick and Foster (1975), Garmager (1976), and Little and Thrailkill (1977).

5. See Garmager (1976), p.688.

6. The *Report of the Commission on Federal Paperwork: The Employee Retirement Income Security Act* of December 3, 1976 runs to approximately 68 pages and includes numerous recommendations for reducing the burden.

7. See for example, Note (1970), Minetz (1972), Rizzi (1975), Johnston, (1975), and Blair and Heggestad (1978).

See, Herbert (1976), pp. 130-131 and 151-154, for a discussion of economic factors that appear to push a pension fund toward a high risk-high return configuration.

9. See Hutchinson (1976), p.17, for these and other abuses such as the dumping of worthless stock into the pension fund by the controlling stockholders of the pension fund's sponsor.

10. These standards are contained in Section 404 of ERISA. Little and Thrailkill (1977) provide an excellent discussion of these standards, including their ambiguities and the possible difficulties inherent in their implementation. In addition, the prohibited transaction rules are examined in an interesting way.

11. A survey conducted by the International Foundation of Employee Benefit Plans reported that ERISA has made it more difficult to find trustees. "Conservatism Grows With Pension Fund Officials. Poll Shows," the Wall Street Journal, August 18, 1977, p.34.

12. Blakinger (1975), p.1118.

13. In addition, if any profits are earned from the illegal use of pension fund assets, they must be deposited in the fund. Blakinger (1975) has examined the enforcement provisions and concluded that civil suits against fiduciaries who have violated ERISA'S prudent man standards offer the primary mechanism for enforcing those standards. To date there have been no suits against a fiduciary. The interpretation of this remarkable statistic is unclear. On the one hand, ERISTA may be serving as an admirable deterrent. On the other hand, the beneficiaries may be impotent in enforcing the provisions of ERISA.

14. In contrast, in England in the early 1800s there was very little government regulation, the tax structure barely touched substantial accumulations of capital, and stability encouraged confidence in the purchasing power of the British pound. In addition, the British government assumed some responsibility for maintaining a viable market for the obligations of the crown. As a consequence, fiduciaries were confined to investing in British consols and other government issues. See Shattuck (1951) and Note (1970).

15. 26 Mass. (9 Pick.) 446 (1830). This statement of the prudent man rule is found on p.461. The absence of safe investments was recognized "Do what you will; the capital is at hazard.

16. 40 New York 76 (1869).

17. See Johnston (1975), pp.491-492. These ten states do not all follow legal lists exclusively. They include states that permit some portions of a trust to be invested in listed securitites.

18. 135 Mt. 103, 197, 835, 838 (1937).

19. This issue is discussed in Posner (1972) and Minetz (1972). In Creed v. McAleer, 275 Mass. 353, 175 N. E. 761 (1931), the court rejected the offset notion: a trustee "cannot offset a loss for which he is liable by a gain not belonging to him..."

20. An efficient market is one in which the price of a security reflects all of the information that exists about that security. Thus efforts on the part of a trustee toward search are fruitless in an efficient market. See E. Fama (1970) for an extensive review.

21. An early empirical effort that supports this view is reported in W. F. Sharpe (1966). On p.138, Sharpe concludes that "good [portfolio] managers concentrate on evaluating risk and providing diversification, spending little effort (and money) on the search for incorrectly priced securities." Further empirical evidence is contained in M. Jensen (1969).

22. Haley and Schall (1973) provide an extremely clear example of this point, pp.115-118.

23. Rizzi (1975), p.421 and footnotes 19 through 23, provides a nice development of this issue.

24. For a particularly clear explanation of the efficiency frontier, see Levy and Sarnat (1972), pp.370-373. In effect the efficiency frontier is the envelope for a constrained minimization problem.

25. See Parzen (1960) pp.226-228.

26. Hutchinson (1975) discusses this point in some detail.

27. In the context of personal trusts, this distinction is examined in Blair and Heggestad (1978). See also Note (1975) for the relevance to ERISA.

28. Joseph E. Miles, vice-president of Lionel D. Edie & Co., Inc., the investment advisory subsidiary of Merrill, Lynch, Pierce, Fenner & Smith, Inc., was quoted by *Business Week,* March 24, 1975, in "Special Report: Pension Reform's Expensive Ricochet," pp.144-152.

29. *Ibid.*

30. See the article by Nancy Ross, "3-Year Old ERISA Faces Serious Problems," in the *Washington Post,* September 4, 1977, MI.

31. Recently this message was received by at least one legislator Senator Charles Mathias suggested that the soundness of investments be judged on the total portfolio. Unfortunately, the significance was lost on one who should know better. Jacob Javits's reaction was most disappointing: "Such a provision, though, should not permit trustees to invest in unacceptable speculative investments." *Ibid.*

32. Markowitz (1970) provides an analysis of the Kuhn-Tucker conditions as they apply to the derivation of the efficient set. Appendix A contains the mathematical conditions under which an asset will be excluded from a portfolio.

33. Hutchinson (1975) noted that of 470,000 pensions plans that reported to the Department of Labor, approximately 77 percent were defined contribution plans.

34. Although Section 404 (c) of ERISA allows an employee to control the assets attributable to his share of the pension fund, this flexibiblity is not free. The economies of scale in portfolio management will be lost if separate portfolios must be maintained for each beneficiary. See Note (1975). Moreover, not all defined contribution pension plans permit employee discretion.

35. The employees bear no risk because their benefits are federally insured through the Pension Benefit Guaranty Corporation.

36. ". . . some companies estimate that pension administration costs have about doubled since the law took effect." See "Many Small Concerns Learn They Can Live With Pension Reform," *Wall Street Journal,* January 12, 1977, p.1.

REFERENCES

Harvey E. Bines, "Modern Portfolio Theory and Investment Management Law: Refinement of Legal Doctrine, *"Columbia Law Review,* vol. 76 (June 1976): 721-798.

Roger D. Blair and Arnold A. Heggestad, "The Prudent Man Rule and the Preservation of Trust Principal," *University of Illinois Law Forum,* vol. 1978 (no. 1, 1978).

Charles B. Blakinger, "Fiduciary Standards under the Employee Retirement Income Scurity Act of 1974," *Georgetown Law Journal,* vol. 63 (May 1975): 1109-1141.

William J. Chadwick and David S. Foster, "Federal Regulation of Retirement Plans: The Quest for Parity," *Vanderbilt Law Review,* vol. 28 (May 1975): 641-709.

Eugene Fama, "Efficient Capital Markets: A Review of Theory and Empirical Work, *Journal of Finance,* vol. 25 (May 1970): 383-417.

Kay G. Finley and Merritt A. Gardner, "The Pension Reform Act of 1974: Brave New World of Retirement Security," *University of Florida Law Review,* vol. 27 (Summer 1975): 1044-1083.

Timothy R. Garmager, "Economic Analysis and the Prudent Man Rule under ERISA: Efficiency Versus the Public Interest," *Loyola University Law Review,* vol. 7 (Summer 1976): 683-713.

Charles Haley and Lawrence Schall, *The Theory of Financial Decisions,* New York: McGraw-Hill Book Company, 1973

Seth Earl Herbert, "Investment Regulation and Conflicts of Interest in Employer-Managed Pension Plans," *Boston College Industrial and Commercial Law Review,* vol. 17 (January 1976): 127-167.

James D. Hutchinson, "The Federal Prudent Man Rule under ERISA," *Villanova Law Review,* vol. 22 (December 1, 1976): 15-59.

Michael Jensen, "The Performance of Mutual Funds in the Period 1945-1964," *Journal of Finance,* vol. 23 (May 1968): 389-416.

Thomas D. Johnston, "Prudence in Trust Investment," *University of Michigan Journal of Law Reform,* vol. 8 (Spring 1975): 491-528.

Haim Levy and Marshall Sarnat, *Investment and Portfolio Analysis,* New York: John Wiley and Sons, 1972.

H. Stennis Little, Jr. and Larry T. Thraikill, *"Fiduciaries under ERISA: A Narrow Path to Tread," Vanderbilt Law Review,* vol. 30 (January 1977): 1-38.

Harry M. Markowitz, "Portfolio Selection," *Journal of Finance,* vol. 37 (March 1952): 77-91.

Harry M. Markowitz, *Portfolio Selection: Efficient Diversification of Investments,* New Haven, Conn.: Yale University Press, 1970.

Robert S. Minetz, "An Examination of the Rule Which Forbids A Trustee to Offset His Investment Losses Against His Investment Gains," *University of Illinois Law Forum,* (No. 4 1972): 784-804.

Note, "The Regulation of Risky Investments," *Harvard Law Review,* vol. 83 (January 1970): 603-62 .

Note, "Fiduciary Standards and the Prudent Man Rule under the Employment Retirement Income Security Act of 1974," *Harvard Law Review,* vol. 88 (March 1975): 960-979.

Emanuel Parzen, *Modern Probability Theory and Its Applications,* New York: John Wiley and Sons, 1960.

Richard A. Posner, *Economic Analysis of Law.* Boston: Little, Brown and Company, 1974.

Joseph V. Rizzi, "Trustee Investment Powers: Imprudent Application of the Prudent Man Rule," *Notre Dame Lawyer,* vol. 50 (February 1975): 519-529.

A.D. Roy, "Safety First and the Holding of Assets," *Econometrica,* vol. 20 (July 1952): 431-449.

William F. Sharpe, "Mutual Fund Performance," *Journal of Business,* vol. 39 (January 1966): 119-138.

Mayo A. Shattuck, "The Development of the Prudent Man Rule for Fiduciary Investment in the Twentieth Century" *Ohio State Law Journal* vol. 12 (Autumn 1951): 491-521.

Jack L. Treynor, "The Principles of Corporate Pension Finance," *Journal of Finance,* vol. 32 (May 1977): 627-638.

Comments on "ERISA and the Prudent Man Rule"

LEWIS A. KORNHAUSER*

As Professor Blair has pointed out, modern portfolio theory suggests a multitude of irrationalities in common law standards for trustees managing investment funds. In elaborating the statutory standards for the "prudent expert" established by the Employee Retirement Income Security Act,[1] these perversities are certainly to be avoided. Using portfolio theory to criticize the current standards, however, is a different and much simpler task than using the theory to promulgate new standards that courts can use effectively.

In the shift from criticism of rules to their reformulation, at least two kinds of difficulties may arise. First, the assumptions underlying the formal economics models — here, the capital assets pricing model and the efficient market hypothesis — may not be robust. In the economic analysis of tort law, for example, we have discovered that elegant efficiency results in the world of complete information, uniform costs, and Nash behavior[2] must be modified substantially when any of the three assumptions is relaxed.[3] Further, the inquiries suggested by the modifications are more complex than those in the simpler world.[4] The second source of difficulty arises if the level of detail necessary for legal decisions is significantly greater than

*New York University School of Law

the analytic power of the economic models. This type of problem arises frequently in antitrust. The courts must determine whether a particular practice or a minute change in the market structure will adversely effect competition; economic theory fails to resolve the question at so microanalytic a level.[5]

A third type of difficulty should also be noted. In both tort law and antitrust law many judges and lawyers maintain that the law is and should remain informed by values other than economic ones.[6] Thus the torts scholar argues that considerations of fairness require rules that deviate from ones that would be strictly efficient. In the analysis of ERISA, however, the goals of the law conform rather closely, if not completely, to goals of optimal economic decision making. Because the difficulty engendered by the need to trade off other values for efficiency seems minimal, I shall restrict myself to suggesting a few problems that may arise in connection with the other two kinds of difficulties. As will become evident, these two kinds of problems interact; the indeterminancy of the theory at some level of specificity arises from the need to distinguish some axioms.

A number of challenges to a manager's decisions can be imagined. ERISA imposes a duty to diversify on the funds' managers.[7] This duty should be elaborated in conformity with the findings of modern portfolio theory. How is this to be done? What questions will courts be likely to confront and in what format? What specific tests will implement the commands of portfolio theory?[8] An employee may object to the inclusion or the exclusion of a particular security from the fund's portfolio.[9] Alternatively, an employee may object to the portfolio as a whole not only because it results in an inappropriate mix of return and risk given the employee's preferences, but also because the manager has not included the proper number of securities in the portfolio and has not followed the best maintenance strategy of the portfolio.[10]

Finally, a pension beneficiary may object to the expenditure of funds on analyzing securities of various types.[11]

Each of these objections can be rephrased in economic terms; each new formulation raises an issue unresolved in the economics literature. First, one must note that court rules will be based not on Markowitz's formulation, which arises from the subjective expectations of the individual investor,[12] expectations that are difficult to observe and to evaluate, but from the Sharpe-Lintner formulation, which compares the movement of the security to the movement of the market as a whole.[13] The evaluation of any security, and whether it should be included or excluded from a portfolio, as well as the evaluation of the portfolio as a whole thus depend on the calculation method of the "betas." Implementing the dictates of modern portfolio theory requires a set of rules to be used to ascertain when sufficient care has been taken in determining a beta. Unfortunately, betas of individual securities are not stable over time;[14] their use in evaluating the choice of particular stocks thus becomes problematic. A recent empirical study of the betas of utility companies, for instance, indicated that the estimate of the beta from historical data — the only means of making the capital assets pricing model operational — did not always lead to accurate estimates of future behavior.[14a] The author of the study concluded that careful evaluation of the adjustment process may allow the use of betas "as one of the many factors to consider" in a rate of return proceeding[14b]

The problems of evaluating the calculation of the beta do not disappear when the focus shifts from the beta of the individual security to that of the portfolio as a whole. Although the beta of a portfolio appears to be relatively stable over time, the beta is somewhat sensitive to the number of stocks used as a proxy for the market and to the time period used in the estimation.[15] How will the courts strike a balance among the filtering out of random, nonrecurring events, the unsystematic risk that one seeks to diversify against, and the likelihood of structural change in the factors underlying the firm, the market, and the economy?[15] [a]

The choice of an appropriate proxy for the market can be interpreted as raising a more fundamental problem. The conventional market for which we have sought a proxy has been the United States stock markets. Thus the Standard and Poor's Index, the Dow Jones Index, or the New York Stock Exchange Index has been used to determine the degree of unsystematic risk to which the ownership of a particular portfolio subjects the investor. Securities and investments not traded on these exchanges exist, however. If the risks that they engender are not systematically linked to those of the better organized, more established exchanges, further diversification may be warranted. Should the pension fund manager be required to diversify into foreign securities exchanges, commodity options, or even into risks that do not trade regularly on any formal market? The courts, I expect, will be loathe toapprove such investments; but some managers may present evidence that the movements of these securities are not well correlated with the ones in the standard market portfolio. How much evidence would the legal system require before approving the investment? How convincing must the evidence be?

A further problem arises when one attempts to evaluate the portfolio as a whole. Given that it is costly to engage in securities transactions and that there appear to be diminishing marginal returns to increased diversification, how many different securities should managers be required to hold?[16] How frequently should a manager be required to reevaluate portfolio holdings and make adjustments in those holdings? In choosing the portfolio initially, how large a list of securities must a manager consider? Suppose the manager wants a portfolio with ten securities. Must he select the optimal portfolio from a list of one hundred, five hundred, one thousand, or two thousand securities? If the cost of the choice did not vary with the length of the list, the answer would be simple. But the longer the list of available securities, the more costly it will be for a manager to make an investigation. What strategy would be followed by a prudent expert? What strategy does portfolio theory recommend?

Portfolio managers, of course, engage in more complex investment strategies than simply determining the length of the list of securities from which they will choose and which they will hold. Legal commentators have focused on the strategic question of whether and what kinds of securities research should be engaged in by fund managers.[17] It has been suggested that managers of funds be required to purchase market index mutuals because the efficient market hypothesis[18] suggests that there are no gains to research.[19] The force of this argument depends on one's beliefs about the mechanisms through which information gets reflected in the market price of a security and the role that the analysis of securities plays in this mechanism. Thus a more fundamental question is broached. Should we prohibit managers from engaging in market strategies other than diversification strategies? If such a prohibition is enforced, will the market continue to behave efficiently? If not, the prohibition will be detrimental to the interests of the fund beneficiaries; fund managers will be prevented from increasing fund yield by discovering undervalued and overvalued securities. Thus courts must answer the perplexing question concerning the dynamics of the securities market: How is information reflected in the price of the security?

Two problems beseige the economist seeking to advise the courts. First, the efficient market hypothesis comes in three forms, at least two of which have different implications for the law. The hypothesis, in summary phrasing, asserts that all prices in the market "fully reflect" the available information. The three forms relate to the nature of the information that is supposed to be fully reflected in stock prices. The weak form asserts that prices reflect all information contained in past prices. The semistrong form asserts that, in addition to the information contained in past prices, the market price reflects all other information that is available publicly. The strong form asserts that no investor or group of investors has monopolistic access to some information and consequently has returns above the expected return.[20]

The weak form of the efficient market hypothesis appears to assert that technical analysis and funds spent on technical research should be proscribed. The semistrong form, if accepted, apparently justifies a ban on or, skepticism about, expenditures for fundamental analysis and research. The strong form may suggest a measure of the efficacy of the insider trader rules.

The second problem explains the temporizing nature of my assertions about the different legal conclusions to which the weak and semistrong forms of the efficient market hypothesis should lead. Without an understanding of how information, past prices, and other available data get reflected in prices, neither lawyers nor economists can predict that there will be no untoward result from the banning of certain research strategies. The efficiency of the market may depend on the search for overvalued and undervalued stocks by managers. The failure of a professional manager to outperform the market by using a single strategy may be consistent with the importance of searching for undervalued and overvalued stock, for the discovery of a successful strategy depends on its concealment. If the strategy becomes public knowledge, competitive forces will bid away the benefits. But the failure to employ a set of established strategies may place the manager at a disadvantage.[21]

The possibility of investing in securities not included in the standard market portfolio — the one used to test the capital assets pricing model and the efficient market hypothesis —

raises in a clear context the question of how much research and of what type a manager may pursue because the importance of a research and investment strategy that extends beyond diversification will depend upon the efficiency of the market. A court must then develop measures of efficiency. Once more the problem of market dynamics must be confronted.

Finally, even in the best of all possible worlds, where the strong form of the efficient market hypothesis is true, the courts would have to resolve a debate in investment strategy; Should managers buy and hold, or should they follow a "fixed investment proportion maintenance" strategy?[22]

Thus in formulating rules consistent with modern portfolio theory, the courts will be presented with difficult economic questions. Economists have frequently noted the gap between a theory and the derivation of some operational test to validate it. Applying a theory to legal problems reveals another gap, one between operational testing and sufficient detail that can be applied to particular problems that the law must confront. The courts will have to deal with criteria for determining the beta of a security, with definitions of the market proxy and the kinds of securities that should be included in it, and with the kinds of research and investment strategies that managers should be permitted to undertake in searching for undervalued and overvalued securities.

In deciding these question, the courts will surely wonder why "realism" failed to inform the assumptions of the model. Such concern will perhaps become most important when a court attempts to apply a model whose predictions are based on an unspecified operational mechanism. Thus a court should be concerned about the realism of the model when it decides the question of appropriate investment strategies, for the mechanism of efficiency is unspecified. Banning certain strategies may alter the mechanism on which the model's predictions are based. Economists frequently examine the robustness of a model's assumptions as a measure of its realism. The capital assets pricing model rests on seven assumptions. I quote from Jensen:[23]

1. All investors are single-period utility of terminal welth maximizers who choose among alternative portfolios on the basis of mean and variance (or standard deviation) of return.
2. All investors can borrow or lend an unlimited amount at an exogenously given risk-free rate of interest R, and there are no restrictions on short sales of any asset.
3. All investors, have identical subjective estimates of the means, variances, and covariances of return among all assets.
4. All assets are perfectly divisible and perfectly liquid, i.e., all assets are marketable, and there are no transactions costs.
5. There are no taxes.
6. All investors are price takers.
7. The quantities of all assets are given.

In fact, the model's results are fairly robust. Jensen cites studies that have relaxed each of the assumptions (except 6, or the competitive market one) and preserved the simpler model's basic results.[24] Unfortunately, robustness for the economist does not resolve the judicial problem. The assumptions are relaxed, naturally, one at a time, and the substituted model, although more plausible than the original, rarely captures the full complexity of actual markets.

No model captures the full complexity of the world, and many models are useful in guiding policy makers' decisions. Courts, however, face peculiar institutional restrictions. Judges and juries have neither the training nor the access to independent experts that would allow complete understanding of the range of applications implicit in a model. Rules must be framed that a judge can manipulate relatively easily and with a fair degree of success. Undoubtedly prudent managers also desire clear, easily understood rules by which to guide their conduct.

Courts are not laboratories in which the truth is diligently sought and revised as new evidence emerges. Instead, courts must decide cases when truth is uncertain and the parties in adversary relations seek to obscure rather than clarify it. When managers face daily decisions that may expose them to liability for vast sums of money certainty and constancy in the rules have added value. We do not want managers to be immobilized by the threat of liability or to undertake unwise strategies.

The thrust of my comments does not denigrate the important contribution that modern portfolio theory can make to the legal rules governing the fiduciary duties of pension fund managers but sketches, in a bit more detail, the institutional framework in which those contributions must be made. Judicial acceptance of the economic model will be accelerated and its decisions will be more compatible with the theory if economists confront the context in which the reforms must be made. Such confrontation may yield benefits to the economist. Attention to legal detail can sometimes provide insight into the economic fuctionings of institutions.

NOTES

1. Act of September 2, 1974, Public Law No. 93-604, 88 Stat. 829. The "Prudent Expert" Rule is established by section 404 (a) (1) (B).

2. Brown, "Toward An Economic Theory of Liability," 2 *Journal of Legal Studies* 323 (1973), sets out one of the basic models.

3. Brown *id.,* criticizes the complete information assumption; Cooter, Kornhauser, and Lande, "Liability Rules, Limited Information and The Role of Precedent," *10 Bell Journal of Economics,* 366 (1979), criticize the informational and behavioral assumptions; Green "On the Optimal Structure of Liability Laws," 7 *Bell Journal of Economics* 553 (1976), investigates the cost uniformity assumption. See also the articles cited in note 4 *infra.*

4. Diamond, "Accident Law and Resource Allocation," *5 Bell Journal of Economics and Management Science* 366 (1924); Diamond & Mirrless, "On the Assignment of Liability: The Uniform Case," 6 *Bell Journal of Economics* 487 (1975).

5. Scherer, "Economies of Scale" in *Industrial Concentration: The New Learning* (Goldschmidt, Mann, and Wester eds.'

6. On tort law, see Fletcher, "Fairness and Utility in Tort Theory," 85 *Harv. L. Rev.* 537 (1972); Epstein, "A Theory of Strict Liability," 2 *J. Legal Stud.* 151 (1973'; Schwartz, "Conctributory and and Comparative Negligence: A Reappraisal," 87 *Yale L.J.* 697 (1978). On antitrust law, see

Blake and Jones, "Toward a Three Dimensional Antitrust Policy," 65 *Colum. L. Rev.* 422 (1965); "Antitrust Jurisprudence: A Symposium on the Economic, Political, and Social Goals of Antitrust Policy," 125 *U. Pa. L. Rev.* 1182 (1977).

7. Act of September 2, 1974. Public Law No. 93-604, 88 Stat. 829 404 (a) (1) (C).

8. Bines, "Modern Portfolio Theory and Investment Management Law: Retirement of Legal Doctrine,"76 *Colum. L. Rev.* 721(1976), begins to confront some of the questions discussed here. See also the sources cited in note 10 *infra.*

9. Bines, *supra* note 8.

10. These challenges are suggested by the discussion in Pozen, "Money Managers and Securities Research," 51 *N.Y.U.L. Rev.* 923, 949-53 (1976).

11. *Id.*

12. Markowitz, *Portfolio Selection: Efficient Diversification of Investments,* New Haven, 1920. Jensen, "Capital Markets: Theory and Evidence," 3 *Bell Journal of Economics* 357 (1972).

13. Sharpe, "Capital Asset Prices: A Theory of Market Equilibrium under Consitions of Risk," 19 *Journal of Finance* 425 (1964); Linter, "Security Prices, Risk and Maximal Gains from Diversification," 20 *Journal of Finance* 587 (1965); , "The Valuation of Risk Assets and the Selection of Risky Investments in Stock Portfolios and Capital Budgets," 47 *Rev. of Econ. & Stat.* 13 (1965); Jensen, *supra* note 12.

14. Pozen, *supra* note 10 at 949-53 and the sources cited therein.

14a. Pettaway, "On the Use of β in Regulatory Proceedings, and Empirical Examination," 9 *Bell Journal of Economics* 239 (1978).

14b. *Id.* at 247.

15. Pozen, *supra* note 10 at 949-59.

15a. *Id.* at note 159.

16. Compare Sharpe, "Risk, Market Sensitivity and Diversification, *Financial Analysts J.,* Jan.-Feb. 1972 at 74-77 (recommending 30-40 stocks as "best") Langbein and Posner, "Market Funds and Trust-Investment Law," 1976 *Am. B. Foundation Research J.* 1, II (recommending a market portfolio.)

17. Pozen, *supra* note 10.

18. Fama, "Efficient Capital Markets: A Review of Theory and Empirical Work," 25 *Journal of Finance* 383 (1920).

19. Langbein and Posner, *supra* note 16.

20. Fama, *supra* note 18.

21. Bines

22. Cohen, "The Suitability Rule and Economic Theory," 80 *Yale L.J.* 1604, note 51 (1971), notes this controversy in the economics literature.

23. Jensen, *supra* note 12, at 358-s9 (footnotes omitted).

24. *Id.,* at 372-91.

Fee Shifting: An Institutional Change to Decrease the Benefits from Free Riding

GORDON L. BRADY, Ph. D.*

The private attorneys general mechanism in the Clean Air Act is an objective institutional change designed to increase the benefits appropriable by an individual for the protection of common property resources. Unlike traditional tort remedies, the private attorneys general mechanism entails no attempt to assess damages or compensate victims. Instead, it relies on fee shifting as a means of decreasing the benefits from free riding, that is, the costs foregone by inaction. Otherwise, the performance of the private attorneys general mechanism depends on such payoffs as the advertising of environmental issues by advocacy groups, quasi-legislative rule changes, and capital building by young attorneys. These kinds of benefits will be more difficult to obtain as the Act moves from implementation into the enforcement phase. The *ad hoc* nature of judicially developed fee shifting criteria has created the expectation of low benefits from undertaking such suits. Consequently, the visability of the private attorneys general mechanism is in question in the enforcement phase because the

---

*Brookings Economic Policy Fellow.

The views expressed in this paper are my own and are not necessarily those of the officers, trustees, or other staff members of the Brookings Institution.

indirect benefits appropriable by private enforcers will be more limited in scope.

Part one of the paper describes the nature of the externality service conceived for the private attorneys general mechanism and discusses the role of fee shifting. Fee shifting was intended to serve as a quality control device. It was meant to encourage actions described by various "public interest" characteristics. Conversely, the taxing of the defendant's fees against the plaintiff was meant to discourage "vexatious or harassing suits." Fee shifting criteria provided for in the act have been developed through interpretative case law. Part Two derives behavioral implications from economic theory to demonstrate the nonviability of the strictly defined private attorneys general mechanism in the absence of fee shifting. Initially a two-person model is used to show the litigant calculus involved in tort actions. This model is expanded to a public context in which free riding is a rational individual choice. Part three discusses the behavioral implications of the private attorneys general mechanism in the absence of fee shifting. Finally, a positive criterion for fee shifting based on the argument that the government should reduce the burden is suggested.

PART ONE: THE NOTION OF A PRIVATE ATTORNEYS GENERAL

One of the most controversial recent developments in federal regulation is the use of private enforcers.[1] The concept of private attorneys general in the Clean Air Act was the first legislatively ascribed private enforcement mechanism to be established in the field of environmental regulation. Although hardly a day goes by in which one does not read about suits brought by advocacy groups, such as the Natural Resources Defense Council, the Environmental Defense Fund, and the Sierra Club, only part of their litigation falls within the prescriptive private attorneys general framework.

As an objective institutional change, the notion of a private attorneys general produces a narrowly defined externality service.[2] It was designed by Congress to identify violators, whether they be bureaucrats charged with implementing the act or polluters. The threat of litigation leading to judicial mandate was intended to deter bureaucratic shirking and violations by firms. Like the private informant, or *qui tam,* the incentive to provide the private attorneys general service is based on a reward.[3] However, unlike the *qui tam* action that guarantees the informant a share called (*moiety*) of the penalty upon conviction, the compensation for performing the private attorneys general service is at the discretion of the courts.

Congress intended fee shifting (the non-punitive and nondamage connected reimbursement of legal fees) to create an incentive structure analogous to that in individual tort actions of nuisance or trespass.[4] Apparently this structure was based on the recognition that individual protection of common property resources is discouraged by the relationship of appropriable benefits and the cost of action. Free riding is a rational, individual choice in instances in which the cost of effecting a claim is high relative to the benefits appropriable by the individual. Such instances in which the "personal interest" does not rise to the dignity of a "cause of action"[5] are important because although subject to diffuse benefits, they produce substantial social costs.

The private attorneys general mechanism represents an institutional fusion of universal standing[6] and fee shifting.[7] Universal standing establishes legal interest without requiring the plaintiff to satisfy traditional criteria of standing that were in force prior to *Sierra Club* v. *Morton*[8] and *Scrap* v. *U. S.* Based[9] on *Scrap,* standing may be construed when economic injury is absent, when alleged injury is not unique to the petitioner, and even when the alleged injury has only faint and uncertain impact on the petitioner. The framers of the act were not attempting to institutionalize a representative for diffuse rights or to create an ideological plaintiff. Instead, their object was to establish an incentive structure for the enforcement of a legislatively ascribed right. The obstacle that they were trying to overcome was the relationship between litigation costs and appropriable benefits. Fee shifting was intended to provide the incentive for private enforcement of the act in the absence of countervailing appropriable gains for the litigant.

The use of paid informants has been a part of Anglo-Saxon law enforcement since the fourteenth century in England and in the United States since its founding.[10] In common law the name given an action of information was derived from the Latin "qui tam pro domino rege quam pro se ipso sequitor," meaning "who brings this action as well for the king as for himself." In essence the *qui tam* "stakes" a claim to moiety by virtue of the action of information. "By commencing the suit the informer has made the popular action his own private action."[11] Other than the entitlement to moiety established by the action, the informant has no legal interest that can be protected by the suit. Motivation is derived solely from penalty splitting with the government.

By virtue of the legal interest in protecting the right to moiety, the qui tam action creates a Hohfeldian plaintiff.[12] As a private inducement, moiety serves in lieu of an injury in fact and provides the basis for an adversarial relationship. Moiety is known, and its award upon conviction is not at the discretion of the court. Because the outcome affects wealth, those bringing the *qui tam* actions are expected to invest resources in additional search until returns are equated at the margin.

The incompleteness of ownership prevents an individual from appropriating the full gains from the protection of *res publica*. Because individual initiative produces spillover benefits for which compensation is impractical from a cost standpoint, one may predict a socially nonoptimal investment in the enforcement of *res publica* by individuals. If one assumes, as does the free rider, that the collective action will be carried forward without his participation,[13] the benefit from free riding is the private cost avoided by inaction. Moiety reduces the benefits from free riding by increasing the expected appropriable benefits. In this way it serves in lieu of a private benefit from compensation for damages or enjoying a nuisance through tort action.

Qui tam is an auxillary enforcer rather than an ideological or a non-Hohfeldian plaintiff. An important use of the *qui tam* mechanism has been to provide a judicial remedy for action wrongfully withheld by government. *Qui tam* action stands on equal footing with action undertaken by the state and may also be directed at the state.[14] In this light it is an exogeneous mechanism for monitoring bureaucratic activity.

Bureaucratic behavior may be explained on the basic of utility maximization subject to constraints.[15] Monitoring by private enforcers circumscribes permissible bureaucratic behavior. Because the benefits from reducing bureaucratic shirking accrue externally and are not subject to appropriation by the bureaucrats themselves, one may expect this kind of monitoring to be unpopular in administrative agencies. On the other hand, monitoring systems that produce appropriable gains through prizes, advancement, or other forms of recognition may be more readily acceptable to bureaucrats. Perhaps for the former reason, *qui tam* action has been neutralized in environmental regulation in the United States.[16]

The notion of a private attorneys general in the Clean Air Act is a variant of the *qui tam* action of information. Like the *qui tam,* the object of the mechanism is to augment the enforcement of a class of injuries characterized by diffuse gains according to individual initiative. The exercise of the private attorneys general right of action leads to judicial mandate compelling resource allocation by firms and bureaucracies. Information is produced about the surety with which expectations may be held by individuals concerning the completeness of control over resources that they own. The threat of mandate acts to constrain future as well as current behavior.

Economics, as the theory of choice under constraints, assumes that property rights are completely specified, privately held, and exchanged at zero information, transactions, and enforcement costs.[17] However, *de jure* and *de facto* rarely coincide. Institutional arrangements act to constrain individual choice by prescribing the harm and benefit that an individual may impose on others. A rational individual can be expected to modify his behavior in order to maximize his welfare subject to socially recognized rights held by others. The system of property rights adopted within a community determines the expectations that an individual can hold in dealing with others.

From a practical standpoint, the private attorneys general mechanism represents a means of establishing and exercising socially recognized rights to common property resources. In particular, it is part of the process by which property rights are established from "political entitlements"; the nominal claims produced through legislative action. The establishment of property rights from political entitlements is an iterative process. Property rights emerge from the resolution of conflict between political entitlements and institutions. The mesh between common law doctrine and political entitlements may be incomplete and necessitate adjudication. Conflict may also arise over bureaucratic interpretations at successive levels and between agencies. Of course, the resultant force of law is subject to legislative redirection, and hence the cycle begins anew.

The notion of a private attorneys general has been the subject of tortuous evolution. It emerged as a common law exception to the American Rule that prohibits the prevailing litigant in federal cases from recovering attorneys fees from the loser in the absence of statutory authorization.[18] By contrast, in England the winning litigant is routinely awarded counsel fees (the Continental Rule). Numerous congressional enactments mandate the award of counsel fees to the prevailing party in the United States.[19] In addition to the Clean Air Act, several federal statutes authorize the federal courts to use their discretion in awarding attorneys' fees.[20]

Common law exceptions to the American Rule have been grounded in the equitable power of the courts, to grant counsel fees to litigants whose actions, vindicate important public policies, protect a "common fund," or discourage vexations and harassing suits. Recently the exception has been expanded to include cases in which a clearly defined right exists and judicial assistance is needed in securing it.[21] The courts have awarded fees to plaintiffs in shareholder derivative suits when their actions protect or maintain a common fund, the benefits from which accrue to fellow shareholders.[22] The fund quantifies the value of spillover benefits accruing to a group of readily identifiable beneficiaries. Its existence provides the basis for recompensating the litigant's legal expense. More recently the common fund doctrine has been held to apply to cases in which a substantial "common benefit" is provided without the creation of an actual fund.[23]

The private attorneys general doctrine is the most recent exception to the American Rule. It has roots in the common fund doctrine and has emerged from the courts as a private initiative that generates spillover effects for a broader and necessarily less well-defined class of beneficiaries. Civil rights and challenges of administrative regulations by taxpayers and environmentalists form the externality context from which the private attorneys general exception has developed. A plaintiff pursuing his own self-interest in these areas has been viewed as acting "not for himself alone but also as a private attorney general vindicating a policy Congress considered of a highest priority."[24] Spillover benefits, however diffuse from such actions have been viewed by the courts and Congress to be in the "public interest."

Descriptively the externality service is identical to that of the *qui tam* action in that information is generated for decision makers. While a common law derivative, the Private Attorneys General concept in the Clear Air Act has been altered through legislative ascription. Congress attempted to graft elements of the *qui tam* construct to establish a mechanism which could be used to mandate action by administrative bureaucrats.

A. The Private Attorneys General Mechanism

The notion of a private attorneys general in the act is reflected in a set of litigation tools and remedies bounded by statute and administrative regulations. It is geared toward identifying violations and producing information for decision makers. Section 304 permits "any person" to bring civil action on his own behalf against "anyone":[25]

1. who is allegedly in violation of emission standards or limitations (including the federal government); or
2. the administrator of EPA for failure to perform a non-discretionary act or duty.

Remedies are limited to a temporary restraining order or a preliminary injunction against violators of an emission standard, limitation, or administrative order. Mandamus may be sought to compel EPA to perform nondiscretionary duties such as adhering to the statutory time frame for promulgating regulations or correcting state implementation plans (SIPs).

In order to encourage agency enforcement, a sixty-day notice of intent to file suit against polluters or EPA is required.[26] Notice must include:

1. the identity and the location of the violation;
2. a brief description of the activity alleged to be violative; and finally,

3. the provision of the law alleged to be in violation. During the waiting period EPA is free to take action against the

violator, correct its own inaction, or intervenue on the side of either party in the suit. Private attorneys general action may be considered by the court even when agency action is pending.[27] Conversely, intervention is permitted in civil suits brought by the administrator seeking compliance with a standard, limitation, or administrative order.[28] However, once action is initiated, the courts maintain complete control over the disposition of the action and may suspend, dismiss, or consolidate private attorneys general petitions. One may describe the mechanism as exogeneous because it is not at the sufferance of EPA.

The transition from the common law enforcement doctrine led to institutional conflict. Universal standing represents one attempt to resolve institutional obstructions to the implementation of the private attorneys general mechanism. In the case of the Clean Air Act,Congress ascribed jurisdiction to the federal district courts without regard to the amount in controversy or the diversity of citizenship.[29] However, the relaxation of traditional standing and damage requirements was limited to the enforcement of emission standards, orders by the states or the administrator concerning standards, and suits to compel nondiscretionary bureaucratic action.

Standing has traditionally been concerned with the characteristics of the "appropriate party" to challenge administrative action in the federal courts.[30] Standing has served as an effective entry barrier against environmental plaintiffs seeking the enforcement of *res publica.*[31] Derived from Article III of the United States Constitution, which limits federal jurisdiction to "case controversies," standing has traditionally been treated as part of the question of "justiciability."[32] It has become a blend of indistinguishable constitutional requirements and policy considerations. In practice, justiciability has been interpreted to include the elements of mootness, political questions, and ripeness, as well as standing. These concepts have been used collectively as a device for rationing judicial resources at the federal level. Indirectly the doctrine of standing has been used to thwart public participation in the judicial process and in many cases has made federal regulatory decisions unchallengable.[33]

In economic terms, universal standing reduces the organizational costs of becoming the proper party to challenge certain types of administrative action in the federal courts. Universal standing avoids minimum damage requirements for federal jurisdiction in class actions and permits judicial scrutiny of a regulation or an action wrongfully withheld without requiring the petitioner to exhaust all administrative remedies.[34] By prescribing jurisdiction to the federal district court in the absence of minimum damage requirements, Section 304 was intended to avoid the problems associated with the identification of parties and the allocation of damages in class actions.[35] The legislative history of the act states emphatically that "(S)ection 304 does not authorize a 'class action.' "[36] Section 304 was phrased to make it clear to the courts that a citizen was not required to establish himself as a member of a class in order to initiate private attorneys general action.[37] Nor did the action restrict "any right which any person (or class of persons) may have under any statute or common law to seek enforcement or to seek any other relief."[38]

Oddly enough, the private attorneys general mechanism has roots in class action legislation. The Environmental Protection Act of 1970 authorized "any person" to bring action in the federal courts without regard to the amount in controversy "in his own behalf or in behalf of a class of persons similarly situated" against those (including government agencies) producing "unreasonable" pollution.[39] The courts were permitted to grant declaratory relief, temporary and permanent equitable relief, or to impose conditions on the defendant to protect the environment.[40]

The private attorneys general concept was introduced by the Senate Public Works Committee in August 1970 and passed in its present form with little debate.[41] Various comments were, however, inserted into the *Congressional Record.* Proponents underscored the establishment of a private right to clean air and viewed public participation as a device for augmenting the enforcement mechanism rather than a detriment.[42] Opposition focused on the impact of multiple litigation and on the applicability of the private attorneys general concept to the enforcement of diverse types of rules.[43]

Basic to the opposition was the criticism that the private attorneys general concept was based on the premise that appropriate officials would fail to administer the act.[44] A deluge of litigation, which would have a number of detrimental effects on policy making, was expected. First, fee shifting and universal standing were thought to encourage multiple litigation.[45] In particular, fee awards to either party were thought to encourage the continuation of suits when settlements were possible.[46] Second, a major deficiency in the act was its lack of administrative or judicial guidelines for consolidating and managing private attorneys general actions. It was feared that the mechanism would become a vehicle for raising complex scientific, factual, and legal questions that the government and the courts were considered ill equipped to handle. For the same reason the notice requirement was considered too short to allow appropriate officials to review the allegations, investigate, and initiate action.[47] The end result of the adoption of the private attorneys general mechanism was thought to be the harassment of governmental and corporate officials. A loss in the government's control over the allocation of enforcement and administrative resources was seen to loom in the future.[48]

The Senate Public Works Committee viewed private attorneys general action as a "useful instrument for detecting violations and bringing them to the attention of the enforcement agencies and courts alike." [48a] "It is the Committee's intent that enforcement of these control provisions be immediate, that citizens should be unconstrained to bring these actions, and that the courts should not hesitate to consider them."[49] According to Senator Muskie, "the idea is to use citizens to trigger the enforcement mechanism. If the enforcement mechanism does not respond, then the citizen has his right to go to court."[50]

As formulated in the act, an alleged "violation" means only that a boundary defined by statute or administrative regulation has been exceeded.[51] The framers intended the act to be crystal clear concerning what constitutes a violation. Air quality goals, emission standards and limitations, and state implementation plans were intended to serve as manageable and precise benchmarks for developing control strategies and for assigning responsibilities. Based on the latest scientific information and subject to EPA scrutiny and limited judicial review once promulgated, the process of proposing and adopting regulation forms an evidentiary standard for enforcement.[52]

There are a number of reasons for paying attention to definition and review. First, well-defined parameters precluded from judicial review prevent enforcement from becoming a technical matter requiring interpretation by the courts.[53] The role of the courts was to provide procedural safeguards and to impose sentence. Second, in order to maintain the integrity of the statutory time frame and to reduce the uncertainty of control strategies, the framers precluded the judicial review of administrative regulations after the thirty-day period following promulgation.[54] This restriction prevents polluters from attacking the scientific basis of the standards at the time of enforcement and also prevents the substitution of a common law definition of air pollution.

The scrutiny of exogeneous monitors was considered integral to maintaining the statutory time frame in the act. Adherence to the prescriptive time schedule was thought essential for achieving the air quality goals in the act. Even a slight modification of a regulation requires EPA to provide time for comment and possibly public hearings and opens the matter to judicial scrutiny.[55]

Acting as an auxillary enforcer with the capacity to produce concurrent and equivalent impact on a narrowly prescribed set of enforcement actions, the concept of private attorneys general serves a coercive function in much the same was as *qui tam* does.[56] Both firms and governmental units are subject to private attorneys general action. By threatening to focus adverse publicity through the courts on recalcitrant local, state, or federal bureaucrats, the framers looked to private attorneys general as a monitoring mechanism to reduce bureaucratic shirking.

Congress intended the private attorneys general concept to supplement, and in some cases supplant, the administrative functions of EPA.[57] Although the role is descriptively "quasi-administrative," it is performed exogeneously rather than in a ministerial capacity. Unlike litigation instituted by the agency, once a private attorneys general suit is initiated, EPA has no authority over its disposition. The outcomes of private attorneys general action and agency initiation display substantive differences.

The Clean Air Act prevents private attorneys general litigation from giving rise to fines or criminal sanctions. Although the act provides for fines of up to $25,000 per day or imprisonment for not more than one year or both, these penalties are reserved for EPA initiative.[58] Although lacking authority to initiate action leading to criminal penalties, it is possible for such sanctions to be imposed for violating court orders generated from private attorneys general action.

Private attorneys general action does not produce revenue for EPA or the Treasury account into which such fines are channeled. Because court-awarded legal fees come from general Treasury funds, EPA stands to suffer no direct monetary damage from private attorneys general action.[59] The cost to EPA of a private attorneys general suit amounts to an internal reallocation of agency resources. Although some litigation may force EPA to reallocate resources and personnel into "nonpriority" areas, some suits may be welcome. Internal or external sources, such as the Office of Management and Budget or the Justice Department (which is required to represent EPA in court) may make it difficult for EPA to reach decisions.[60] In such instances, private attorney general action shifts the decision-making burden to the judiciary. Similarly, the threat of litigation may force a solution before a case can be initiated or an internal decision can be reached.[61]

The evidentiary standard, the closely circumscribed set of tools and remedies, and the prescriptive right to judicial review indicate congressional intent to establish an action of information. The narrow definition of tools and remedies was intended to prevent quasi-legislative activity by use of the private attorneys general mechanism. This action was also aimed at the courts. Quite plainly, the courts were intended to provide procedural safeguards and to impose sentence. Because private attorneys general action does not give rise to fines, the role of the private enforcer is limited to indentifying violators for judicial or administrative scrutiny. Generating court orders or consent decrees from which penalties could issue was considered integral to the accomplishment of the statutory time frame.

But what incentive motivates private attorneys or citizens to produce the kinds of information required? The nondamage nature of the injunctive or mandamus remedy does not produce monetary judgments from which compensation may be obtained. Enjoining an action or compelling administrative performance is characterized by diffuse benefits and the inability to force payment for spillover benefits. In order to overcome the benefits from free riding, Congress authorized the courts to award reasonable attorney and expert witness fees to "any party whenever the court determines such an award is appropriate."[62]

B. Fee Shifting as a Quality Control Device

Fee shifting in the act was intended to serve as a quality control device. Because it was feared that the private attorneys general mechanism could become a vehicle for bringing "frivolous and harassing" actions, the courts were allowed to tax fees against either party.[63] Although intended to discourage the abuse of private attorneys general action, fee shifting was also permitted to encourage "legitimate" actions.[64] Senator Hart thought that, in the absence of a damage remedy, an individual who brought a private attorneys general action had no incentive other than to protect the health and welfare of those involved and of others similarly situated.

> It will be the rare, rather than the ordinary person, I suspect, who, with no hope of financial gain and the very real prospect of financial loss, will initiate court action under this bill. For the most part, only in the case where there is a crying need for action will action in fact be likely. In such cases, I could argue that action must be in the *public interest*.[65] (Emphasis added.)

Benefits were recognized to accrue to the public "without regard to the outcome of the litigation" in cases that resulted in the successful abatement of the infraction but failed to reach a verdict.[66] Successful and unsuccessful suits were considered to qualify under this criterion.[67]

The reimbursement of legal fees is *de jure* at the discretion of the courts.[68] For this reason the judicial implementation of the incentive structure of the private attorneys general mechanism determines the countenance of the private enforcement in the act and hence will affect policy formation. Fee shifting criteria developed by the courts does not mesh with arguments used for *pro bono* rates.

Approximately ninety separate actions have been brought

under the Clean Air Act. Of these only fifteen actions have been initiated within the private attorneys general framework.[69] Most have concerned the setting of standards or the failure to perform nondiscretionary duties in issuing or revising various regulations. The few suits that were aimed directly at enforcing an emission standard or at a limitation were charged with being premature while the implementation of the act was still in the standards-setting stage.[70] Fees have been sought in five actions. Awards were made in four cases, one of which was later reversed. Several fee petitions are pending.[71]

C. "Public Interest" and Fee Awards at Noncommercial Rates

In *Citizens Association of Georgetown* v. *Washington* the D.C. circuit court ruled that although ultimately unsuccessful, the plaintiff had "benefitted the public interest" by demonstrating the failure of the government of the District of Columbia to implement the act.[72] The court held that the plaintiff had acted in the "public interest" by documenting inaction and delay.[73] A detailed bill of costs amounting to $38,698 was submitted by the plaintiff. Because the two nongovernmental codefendants were found innocent, a pro rata award of $12,899 was made.[74] This award represented $40.00 per lawyer hour. The award was later reversed on other grounds.[75]

In *Citizens for a Better Environment* v. *Train* the court ruled that the plaintiff had "vindicated a congressional purpose which has resulted in the performance of a meaningful duty which otherwise would not have been done."[76] In February 1975 Citizens for a Better Environment sought mandamus requiring the administrator to issue a notice of violation to Cooke County for failing to implement the Illinois Transportation Control Plan.[77] The action resulted in an announcement by the administrator that he had decided "as a matter of discretion" to issue notices of violation against

Cooke Country and Chicago. Citizens for a Better Environment pctitioned the court for an award of $7,098 and received $1,250.[78]

A successful fee petition was entered in *Natural Resources Defense Council* v. *EPA*.[79] The suit was brought under Section 307 of the act. But the first circuit construed that the nature of the suit made it pursuant to a private attorneys general action under Section 304. Although the plaintiff did not win the case, a public service was held to have been rendered because the plaintiff's action led to the "achievement of urgent statutory goals."[81] The court noted that Section 304 permits fee awards "to any party whenever the court determines such award appropriate."[82]

Although ultimately unsuccessful, the court viewed Natural Resource Defense Council's challenges as "mainly constructive and reasonable."[83] Noting that the petitioner had been upheld in several major respects, the court ruled that Natural Resource Defense Council "should not be penalized for having also advanced some points of lesser weight."[84] Although the court acknowledged that the award was at *pro bono* reduced rates, it viewed the award as an encouragement to other "serious" plaintiffs to undertake similar actions. The plaintiff received $7,863 in fees for 346 hours billed and $1,047 in costs.[85] The hourly rate is $22.72.

A fee petition was denied in *Delaware Citizens for Clean Air, Inc.* v. *Stauffer Chemical Company*.[86] The plaintiff charged that its members had suffered damages from sulphur dioxide emissions in excess of allowable concentrations prior to EPA's approval of a one-year variance for Stauffer. The petition was denied on the grounds that the Clean Air Act does not provide a remedy for damage.[87] Delaware Citizens' petition for $10,000 in fees was based on the argument that it had provided a public service in identifying the failure of the administrator to take action. Its petition was denied by the court based on the reasoning that a fee award to a losing party was "reserved for those cases in which . . . the litigation, though ultimately unsuccessful, serves the objectives of the Act in some substantial way. . . ."[88] in this instance a fee award was viewed as unwarranted because the plaintiff's action did not lead to a change in the behavior of either the government or of Stauffer Chemical.[89]

The judicial construction of "public benefit" or "public service" appears incongruous with the arguments for noncommercial or *pro bono* compensation. The criteria for fee shifting — the identification of violators, aid in the achievement of urgent statutory goals, and modification of the behavior of principal polluters and bureaucrats — do not mesh with the arguments advanced by the courts concerning the level of fees.

D. Judicial Arguments for Noncommercial Fees

The first and to this date the largest fee award was made in *Fri* v. *Sierra Club.*[90] The district court of the District of Columbia held that EPA must disapprove any portion of a state plan that fails to prevent "significant deterioration of existing air quality."[91] By a 4–4 tie vote, the Supreme Court affirmed the lower court.[92] In a separate action the Sierra Club petitioned the district court for $100,000 in attorneys' fees and $4,366 in costs.[93] The government succeeded in whittling down the award by 50 percent by challenging the sum charged to billable hours based on the age and experience of the attorneys. The court awarded $48,500 for 980 hours billed. This sum is equivalent to an hourly rate of $49.50.[94] Although the size of the award was said to be significant because it was commensurate with commercial rates, this argument is not compelling.

Pro bono litigants often receive considerably larger fee awards than those in *Sierra Club* and *Citizens of Georgetown.* For example, in a school desegregation case in 1975 the court awarded attorneys' fees of $175,000 for 2,700 hours of time.[95]

This sum amounted to $65.00 per hour. In 1974 the D.C. circuit court awarded $50.000 and a "bonus" of $15,000 in a case concerning the impoundment of federal funds.[96] The plaintiff, the National Council of Community Mental Health Centers, Inc. billed the government for 355 hours and received an average of $190 per hour.[97] In 1974 Western Addition Community Organization received $240 per hour for 841 hours billed by four attorneys.[98] The petition had been for $100 per hour.

In the Natural Resources Defense Council action the court's memorandum referred to the $22.72 hourly rate as a *pro bono* reduced rate.[99] Perhaps the first circuit court provides the most explicit statement of the court's fear of private attorneys general action. The court noted that "(I)n light of the complexity of the case and novel nature of the legal issues presented, we find the requested fees to be reasonable."[100] Because taxpayers' money was involved, however, special considerations were thought to be in order. The private attorneys general concept was thought to create a surrogate attorney for an involuntary client.[101] The institutional structure of the act, it was argued, allowed the imposition of services on "clients" that had never contracted for them. Based on the involuntary client argument, the court reasoned that fee awards should be less than those obtainable from private practice. Commercial rates were viewed as a subsidy that could lead to "needless or excessive" litigation.[102]

In *Citizens Association of Georgetown* the court noted with approval that the plaintiff's fee request was based on an hourly rate of $40.00, which was below the commercial rate in Washington and also below that used by the district court in other cases.[103] It was also noted that the plaintiff had raised legal issues that had not previously been brought before the D.C. circuit court and its case was acknowledged to be both novel and complex. Although the heavy burden of proof incumbent upon the plaintiff was recognized, the court plainly considered the meagerness of the fee petition to be an important factor in its decision.

In *Citizens for a Better Environment* EPA argued that a fee award was not in order because no benefit accrued to the republic by virtue of the plaintiff's action. No order had been issued, and the notice of violation was argued to be a discretionary act. But if an award were to be made, the government argued that it should be small because the pleadings in this case were "practically carbon copies of the pleadings" that Citizens for a Better Environment had filed in other cases dealing with similar situations.[104] The government maintained that "if it awarded anything at all (and it should not), no more than $20.00 an hour was appropriate."[105] The court ruled that the plaintiff had "vindicated a congressional purpose which has resulted in the performance of a meaningful duty which otherwise would not have been done."[106] Apparently, on reasoning set apart from that quoted above, an 80 percent reduction in the fee request was deemed in order.[107] An award of approximately $22.00 per hour was granted.

Judicially ascribed "public interest" characteristics have centered on the information generated, polluter and governmental behavioral modification, and the vindication of urgent public goals. In evaluating results within a public benefit rubric, the courts have been in substantive agreement that the outcome need not be a necessary condition for fee shifting. Fee awards have been made when results were obtained that would not otherwise have been possible without the suits. On the other hand, when setting the rate of recompensations, the reasoning has shifted implicitly toward the involuntary client relationship. The prescriptive limitations placed on the private attorneys general concept renders the involuntary client argument unsupportable. Legislative history clearly states the intent that fee shifting provide an incentive to the exercise of the private right of action by its holder. The involuntary client argument may be forcefully mounted in the case of quasi-legislative activity because in that case the argument is ideological and the plaintiff of necessity becomes non-Hohfeldian.

Part Two focuses on the role of expected appropriable gains and legal costs in litigant calculus. It is shown that discounted benefits, whether received directly as monetary compensation or indirectly, must exceed the cost of litigation before action will be undertaken. The diffuseness of individual gains from private attorneys general action in comparison with the costs of litigation discourages such suits. In the following section fee awards are shown to increase the expected appropriable benefits from performing the private attorneys general role.

PART TWO: PRIVATE ENFORCEMENT OF THE LAW

The objective of Part Two is to show that fee shifting will encourage litigation by increasing expected private gains. This observation becomes an important consideration in the context characterized by diffuse benefits and high litigation costs. Let us look first at a simple two-person model in which the defendant emits smoke that fouls the plaintiff's laundry.[108] A damage remedy is sought. Litigation calculus is a function of P, W, J, and C and is denoted by subscripts p and d for the plaintiff and defendant respectively.

Pp is the plaintiff's subjective probability estimate of prevailing at bar. Similarly, Pd is the defendant's estimate of the plaintiff's chances of winning. (1-Pp) represents the plaintiff's estimate of the probability of losing. Because P is a subjective evaluation made by each party, Pp and Pd need bear no specific relationship to each or sum to unity. Although P incorporates knowledge of outcomes in similar actions and the likelihood of judicial error, it is assumed independent of the judicial resources purchased by each party. In other words, neither party can affect the outcome by purchasing additional legal resources.

W represents the pretrial wealth of each party. It is the litigant's endowment with which he enters the game, and it will affect his strategies. An individual derives utility from wealth according to a function U(W). Utility is assumed to vary directly with W and to have a negative second derivative.

J represents the plaintiff's monetary stake or damages. It is the value of the externality created by the defendant. Also ignored is the effect on J from expected behavioral or technological changes that a decision may dictate. C is litigation expense, including attorneys' fees and various court-related costs. However, C does not reflect the time costs of the litigants. Because these factors will affect wealth at the margin, the calculus is best approached in terms of expected utilities.

At this point let us assume that the parties are risk neutral and that the American Rule is in effect. For the plaintiff the expected utility of going to trial is

$$V_p (W_1, W_2) = P_p U(W_1) + (1 - P_p) U(W_2) \text{ where}$$
$$W_1 = J - C_p \qquad \text{(win)}$$
$$W_2 = -C_p \qquad \text{(loss)}$$

For a win (W^2), the plaintiff receives his monetary stake less his litigation expenses Cp. A loss (W^2) reduces his pretrial wealth by Cp only. In the same fashion the defendant's calculus is guided by the expected utility of litigation as indicated by

$$V_d(W_1, W_2) = P_d U(W_2) + (1 - P_d) U(W_1) \text{ where}$$
$$W_2 = J - C_d \qquad \text{(loss)}$$
$$W_1 = -C_d \qquad \text{(win).}$$

If the defendant wins (W_1), his pretrial wealth is reduced by litigation expenses C_d. On the other hand, a loss (W_2) requires that he transfer J, as well as lose the right to shift these costs (we ignore this effect), and he must again pay C_d.

For both parties the outcome of gaming within the litigation context entails uncertainty. The courts function as a market in which certain kinds of exchanges are allowed. One would expect the parties to make trades as dictated by their self-interests. Out-of-court bargaining inherently provides greater latitude to the litigants. An additional gain is possible by eliminating judicial uncertainty through settlement that involves a transfer of wealth. On the other hand, the predisposition of judges or the general attitudes of the parties toward risk and gaming may make the court the preferred forum.

In the pretrial bargaining context expected utility values represent the bids and the offers of the parties. Adversaries will be expected to go to court when the plaintiff's minimum bid exceeds the defendant's maximum offer. The condition for litigation is

$$\text{(1a)}\quad P_pU(W_1) + (1 - P_p)U(W_2) > P_dU(W_2) + (1-P_d)U(W_1).$$

Similarly, a nonjudicial resolution is possible when the plaintiff's bid is smaller than the defendant's offer, and a settlement will occur when

$$\text{(1b)}\quad P_pU(W_1) + (1-P_p)U(W_2) < P_dU(W_2) + (1-P_d)U(W_1).$$

One may expect the optimism of the parties with respect to P and the size of J to loom importantly. Although the C and S would not be expected to display marked differences for the plaintiff and the defendant, C will be extremely important in the enforcement of *res publica* through private attorneys general actions. Self-interest will ensure that it will occur but only for those rights characterized by a low C relative to appropriable J benefits or if the litigation is attractive from an expected utility standpoint because of P. The enforcement of private rights through tort action provides appropriable benefits, and as a by-product, externalities are created. Among them, information and legal precedents achieve importance as additions to social capital.

Law embodies a general agreement to respect a set of rights of disposition over physical property. The implicit agreement embodies in the law allows the use of the contractual framework as an analytical device.[109] In this setting the invidivuals in a group are assumed to recognize that the uncertainty of interpersonal transactions may be reduced by an agreement among group members to abide by certin modes of behavior. The agreement torecognize property rights represents a trade among members of the group having both public and private good benefits. Such agreements are Pareto-relevant externalities and allow all of the gains from trade to be exhausted. The agreement itself internalizes the externalities.

The private good is the increase in the value of private property resulting from the reduction in the uncertainty of its disposition. Direct private benefits are limited by the extent to which enforcement is actually used. Given the existence of an enforcement system, an individual incurs private costs in seeking compliance or damages when contract default occurs. The willingness to incur the private costs of using the enforcement system generates two types of private benefits. First, there is the direct benefit received from enjoining the actions. Second, and perhaps more important from a long-term perspective, the willingness to enforce contracts reduces the probability of future defaults against that particular enforcer.

To the extent that gains from this type of trade are not fully appropriable, there are spillovers or public goods generated. The public good aspect is the increase in the well-being of the groups resulting from the reduction in resources allocated to the protection of property. Property rights are defined and clarified through legal precedent and case law. The exercise of property rights generates information for use in decision making. By acting as a deterrent, the threat of enforcement in general provides purely joint and nonexcludable benefits for the entity as a whole. To the extent that over time the members of the group recognize that private rights are enforced, even though it is not possible to determine beforehand when enforcement will take place, the threat of enforcement is a pure public good.

The technical attributes of law enforcement make it impossible or inefficient to exclude noncontracting persons from benefits.[110] The collective good as produced is necessarily nonexcludable. According to law, conceived in this public context, that which is produced tends by its nature to be selective, and self-interest will ensure its presence.[111] The ability of enforcers to become readily identifiable through reputation reduces the expected private gain from defaulting against them. To the extent that nonenforcement is perceived by defaulters, the number of defaults will increase. Current enforcement reduces the need for future enforcement if the enforcer is readily identifiable. Similarly, the cost of future enforcement is increased for parties readily identifiable as nonenforcers. However, the fact that private remedies are sought reduces the expected benefits from defaulting within the group. Enforcement is a gain to nonenforcers produced by enforcers for which compensation is not possible.

Specialization may occur because of personal distaste for particular kinds of default or because of comparative advantage in enforcement. Based purely on private benefits, we should expect enforcement as well as specialization among enforcers. But behavior is predictable only when the appropriability of J is sufficient to counterbalance a pessimistic P or a large C factor. The private attorneys general mechanism was designed to protect *res publica,* or those rights characterized by diffuse appropriable benefits. The Cp of expressing environmental concern through litigation and the small J from individual action encourage free riding.

The "publicness", or the joint consumption interaction among the "separate" consumers of the externality, provides the incentive for free riding.[112] Free riding may be present in either the large or the small number setting. The important condition is that the individual feels that he can escape censure for not paying for spillover benefits. The organizational and bargaining costs of forming a cost-sharing group would be expected to be high based on the diffuse benefits characterizing *res publica.* In the absence of "publicness," or institutional prohibitions against joint production, the emergence of voluntary contractual arrangements can be relied on to produce tolerably efficient outcomes.[113]

With the effects of individual action spilling over mainly to others and the inability to censure nonpayers in the large number setting, public goods theory predicts that the private attorneys general externality service will be underfinanced, short-lived, and hence supplied in nonoptimal quantities. In the absence of a coercive financing scheme for providing goods characterized by jointness efficiencies in consumption, rational individuals will be expected to invest less in "negotiating" with polluters or EPA through the courts than is socially optimal. Improvements in environmental quality through private action will be incurred only to the point where marginal private benefits equal marginal private costs.

Fee shifting is an institutional change to decrease the benefits from free riding in the publicness setting characterized by high cost relative to expected appropriable benefits. Let V_i be the gain appropriable by the individual *i* for a successful action of information resulting in a mandate to compel bureaucratic performance.[114] The cost of the private attorneys general service as a collective good is *G,* and there are *n* individuals in the group. Clearly, the joint action makes the group better off when V_i for all individuals in the collective exceeds the group expenditure *G.*

$$(3)\ n\,V_i > G$$

In the small number setting nonpayers may be censured, and i is better able to gauge the viability of a project without his contribution. In this setting, one may expect the project to be undertaken and optimal resources to be allocated to the activity. However, in the publicness context the individual will refrain from joining the collective if *n* is of some dimension so that the large number setting is operative. If this stance is adopted by "enough" individuals, the collective action will not be taken.

Olson has shown that in order for an action to be provided collectively, the condition in equation (4) must be satisfied.[115]

$$(4)\quad \frac{dV_g}{dG} - \frac{dC_i}{dG} > V_i$$

where Vg = group gain

The rate of gain to the group (dV_g/dG) from incremental expenditure must exceed the rate of increase in the individual's cost share (dCi/dG) by some multiple so that Vg exceeds V_i. The individual obtains optimal net benefits from collective action when the condition below is satisfied:

$$(5)\quad \frac{dA_i}{dG} = \frac{dV_i}{dG} - \frac{dC_i}{dG} = 0 \quad \text{where}$$

$$A_i = V_i - C_i$$

since $dV_i/dG = F_i(dV_g/dG)$ where $F_i = V_i/V_g$, it follows that:

$$(6)\quad F_i\left(\frac{dV_g}{dG}\right) - \frac{dC_i}{dG} = 0 \quad \text{and, therefore}$$

$$(7)\quad F_i\left(\frac{dV_g}{dG}\right) = \frac{dC_i}{dG}$$

Equation (4) indicates that the optimal purchase of the collective good by the individual *i* occurs when the product of the rate of gain (dV_g/dG) and V_i, the fraction of gain appropriable by individual *i*, are equal to the rate of change of C_i.

Because $dC_i/dG = 1/n$, it follows from equation (4) that

$$(8)\quad \frac{dV_g}{dG} - \frac{1}{n} > V_i.$$

This implies that the collective action becomes more likley as *n* rises because the cost-sharing arrangement becomes more attractive. However, the diffuseness of the benefits appropriable from the action of information discourages individual participation in the collective action.

Individual *i* will provide the collective good without compensation for the spillovers that he produces if $V_i / V_g > C_i / V_g$. From this it follows that the private provision of the collective good is rational when $V_i > G$. This implies that the collective good will be provided by *i* if C_i is at the optimal point for him and is so small in relation to V_g that the total gain exceeds C_i by as much or more than the V_g exceeds V_i.

Now let us consider fee shifting as a means of increasing the appropriable benefits V_i from the private provision of the private attorneys general service. (A possible alternative that shall not be pursued in this paper would be to decrease C_i.) For the collectively provided good, *i* would pay C_i and appropriate V_i benefits. In order for fee shifting to be effective as an incentive, it must increase expected benefits F_i to exceed G, the group expenditure.

B. Behavioral Implications of Fee Shifting

With indemnity of legal fees to the prevailing litigant the plaintiff's calculus in equation (2) becomes[116]

$$(9)\quad V_p(W_1, W_2) = P_p U(W_1 + C_p) + (1 - P_p) U(W_2 + C_d).$$

Note that for a win (W_1) the plaintiff maintains W_p, his J stake, and receives C_p from the defendant. Unlike litigation under the American Rule, he incurs no litigation expenses. However, for a loss the plaintiff pays C_d as well as C_p.

The defendant's expected value from litigation becomes:

$$(10)\quad V_d(W_1, W_2) = P_d U(W_2 - C_p) + (1 - P_d) U(W_1).$$

With indemnity to the prevailing party, a loss means that the defendant must reimburse the plaintiff's legal expenses in addition to paying for damages and his own expenses. For a win (W_2) the defendant maintains the right to impose costs on the plaintiff and is reimbursed C_d by the plaintiff. His W remains unchanged by litigation.

Again, this can be discussed in terms of bids and offers. If the plaintiff's bid $V_p(W_1, W_2)$ exceeds the defendant's offer $V_d(W_1,W_2)$, litigation will ensue as shown below:

(11) $P_pU(W_1+C_p)+(1-P_p)U(W_2+C_d) > P_dU(W_2-C_p)+(1-P_p)U(W_1)$.

Similarly, a settlement resolves the conflict if the opposite occurs.

(12) $P_pU(W_1+C_p)+(1-P_p)U(W_2+Cd) > P_dU(W_2-C_p)+(1-P_p)U(W_1)$.

The expansion of the Vp term acts to increase the expected returns from litigation. Posner has shown that fee shifting will increase both the variance of expected returns and expected returns from litigation.[117] Introducing risk into the analysis indicates that fee shifting leads to more litigation risk averters as well as preferers.

The importance of the litigant's attitude toward risk is shown in Figure 1.

Although the shape of the utility function will be decisive in litigation calculus, it is obvious that fee shifting increases the range of postlitigation outcomes W. By increasing both the size and the variance of expected utility from litigation, fee shifting will reduce the importance of P in the litigant's calculus.

The importance of fee shifting as an incentive to litigate may also be illustrated in the following way. If we ignore initial W, equation (1a) becomes:

(13) $J(P_p-P_d) > C_p+C_d$

If C_p is assumed equal to C_d, equation (11) becomes

(14) $J(P_p-P_d) > 2[(P_d+1-P_pC]$

The only difference in (13) and (14) is the term Pp+1-P. This also suggests that more litigation will occur with fee shifting than under the American Rule if Pp exceeds P_d. With this

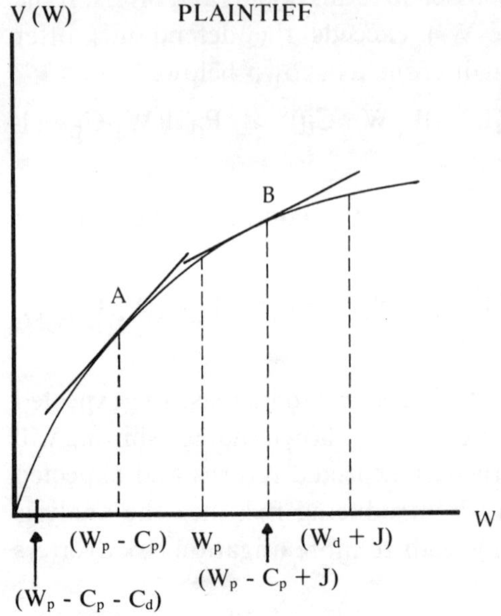

FIGURE 1

American Rule

Loss U′(Wp-Cp) ' 1

Win U′(Wp—Cp+J)

Fee Shifting

Loss U′(Wp-Cp-Cd)

u′ 9wp+J)

where U′ = dU/dW

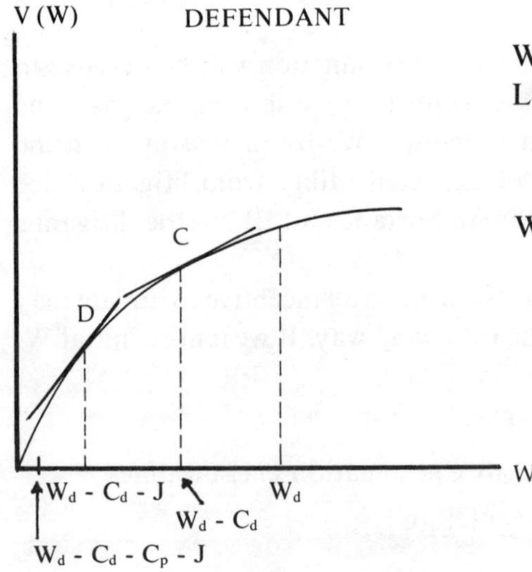

Win U′(Wd-Cd) ' 1

Loss U′(Wd-Cd-J)

Win U′(Wd)

U′(Wd-J-Cd-Cp)

designation the right-hand side of (14) will be smaller than (13).

Part Two has demonstrated the importance of fee shifting as an incentive. By increasing the appropriable gains from performing private attorneys general services, the benefits from free riding may be reduced. Part Three focuses on fee shifting as a determinant of the type of policy formed in the enforcement of the act.

PART THREE: FEE SHIFTING DETERMINES THE COUNTENANCE OF THE ACT

Part Two of this paper assumed that because the Clean Air Act is a majority rule collective decision, the augmentation of its enforcement through private attorneys general actions produces spillover benefits or public goods. However, it is not altogether clear that the impact of private attorneys general action is not equivalent to random enforcement of tort actions. The information generated by bringing the action produces spillover benefits that can be used in decision making by others. Part One and Part Two ignored the normative aspects of private attorneys general action in order to focus on the importance of fee shifting in the performance of private attorneys general action. Part Two demonstrated that the appropriability of benefits from action is the key to undertaking the private attorneys general externality service. The nondamage remedy and the diffuseness of benefits from injunction make fee shifting essential to the performance of the prescriptive enforcement role.

In point of fact there have been very few private attorneys general suits during the first six years of the act. Part Three proceeds under the assumption that fee shifting might have been of inframarginal importance during the implementation phase of the act. In the period in which the legislative framework for enforcement was fleshed out, it is possible that other incentives might have counterbalanced the low expected value of fee awards. Quasi-legislative activity, individual and group advertising, and the building of human capital by young attorneys are advanced as possible explanations for performing the private attorneys general role. Finally, an argument based on the reduction of burdens by the government is advanced as a positive criterion for fee shifting.

The tax treatment of environmental advocates and public interest law firms has had an unqestionable effect on the selection, based on relative costs, of tools for policy input.[118] Performance of the private attorneys general role has become the exclusive domain of publicly subvented environmental advocates. Contributions to these groups are tax deductible for the donor, and subsequent income is exempt from federal income tax.[119] The Natural Resources Defense Council, the Environmental Defense Fund, Friends of the Earth, and the Sierra Club have established reputations for bringing air pollution cases. The Internal Revenue Service's construction of regulations governing these groups has been subject to uncertainty concerning permissible lobbying activities and the acceptability of court-awarded legal fees.[120] However, the IRS has not prevented such groups from using litigation to effect their missions.

"Gray areas" or ambiguities in the act or in agency procedures may provide the basis for private attorneys general action. Quasi-legislative activity may also represent a lower cost method of establishing a rule than going through the traditional legislative channels would constitute. Interstitial gaps are present until the implementation phase of a new law is fleshed out. Consequently, there is greater latitude for private attorneys general action. One would also expect to find areas of input with potentially large impacts in establishing the procedures of a new agency.[121] Although the object of the framers was to ensure enforcement of substantive rules, the incentive may involve looking for areas in which to "make" law.

A danger inherent in quasi-legislative activity is that by definition such changes are not backed by a majority rule collective decision. There is very little difference between case law and statutory law in the sense that their ability to shape results is virtually indistinguishable. It may indeed be argued that interpretive case law that violates legislative intent can be overturned though statutory clarification. But it is not difficult to make a case — based on such factors as the transactional cost of political coalition formation — that the status quo occupies a strongly favored position in collective decision-making processes. Because of inertial considerations bills that engender opposition in the course of legislative passage may be incapable of repeal.

The use of the private attorneys general mechanism as a policy-making tool may serve additional functions. The media publicity surrounding litigation provides valuable advertising for the mission of the advocacy group. Through effective use of the media, environmentalists were probably instrumental in awakening public opinion to environmental issues during the late 1960s and early 1970s. Moreover, the generation of publicity is often an extremely low-cost by-product that is open even to a small local organization that chooses to bring litigation as a means of effectuating its mission. This mobilization of public opinion, analogous to the institutional advertising campaign in the private sector, is probably the most cost-effective tool available to environmentalists.

In a similar light, the private attorneys general mechanism offers an opportunity to avoid institutional proscriptions against advertising by lawyers. Quite obviously, media coverage of cases conveys information to the public concerning the characteristics of lawyers. Such cases may represent an intra-industry device for generating referrals. After all, undertaking a certain amount of *pro bono* cases may be viewed as the "price" of admission to an elite club. Several prominent law firms, such as Arnold and Porter, handle a limited number of cases in this field of litigation.[122] There are forty-four private law firms that concentrate 50 percent or more of their case loads in the public interest field.[123]

Less well established firms would tend to receive the greatest gains from this type of advertising. The Council for Public Interest Law determined that 60 percent of the private attorneys engaged in public interest law earned $20,000 or less per year.[124] Sixteen percent of the lawyers surveyed earned more than $30,000 and only six lawyers earned in excess of $40,000.[125] These sums contrast with the average compensation of private attorneys engaged in "general litigation." In this admittedly broad category the average compensation for an associate was $20,532 in 1975. A partner/shareholder received $63,068.[126] The lower quartiles were $16,250 and $41,500 respectively.

The hourly rate charged to clients by private attorneys engaged in public interest litigation varies substantially and is sometimes as low as $10 per hour.[127] The more typical rates range from $25.00 to $40.00 per hour. By contrast the mean hourly billing rate for lawyers with from two to four years' experience in the Northeast was $41.00.[128] Those having from four to five years' experience averaged $48.00

The opportunity to build human capital in a new law, the novelty of the private attorneys general mechanism, and perhaps shaping the implementation of a new law would be expected to appeal to young attorneys.[129] Recent law school graduates would also be more aware of the possible impact of these new areas. Because the value of their time is low relative to that of more experienced attorneys, we would expect them to respond positively to the private attorneys general mechanism despite its low direct monetary payoffs.

Although non-monetary benefits may be important in the calculus of private attorneys who undertake *pro bono* work, a number of explicit institutional arrangements have emerged for the employment of private attorneys by tax-exempt public interest law firms. Loans, contingency fees, contracts, and grants are frequently used.[130] For example, the Open Space Institute and the Project Environmental Foundation have been willing to underwrite the participation of private attorneys. The rate of subsidy is approximately $15.00 per hour.[131]

Citizen interest groups and public interest law firms constitute a large and growing force in environmental litigation, acting as principal plaintiffs in 24 percent of the 1,145 major environmental cases reported in the period May 1970 to October 1974 and in 45 percent of the 181 cases reported during the last ten months of that period.[132] Approximately one-third of those cases were concentrated among three major national groups, the Environmental Defense Fund, the Natural Resources Defense Council, and the Sierra Club, all of which employ private attorneys in addition to their own staffs.[133]

It has been argued that the primary motivations for private attorneys general action might have been quasi-legislation, the building of human capital by young attorneys, and the advertising of environmental issues by advocacy groups. During the enforcement phase, private attorneys general action will obtain less national publicity because it will be focused primarily on the identification of local violators. Implementation has been marked by a national focus stemming from the scrutiny of EPA actions. From the legislative history it is clear that the mechanism was intended to deter violators by producing information about their actions or inactions.[134] The exogeneous enforcement mechanism was not intended to punish violators by criminal sanction or penalty.[135] Nor was it to be a compensatory damage remedy based on the social cost of a violation as in a nuisance, trespass, or class action.[136] Instead, the objective was to encourage compliance by providing a threat that judicial scrunity and its attendant publicity would be directed at polluters and bureaucrats.[137]

On the basis of differentials in the cost of detecting procedural violations, one would expect EPA to become the principal defendant in private attorneys general suits. Its prominence would be apparent both in the fleshing out of a new law and in defining or clarifying its duties. Failure to perform procedural duties associated with the SIP process or, for example, to classify hazardous pollutants would result in a low cost of detection. In this case failure to publish agency action in the *Federal Register* by a required date provides grounds for action. Because a successful action is not required for fee shifting, one would predict that profit-maximizing private attorneys would select violations that have low detection costs and would file on a large number of them.

However, once the act is defined through statute and administrative regulation, the payoffs from private attorneys general action will be confined primarily to actions against individual polluters. In the enforcement stage the detection of emission violations will be more costly than for procedural noncompliance. Although emissions inventories are nominally public information, trade secret restrictions, coupled with the reluctance to state and local governments to release such information, will make this type of information more difficult to obtain. With the opportunity for quasi-legislative activity circumscribed and publicity limited in most cases to the state and local levels, the performance of the narrowly prescribed private attorneys general role will hinge on the incentives from fee shifting.

Fee awards represent only part of the cost of instituting an action. The act provides that awards may cover fees for lawyers and expert witnessses. For this reason awards cannot be based on the cost of detecting violations nor can they provide recompensation for research undertaken by the plaintiff. The emergence of fee award criteria based on *pro bono* rates during the implementation phase will have serious effects on the incentives for research and investigation in private enforcement suits. If private enforcement is to be effective, the criteria for fee awards must be clarified. In the following section an economic argument is advanced for fee shifting that would provide a means of avoiding emotion-laden terms such as *public interest.*

3B. POSITIVE CRITERION FOR FEE

By approaching the fee award question strictly from the standpoint of modern welfare economics and public finance, a rationale for government awards can be elaborated that is conceptually independent of the ambiguous notion "public benefit" or "in the public interest." Fundamental to this approach is the concept of an activity that produces positive externalities or spillovers to persons other than those carrying on the activity. When private activity provides both a direct private good and also an indirect spillover benefit to others, the collectivity may have an economic interest in stimulating the provision of this quasi-public good. The clearest case arises when the privately-provided good supplants an activity that might otherwise have been provided at government expense. Legislative history argues for the private attorneys general mechanism as a means of reducing the burden of government enforcement. That argument is a sufficient but not a necessary condition for government encouragement of private attorneys general action through institutional changes such as fee shifting and universal standing. It would be overly restrictive to require that the government carry on a similar activity itself, for government intervention, as opposed to private enforcement, may be much less cost effective.

The object of the private attorneys general mechanism is to generate an externality service that decreases EPA's cost of identifying violators and monitors bureaucratic shirking through the threat of judicial mandate. As previously noted, a successful judicial outcome is not decisive in fee awards. Someday we may confront a situation in which a private attorney's general action produces substantial public benefit by virtue of its informational content, but yet the plaintiff is ultimately unsuccessful. In this instance, should the nongovernmental defendant be liable for the fees against the defendant even when substantial aggregate benefits may be possible.

Judicial protection of diffuse right was established in *Eisen* v. *Carlisle and Jacquelin.*[138] In this case the lower court ruled that it was an impossible burden on the plaintif to notify identifiable persons in the class of harmed individuals and ruled that the defendant was required to pay those costs. In its reversal the Supreme Court held that the costs of notice, in the absence of a fiduciary relationship between the parties, had to be borne by the plaintiff with the possibility of reimbursement only if he prevailed in the suit.[139]

In conclusion, the narrowly defined private attorneys' general concept produces an externality service. Because the object is to reduce the burden on the government, the incidence of compensation should be placed on the government.The question of legal entrepreneurship in the Clean Air Act is a collective decision, and the rate of compensation is crucial to the development of the enforcement policy of the act.Treble damages have proved effective in motivating legal entrepreneurs in antitrust action.[140] The experience in this area is indicative of the kind of enforcement zeal that is possible in environmental laws. Penalty splitting is another alternative. Its advantage is that the process of compliance may be controlled by the size of the penalty. Violations invoking large penalties would encourage rapid compliance by firms because of the possibility of private enforcement emanating from exogeneous agents.

Its advantage is that the process of compliance may be controlled by the size of the penalty. Violations invoking large penalties would encourage rapid compliance by firms because of the possibility of private enforcement emanating from exogeneous agents.

The optimal supply of private enforcement as a collective good may be obtained by (1) failing to prosecute some defaulters through random enforcement, or perhaps by (2) creating the impression that overenforcement can be achieved by private enforcers. Of course, it is true that for any enforcement system the greatest potential threat, and hence the largest public good, is obtained when the facility is not used. But without enforcement, there is no deterrent, even though more of the enforcement mechanism is available. Without the assurance that financial consideration will be given to private attorneys who perform the private attorneys general role, the mechanism depends on those who are able to subsidize such activities from other sources of revenue or expect different payoffs.

NOTES

1. See Schellhardt, "U. S. Mulls Enlistment of Private Lawyers to Prosecute High-Level Antitrust Suits" *the Wall Street Journal,* May 2, 1977, p. 19, col. 2; Paul, "Power Play," *the Wall Street Journal,* Jan. 11, 1977, p. 48, col. 1; *the Wall Street Journal,* June 16, 1977, p. 1, col. 5; Schmedel, " SCM's $1.47 Billion Suit against Xerox to go to Trail in Federal Court Monday," *the Wall Street Journal,* June 16, 1977, p. 8, col. 2; *the Wall Street Journal,* March 3, 1977, p. 14, col. 1; and *the Wall Street Journal,* March 17, 1977, p. 14, col. 3.

2. The mechanism is defined at 42 U. S. C. Section 1857h-2. Legislative history is provided in H. R. Rep. no. 91-1196, 91st Cong., 2d Sess., (1970); S. Rep. no. 91-1196, 91st Cong., 2d Sess., (1970); H; R. Rep. no. 91-1783, 91st Cong., 2d Sess. (1970); 116 *Cong. Rec.* 19200 (daily ed., June 10, 1970) and 116 Cong. Rec. 32900, 33072 (daily ed., Sept. 21, 23, 1970).

3. *Qui Tam Actions and the 1899 Refuse Act: Citizen Lawsuits Against Polluters of the Nation's Waterways.* Conservation and Natural

Resources Subcommittee of the Committee on Government Operations, 91st Cong., 2d Sess. (1970).

4. S. Rep. 91-1196, 91st Cong., 2d Sess. 36 (1970).

5. Berger, "Standing to Sue in Public Actions: Is It a Constitutional Requirement?" 78 *Yale L. J.* 816, 824 (1969).

6. 42 U. S. C., Section 1857h-2(a) (2).

7. 42 U. S. C., Section 1857h-2(d).

8. 405 U. S. 727.

9. *Students Challenging Regulatory Agency* v. *U. S., 422 U. S. 289.*

10. Qui Tam Actions and the 1899 Refuse Act, 91st Cong., 2d Sess. 2 (1970).

11. Berger, note 113 (1969).

12. Jaffe, "The Citizen As Litigant in Public Actions: The Non-Hohfeldian or Ideological Plaintiff," 116 *U. Penn. L. Rev.* 1033 (1968).

13. See, for examples, Buchanan and Tullock, *The Calculus of Consent,* III (1965), and Buchanan, *The Demand and Supply of Public Goods,* 96 (1968).

14. *Qui Tam Actions and the 1899 Refuse Act,* 91st Cong., 2d Sess. 11 (1970).

15. See, for example, Niskanen, "The Peculiar Economics of Bureaucracy," *Am. Econ. Rev.* 293 (1968), and Tullock, *The Politics of Bureaucracy* (1965).

16. In *Bass Anglers* v. U. S. Plywood, 324 F. Supp. 302, the court held that the statute provided that a private information had the right to a portion of the statutory fine, that the fine could be imposed only after a criminal conviction, which could only be obtained in a criminal procceding brought by the Department of Justice.

17. Furubotn and Pejovich, "Property Rights and Economic Theory: A Survey of Recent Literature," 10 *J. Econ. Lit.* 1137 (1972).

18. See 6, J. Moore, *Federal Practices,* Section 54.71(2), at 1703, and note 2 (2 ed., 1972); *N. Y. Civ. Prac. Law Section 8101* (McKinny, 1963); Note, "The Allocation of Attorney's Fees after *Mills* v. *Electric Auto Lite Co.,"* 38 *U. Chi. L. Rev.* 316, 324 (1971); Note, "Awarding Attorney and Expert Witness Fees in Environmental Litigation," 58 *Corn. L. Rev.* 1222, 1230 (1973); Kuenzel, "The Attorney's Fee: Why Not a Cost of Litigation?" 49 *Iowa L. Rev.* 75, 78 (1963); Ehrenzweig, "Reimbursement of Counsel Fees and the Great Society," 54 *Calif. L. Rev.* 792, 793 (1966). Dawsons, "Lawyers and Involuntary Clients: Attorney Fees from Funds," 87 *Harv. L. Rev.* 1597 (1974).

19. There are forty-six laws that provide for fee awards.

20. Clean Air Act, 42 U. S. C., Section 1857h-2 (1970); Federal Water Pollution Control Act, 33 U. S. C. 1365 (Supp. II, 1972); Marine Protection Research and Sanctuaries Act of 1972, 42 U. S. C., Section 1415 (g) (1972); of 1974, 33 U. S. C., Section 1515; Safe Drinking Water Act, 42 U. S. C., Section 200j-8; Endangered Species Act of 1973, 16 U. S.

C., Section 1540(g).

21. See for example *Bell* v. School Board, 321 F. 2d. 494 (4th Cir., 1963); *Cato* v. *Parham,* 293 F Supp. 1375 (T. D. Ark.), aff'd, 403 F. 2d 12 (8th Cir., 1968). See Dawson, ":qwyers and Involuntary Clients in Public Interest Litigation," 88 *Harv. L. Rev.* 849, 894 (1975).

22. See, for example, *Bosch* v. *Meeker Coop. Light & Power Ass'n,* 257 Minn. 362, 101 N. W. 2d 423 (1960).

23. *Mills* v. *Electric Auto-Lite Co.,* 396 U. S. 375, 392 (1970).

24. *Newman* v. *Piggie Park Enterprises, Inc.,* 390 U. S. 400, 402 (1968).

25. 42 U. S. C., Section 1857h-2(a).

26. 42 U. S. C., Section 1857h-2(b) (1) (A).

27. 42 U. S. C., Section 1857h-2(c) (1).

28. 42 U. S. C., Section 1857h-2(b) (1) (B).

29. 42 U. S. C., Section 1857h-2(a). S. Rep. 91-1196, 91st Cong., 2d Sess. 36, 37 (1970).

30. See, for example, "Recent Decision," 40 *Brooklyn L. Rev.* 421 (1973); Van Horne, "Citizen Organizations Intervening in Federal Administrative Proceedings: The Lingering Issue of Standing," 51 *Bost. L. Rev.* 403 (1971); Jaffe, "Standing Again," 84 *Harv. L. Rev.* 633 (1971); Davis, "The Liberalized Law of Standing," 37 *U. Chi. L. Rev.* 450 (1970); and Scott, "Standing in the Supreme Court-A Functional Analysis," 86 *Harv. L.Rev.* 645 (1973).

31. "The first, and perhaps the greatest hurdle in a suit with the federal government is the motion to dismiss for lack of jurisdiction. Because the government puts so much of its litigation effort into such motions, he who defeats one may consider himself to have won a major victory. In fact, establishing the right of the citizen to sue to protect the environment by defeating such motions is of the first priority. Precedents in the field are to be sought after." Note, "Project Rulison Brief," 55 *Com. L. Rev.* 761 (1970).

32. U. S. Cobst., Art. III, Section 2. See McCann, "Standing: Who Speaks for the Environment?" 32 *Mont: L. Rev.* 130, 131 (1971).

33. Van Horne, "Citizens Organizations Intervening in Federal Administration Proceedings: The Lingering Issue of Standing," 57 *Boston U. L. Rev.* 403, 411 (1971).

34. Bolbach, "The Courts and the Clean Air Act," 5 *Envir. Rep.* 11, 4 (1974).

35. S; Rep. 91-1196, 91st Cong., 3d Sess. 37 (1970).

36. *Id.*

37. Continuing Senate Debate on S. 4358, September 22, 1970. *A Legislative History of the Clean Air Amendments of 1970.* Congressional Research Service fot the Senate Public Works Committee, January 1974, Serial No. 93-18 at 355, (Statement by Senator Edmund Muskie). Hereinafter the work will be cited *Legislative History.*

38. 42 U. S. C. Section 1857h-2(e). S. Rep. 91-1196, 37 (1970).

39. S. 3575, 91st. Cong., 2d Sess., entered in the *Cong. Rec.* at 33112, September 22, 1970, by Senator Robert P. Griffin. *Legislative History* 375.

40. *Id.,* Section 5.

41. Senator Roman Hruska requested withdrawal of the provision because time did not permit adequate debate. Sen. Debate on S. 4358, Sept. 21, 1970. *Legislative History,* 277.

42. Governor Thomas argent of Massachusetts, speaking on behalf of the National Governor's Conference, endorsed the concept. Ramsay Clark, speaking before the Senate Subcommittee on Energy, Natural Resources, and the Envirinment, cited the need for the creation of such a right. Paul Treush, president of the Federal Bar Association, endorsed Section 304. Jamis Jeans endorsed the provision for the American Trial Lawyers Association on the basis of the "recognation of the value of private enforcement actions in a democratic society." *Legislative History,* 355, 352.

43. Union Carbide; the Automobile Manufacturers Association endorsed the concept for the enforcement of emission standards against stationary sources. It was argued that a two-year lead time was necessary, however, for the automobile industry. *Legislative History* 788, 725.

44. A letter from Standard Oil of Indiana suggested that "the proper solution would be for Congress through its oversight powers to determine the cause of such breakdown." The Automobile Manufacturers Association and Ford Motor Company expressed similar views. *Legislative History* 783, 748, 751.

45. Collier, Channon, Rill, and Edwards, *Legislative History* 727, 732.

46. Senator Roman Hruska, *Legislative History,* 278.

47. Collier, Shannon, Rill, and Edwards, *Legislative History* 727, 731.

48. Manufacturing Chemist Association; letter from James D. Kittleton, Director, Environmental Activities, American Mining Congress, to Richard Grundy, Senate Public Works Committee; Douglas Head, attorney general of Minnesota, endorsed the concept but noted the possibility of the additional cases slowing down efforts to enforce the law. *Legislative History,* 751, 717, 351.

48a. 116 *Cong. Rec.* 33927.

49. Statement by Senator Edmund Muskie, *Legislative History* 280. S. Pep. 91-1196 37 (1970). 116 *Cong. Rec.* 33103.

50. *Legislative History,* 353.

51. S. Rep. 91-1196, 35 (1970).

52. S; Rep. 91-1196, 37 (1970).

53. "Standards provide manageable and precise benchmarks for enforcement." S. Rep. 91-1196, 37 (1970).

54. S. Rep. 91-1196, 40 (1970).

55. *Id.*

56. The notice requirements for filing private attorneys general suits were expected to have the effect of prodding agencies to act. Statement by

Senator Phillip Hart, *Legislative History* 355.

57. "The standards for which enforcement would be sought either under administrative enforcement or through citizen enforcement procedures are the same." S. Rep. 91-1196, 36 (1970).

58. 42 U. S. C., Section 1857c-8(c) (1).

59. Interview with Jerry Ostrov, EPA, Washington, D. C., by telephone, February 18, 1977.

60. Downing and Brady, "A Case Study of Oxidant Control in Los Angeles," *Natural Resources Journal* (1978).

61. In July 1973 EPA instiued an *ad hoc* emergency episode procedure based on predicted hight smog levels. The action was in response to a threatened private attorneys general suit by the Center for Law in the Public Interest in Los Angeles. Downing and Brady, *The Clean Air Act Is Dead,* manuscript under review for publication.

62. 42 U. S. C., Section 1857h-2(d).

63. S; Rep. 91-1196, 37 (1970).

64. Taxing fees against either party". . . should have the effect of discouraging abuse of this provision (Section 304), while at the same time encouraging the quality of the actions that will be brought." S; Rep. 91-1196, 37 (1970).

65. Statement by Senator Phillip Hart, Continuing Senate Debate on S. 4358, September 22, 1970, *Legislative History* 355. See also, S. Rep. 91-1196, 65 (1970).

66. S; Rep. 91-1196, 37 (1970).

67. *Id.*

68. "The court, in issuing any final order in any action brought pursuant to subsection (a) of this section, may award costs of litigation (including reasonable attorney and expert witness fees) to any party, whenever the court determines such award is appropriate." 42 U. S. C., Section 1857h-2(d).

69. *City of Reverside* v. *Ruckelshaus,* 3 ELK 20043; *Sierra Club* v. *Ruckelshaus,* 344 F. Supp. 253, (D. D. C., 1972), aff'd per curiam, 2 ELR 20656 (D. C. Cir., 1972), aff'd by an evenly divided court sub nom *Fri* v. Sierra Club, 412 U. S. 541, 3 ELR 20684 (1973); City of Highland Park v. *Train,* 374 F. Supp. 758, 4 ELR 20677 (N. D. III., 1974), aff'd 519 F. 2d 681, 5 ELR 20408 (7th Cir., 1975); *Olijato Chapter of the Navajo Tribe* v. Train, 515 F. 2d 654, 5 LR 20481 (D; C. Cir., 1975); *West Penn Power* v. *Train,* 378 F. Supp. 941, 4 ELR 20812 (W. D. Pa., 1974), aff'd 522 F. 2d 302, ; *Friends of the Earth* v. *Carey,* 522 F 2d 25; *Friends of the Earth* v. *James J. Lacey, Citizens Association of Georgetown* v. *Wahington,* 370 F. Supp. 1101; *Sierra Club* v. *Hodel,* 5 ELR 20031 (W. D. Wash., Oct. 3, Noq. 15, 1974).

70. *Citizens Ass'n of Georgetown* v. *Washington,* 370 F; Supp. 1101 (D. D. C., Jan. 2, 1974); *Sierra Club* v. *Hodel,* 5 ELR 20031.

71. *Sierra Club* v. *Train.* 7 ER 62 (May 21, 1976); *Sierra Club* v. *Train,*

California Lung Association v. *Train,* -; *Friends of the Earth* v. *PEPCO,* No. 75-747 (7 ER 683, Sept. 3, 1976); *Friends of the Earth* v. D. C. -; *Friends of the Earth* v. *City of Alexandria,* Civ. A. no. 75-715-A; *Friends of the Earth* v. *James J. Lacey,* Civ. A. no. M-75-1394.

72. *Citizens Ass'n of Heorgetown* v. *Washington,* 386 F. Supp. 136 (D. D. C., Sept. 30, 1974), 4 ELR 20860.

73. 4 ELR 20860.

74. *Id.*

75. *Citizens Ass'n of Georgetown* v. *Washington,* 6 ELR 20524.

76. Civ. A. no. 75-1698 (D. D. C., June 9, 1976), 6 ELR 20588.

77. *Id.*

78. *Id.*

79. 484 F. 2d 1331.

80. It should be noted that the Natural Resources Defense Council filed two unsuccessful petitions based on the same argument under Section 307. In Natural Resources Defence Council (512 F. 2d 1351) a petition for $13,000 ($70.00 per lawyer hour) was denied by the D. C. circuit Court. In *Natural Resources Defence Council v. EPA* (6 Elr 29777) the fifth circuit denied a fee petition for $40,000 concerning litigation brought in 1974 and 1975 that contested tall stack provisions in the Georgia Implementation Plan.

81. 3 ELR 20805.

82. S. Rep. 91-1196, 65 (1970). ELR 20805.

83. 3 ELR 20806.

84. *Id.*

85. Interview with Thomas Arnold, Esq., by telephone, February 1977.

86. 4 ELR 20129.

87. 4 ELR 20551.

88. 4 ELR 20553.

89. *Id.*

90. 412 U. S. 541 (1973).

91. *Sierra Club* v. *Ruckelshaus,* 344 F. Supp. 253 (1972).

92. 412 U. S. 541 (1973).

93. Interview with Martin J. Green, Justice Department, by telephone, June 24, 1977. Fee award petitions are filed as separate briefs. In many instances the decisions will not be reported in the federal reporters. For this reason personal interviews with the attorneys involved represent the only means of obtaining information about fee awards.

94. *Id.*

95. *Swann* v. *Charlotte-Mecklenburg Bd. of Ed.,* Civil No. 1974, Order, Feb 14, 1975 (W. D. N. C.).

96. *National Council of Commumity Health Centers, Inc.* v. *Weinberger,* Civil No. 1223 - 73(D. D. C., Dtc. 2, 1974).

97. *Id.*

98. Civil no. C-70-1335, (N. C. Cal., Sept. 19, 1974).

99. 3 ELR 20806.
100. *Id.*
101. *Id.*
102. *Id.*
103. 386 F. Supp. 126 (D. D. C., Sept. 30, 1974).
104. Brief for defendant at 12, *Citizens for a Better Environment* v. *Russell E. Train,* No. 75-c-483.
105. *Id.* at 14.
106. See note, 104 at 14.
107. *Id.*
108. Part Two is based primarily on analytical tools developed in Posner, *Economic Anakysis of the Law,* Chapter 21, (1977), and Gould, "The Econimics of Legal Conflict," 2 *J. Legal Studies* 279 (1973).
109. Buchanan, *The Limits of Liberty Between Anarchy and Leviathan,* Chapter 7 (1965).
110. *Id* at 111.
111. *Id.*
112. Buchnnan, *The Demand and Supply of Public Goods,* 174 (1968).
113. *Id.*
114. See Olson, *The Logic of Collective Action,* Chapter 1 (1965).
115. *Id.* at 28.
116. Posner, *The Economic Analysis of the Law,* 451 (1977).
117. *Id.* at 453.
118. Goetz and Brady, "Environmental Policy Formation and the Tax Treatment of Citizen Interest Groups," 39 *Law and Contemporary Problems* 211 (1976).
119. Treas. Reg. Section 1.501 (c) (3) (1967).
120. See, for example, Goetz and Brady, onte 118 *supra;* Hobbet, "Public Interst Law Firms — To Fee or Not to Fee, 27 *Nat'l Tax J.* 45, 46 (1974); Note, "The Tax-Exempt Status of Public Interst Law Firms," 45 S. Cal. L. Rev. 228, 232 (1972).
121. See Posner, "Economic Analysis of the Law," Chapter 20 (1977).
122. Note, "Public Interst Law," 79 *Yale L. J.* 979 (1970).
123. *Balancing the Scales of Justice: Financing Public Interst Law in America,* Council on Public Interest Law (1976) at 138. Hereinafter cited *Council.*
124. Id.
125. Id.
126. *The 1976 Survey of Law Firm Economics* Altman and Weil, Inc., Management Consultants, Ardmore, Pa. Average *pro bono* hours reported for associates and partner /shareholders were 146 and 148 respectively, at 85. Hereinafter cited *Altman and Weil.*
127. *Council* at 138.
128. Altman and Weil at 148.
129. Tollison and Leibowitz, ::Free Riding, Shirking, And Team

Production in Legal Partnerships," unpublished paper, Law and Economics Center (1977).

130. *Concil* at 139.

131. *Id.* Bruce Terris, the private attorney who brought Sierra Club v. *Ruckelshaus,* was paid $25.00 per hour while the case was in progress. At the time of the fee award, he was reimbursed the difference between that figure and the $50.00 per hour rate granted by the court. Interview with Bruce Terris, Esq., Washington, D. C., by telephone, February 22, 1977.

132. This tabulation is based on the cases reported in 1 ERC (1970) and 6 ERC (1974).

133. *Id.*

134. See note, 49 *supra.*

135. See note, 58 *supra.*

136. See note 38 *supra.*

137. See note 57 *supra.*

138. See Note, "Managing the Large Class Action: *Eisen* v. *Carlisle and Jacquelin,"* 87 *Harv. L. Rev.* 426 (1973).

139. *Id.* at 431.

140. See Landes and Posner, "The Private Enforecement of the Law," 4 *J. Legal Studies* 1 (1975).

Comments on "Fee Shifting: An Institutional Change to Decrease the Benefits from Free Riding"

MICHELLE J. WHITE*

Gordon Brady starts his paper on fee shifting by examining the legislative history of the Clean Air Act of 1970 that established a private attorneys general (PAG) mechanism for litigation in environmental cases. The act provided that any person could bring a civil action on his own behalf against (1) anyone violating emission standards, including the federal government, or (2) the administrator of the Environmental Protection Agency (after sixty days notice) for failure to perform a duty. Some of the concerns of the legislators who shaped the private attorneys general provision were:

1. to provide an alternative and additional means of identifying violators and of enforcing the Clean Air Act through the use of the judicial forum as well as through the administrative process; and
2. to speed the timing of enforcement of environmental regulations and to reduce bureaucratic shirking.

The legislators, particularly Senator Muskie, appeared to be concerned that the Environmental Protection Agency (EPA)

*Associate Professor of Economics, Graduate School of Business, New York University.

was too slow in enforcing environmental legislation and did not enforce its sanctions uniformly against all violators. I find these concerns somewhat ironic coming from the senator. Presumably the EPA could prosecute more cases if Congress gave it more money. Also the delay in enforcement probably stems to some extent from requirements for notice and public hearings. The senator seems to favor slow procedures when they allow citizens and local communities to challenge a proposed highway or a dam but to object to them when they allow firms to challenge EPA's rules.

The legislative history suggests that the PAG provision was intended to increase the resources devoted to the enforcement of environmental legislation by a kind of competitive industry model: the EPA's monopoly on enforcement would be broken by allowing private parties to participate. The fiscal incentives specified in the act are, first, to reduce the requirements for standing; second, to allow the use of the courts before administrative remedies are exhausted; and, third, to provide for fee shifting (although not for damages or criminal sanctions) to private litigants.

Brady presents a conventional analysis of the incentives to litigate along lines developed by Posner.[1] Posner's analysis is geared toward conventional tort actions in which the incentive for bringing suit is the possible payment. Brady discusses the distinction between conventional tort cases and environmental cases in which there are many potential victims, each of whom suffers relatively small damages. He quotes from Mancur Olson[2] on public goods and appropriability but his analysis basically follows Posner's. We learn, not surprisingly, that when fee shifting is permitted, environmental litigation is encouraged. Because Olson's analysis of free riding and collective goods provision suggests that environmental litigation and environmental precedents will be underprovided, Brady concludes that fee shifting is a good thing.

I have no particular qualms about this analysis as far as it goes, but I think that it neglects the most interesting questions. My preferred agenda for research on the subject of PAG actions in the area of environmental law would include three general sets of issues:

First, what are the implications of shifting environmental cases from the administrative to the judicial arena? One important question would be what are the relative cost of pursuing remedies through one forum versus the other? This question is basically empirical. A second question would be what factors are weighted most heavily in each of the two forums? For example an administrative law judge is likely to have more technical expertise than the average (judicial) judge, but the latter may be better equipped to deal with questions of due process and equity. This question raises "lawyerly" issues. Further, how does the timing of the two procedures compare? Senator Muskie is concerned about speedy enforcement and perhaps so should we.

Second, what is the effect of allowing environmental competition between the two arenas? We can ask what types of cases are brought in PAG actions and how they compare with the types of cases that would be brought by the EPA. What are the effects of allowing PAG actions to dictate EPA's agenda? Does the effect of allowing PAG actions increase the enforcement of the Clean Air Act? Or does it merely dilute EPA's enforcement efforts?

Third, to return to fee shifting, an interesting question is why the courts have displayed such resistance to it. Brady documents a long series of PAG actions in which no awards were made or awards were made that were much below commercial rates and even below the usual level prevailing in other areas in which fee shifting is standard practice, such as school desegregation cases. But he provides no explanation for the courts' behavior. Finally, Brady does not consider the effect of fee shifting on incentives for settlement or the relation between the PAG mechanism and class action litigation as alternative means of overcoming the free rider problem. Posner raised both these issues in his book. Also an issue that neither Posner nor Brady raises (but interesting nonetheless) is whether nonprice allocation devices, such as the PAG mechanism, cause excessive resources to be devoted to queuing or being there first. Perhaps we may want to worry (as the senators did) that too many young lawyers may attempt to make their reputations in PAG cases by being the first to file environmental cases. It may drive up the price of divorce.

NOTES

1. Rechard A. Posner, *Economic Analysis of Law* (1977).
2. Mancur Olson, *The Logic of Collective Action* (1965).

The Optimal Size of the Criminal Court System

Eli M. Noam [1]

Court congestion is not a recent phenomenon. It seems that throughout history courts have rarely been able to cope with their case loads; their sorry state was mocked, in different generations, by Goethe and Shakespeare, Dickens and Balzac. Yet despite the long-standing dissatisfaction with the inability of the court system to handle its cases with dispatch, there is little discussion of what the proper size of a court should be in relation to its case load.

How is court size determined? Additional judges are usually appointed when the old ones cannot cope with their case loads. When congestion seems to become intolerable, a few judgeships are added. Some jurisdictions attempt to go beyond such an *ad hoc* approach and have adopted systems that are called, with certain exaggeration, "scientific". Ohio, for example, allocates judgeships by population at the statutory rate of one judge per 30,000 inhabitants.[2] Others allocate judgeships according to cases. Iowa, for example, assigns one judgeship per 450 or 550 "filings."[3] California has refined that system and uses a "weighted" case load system that takes into account the length of a trial.[4] For the federal court system there is no statutory rule, but an unofficial standard exists, endorsed cautiously in a Senate report.[5] Four hundred per judge are used as a threshold indicator of the need for additional judicial manpower within a district.

What these guidelines have in common is their lack of analytical content. They follow essentially a containment strategy: Yesterday's congestion, in retrospect bearable, is to be preserved for tomorrow. The goal is to make the judges' workload manageable by increasing judgeships. Yet there is no reason to believe that the demand for court time is independent of its supply. A speedier access to the courts will affect the litigating behavior of parties to a conflict and the conduct of the proceedings. If the experience of court expansions and managerial reforms is any guide for the future, one should not expect that the supply of court time will match or exceed the demand for it. Many courts will probably be *always* overburdened, which raises a fundamental problem: If there is no obvious end to congestion, how large or how small should one make the court? The real question is not whether one can succeed in preventing congestion by adding some judgeships, but what the right solcial investment in the court system should be. This is a problem that to the best of my knowledge has never been addressed. One reason for that omission is that it was not possible to conceptualize in an operationally useful way the benefits of changes in the courts system.

This paper is an attempt to deal with the question of the optimal size of the criminal court system. To solve the problem, a model of several equations is specified, which is used in analyzing the effects of capacity changes in the court system. The empirical results suggest that, at least in the District of Columbia, the optimal size of the court system is approximately four times its current size. Other results show that the unofficial federal guidelines require far too many additional cases for the creation of new judgeships and that the marginal benefits of an expansion of the court system are considerable.

THE BASIC MODEL

Besides its other functions, a criminal court is concerned with the enforcement of law; its operation will effect crime, either directly or indirectly. How many resources should be spent on this function? Despite society's periodic ardor for law enforcement, it seems unrealistic to expect the courts to be financed without limits, or to the point of minuscule marginal benefits. The operation of the courts is not cost free. From an *economic* point of view, the criminal court system should be financed up to the point where the benefits of additional resources, in terms of their reduction of crime-related losses Z, are not exceeded by their cost B. This occurs where marginal cost is equal to marginal benefits, $dZ/dB=-1$. At that point the sum of crime losses Z and court cost M are at a minimum. Of course, there are other benefits that can be derived from an expansion of the court; an economic analysis can only deal with the lower boundary of optimal court size.

The objective is defined as finding the court size M that fulfills the optimization requirement (1) $dZ/dB=-1$ subject to the following relations:

$$Z = f(C,r,k) \quad (2)$$
$$B = g(M,E) \quad (3)$$
$$C = h(\alpha, W, \beta, P) \quad (4)$$
$$W = \phi(M, \mu, \lambda, V) \quad (5)$$
$$\lambda = \Psi(C) \quad (6)$$

where

Z = total losses caused by crime

B = budget cost of court system

C = reported crime rate

k = loss caused by an average crime

r = adjustment factor for unreported crime

E = cost per judgeship

W = average sentence

μ = average trial capacity per judge per year

α = other factors influencing crime

λ = case fillings per year

β = elasticity coefficient of sentencing effect

V = average jury trial sentence

P = population in jurisdiction

M = number of full-time judgeship equivalents

These equations will now be described in detail. The first two are simple definitions. Let the cost to society be defined as

$$Z = Crk \tag{2}$$

C is the reported crime rate; because many crimes remain unreported, a factor r adjusts for the real crime rate; k is the average loss that is associated with a crime. A marginal benefit to society in terms of impact on crime can then be defined as the negative change dZ; the marginal cost of crime is

$$\frac{dZ}{dC} = rk \tag{2'}$$

Looking at the cost side of the court system, E is defined as the average cost per additional judgeship (including a pro rata share of support staff, overhead, and so on), and M is the number of full-time judgeships or their part-time equivalents. The marginal effect of an increase in the budget B on available judgeships M is then

$$\frac{dM}{dB} = \frac{1}{E} \tag{3}$$

The next equation, $C = h(\alpha, W, \beta)$, refers to the relationship between the reported crime rate C, sentencing severity W, and other factors. There are many determinative factors that go into C and explain a given crime rate; poverty and unemployment are two examples. One can also assume that there is at least *some* effect of the risk element, that is, the expected magnitude and probability of punishment for committing a crime. The concept of deterrence is controversial, but for "crimes of property" (as opposed to "crimes of passion") its existence does not appear implausible. A professional burglar, on the margin, may well reduce his activity level if its riskiness increases. To express this effect, let β be defined as the elasticity of the crime rate with respect to sentencing severity W so that.

$$\frac{C}{P} = \alpha W^{\beta} \tag{4'}$$

This relationship expresses per capita crime C/P as a function of sentence severity W; other factors that influence crime are included in the α and are assumed to be given exogenously. The marginal effect of changes in sentencing is then

$$\frac{dC}{dW} = \alpha \beta W^{\beta-1} P \tag{4''}$$

A further equation asserts a relationship between the average sentence W and the state of court congestion: $W = (M, \mu, \lambda, V)$. It is difficult to conceptualize the impact of increased court capacity, and this problem has prevented the analysis of court size. Most criminal courts in urban areas are heavily congested, and therefore only a small fraction of all cases can be tried. The remaining cases must be disposed of either by dismissal or by inducing the defendant to plead guilty. Such a plea will be offered by a defendant in return for a reward: a promise of a reduced sentence compared with what he could expect to receive after a trial. This process, known as plea bargaining, has become by far the major form of case disposition. The average reward that is necessary to induce defendants to plead guilty can be considered the price paid by the prosecutor. This price will tend to be related to the relative quantity of guilty pleas that is demanded, just as other prices are usually associated with some quantities. In other words, if the prosecutor needs more guilty pleas to reduce the case load, he will have to offer, on the average, better terms. It is now hypothesized, and later empirically verified, that there is a direct relation between the degree of congestion of a court system and the substantial sentence "discount" that is given for pleading guilty. The degree of congestion can be expressed as the ratio of court trial capacity $M\mu$ and the rate of case flow λ. The entire functional relationship can be expressed as follows: The average effective sentence W, including trial and plea bargain sentences, is related to average trial sentence V according to

$$W = b\frac{M\mu}{\lambda} V \qquad (5')$$

where b is a coefficient.

The existence of this relationship is confirmed in the empirical part of the paper. If it is true, then the impact of a change in court capacity on sentencing is expressed as the derivative

$$\frac{dW}{dM} = \frac{b\mu}{\lambda} V \qquad (5'')$$

Finally, the case flow is constant. This assumption will be relaxed shortly.

It is now possible to put all of these elements together and solve for the optimization criterion

$$\frac{dZ}{dB} = -1.$$

By the chain rule it is

$$\frac{dZ}{dB} = \frac{dM}{dB} \cdot \frac{dW}{dB} \cdot \frac{dC}{dW} \cdot \frac{dZ}{dC} \qquad (3)$$

and, from before

$$\frac{dM}{dB} = \frac{1}{E}$$

$$\frac{dW}{dM} = \frac{b\,\mu}{\lambda}\ V \qquad (5'')$$

$$\frac{dC}{dW} = P\alpha\beta W^{\beta\text{-}1} = P\alpha\beta\ (\frac{bM\,\mu}{\lambda}\ V\ )^{\beta\text{-}1} \qquad (4'')$$

$$\frac{dZ}{dC} = rk \qquad (2')$$

so that

$$\frac{dZ}{dB} = \frac{rkP\alpha\beta}{E}\ (\frac{b\mu\ V}{\lambda})^{\beta}\ M^{\beta\text{-}1} \qquad (7)$$

Solving this equation for the M that fulfills the condition

$$\frac{dZ}{dB} = \text{-}1$$

one obtains as the optimal M

$$M^* = (\frac{\text{-}rkP\alpha\beta}{E})^{1/1\text{-}\beta} \quad (\frac{b\mu V}{\lambda})^{\beta/1\text{-}\beta} \qquad (7')$$

This equation expresses the optimal court size M* when the case inflow is given.

SIMULTANEOUS EQUATIONS MODEL

The previous model assumed that the total number of criminal cases filed, λ, is constant. This assumption will now be relaxed. The number of criminal cases can be expected to have a functional relationship to crime

$$\lambda = f(C).$$

This relation can be linear, such as

$$\lambda = tC \tag{6'}$$

or exponential, as in

$$\lambda = \delta C^{\gamma} \tag{6''}$$

The introduction of this new element change the model into a system of simultaneous equations; court size is a function of crime, and crime is also a function of the court size, namely,

$$M = g(C)$$
$$C = h(M)$$

To solve this system is again a question of finding an optimal court size so that

$$\frac{dZ}{dB} = -1$$

let

$$Z = f(C)$$
$$B = g(M)$$
$$C = h(W)$$
$$W = \phi\,(M,\lambda)$$
$$\lambda = \psi\,(C)$$

Then

$$dZ = f'dC \tag{2*}$$
$$dB = g'dM \tag{3*}$$
$$dC = h'dW \tag{4*}$$
$$dW = \phi_1 dM + \phi_2 d\lambda \tag{5*}$$
$$d\lambda = \psi' dC \tag{6*}$$

Substituting from (6*) into (5*)

$$dW = \phi_1 dM + \phi_2 \psi' dC \tag{8*}$$

and (4*) into (8*)

$$dW = \phi_1\, dM + \phi_2 \psi' h' dW$$

Therefore

$$dW = \frac{\phi_1}{1-\phi_2\psi'h'}\, dM$$

and, from (3*)

$$dW = \frac{\phi'}{g'(1-\phi'\,\psi'h')}\, dB \tag{9*}$$

Similarly, from (2*), (3*), and (9*)

$$dZ = \frac{f'h'\phi_1}{g'(1-\phi_2\,\psi'h')}\, dB \tag{10}$$

Substituting the partials, one has

$$\frac{dZ}{dB} = \frac{rk \cdot \alpha\beta PW^{\beta-1}\,\frac{b\,\mu V}{\lambda}}{E\,(1-\frac{-bM\,\mu V}{\lambda^2}\,t\,\alpha\,\beta\,PW^{\beta-1})} = -1 \tag{10'}$$

Substituting $\lambda = tC$, $W = \frac{bM\,\mu\,V}{\lambda}$, and defining $a = \frac{b\,\mu V}{t}$, this becomes

$$\frac{dZ}{dB} = \frac{rk\;\alpha\beta P\,(\frac{a}{C})\;M^{\beta-1}}{E\,(1+(\frac{a}{C}M)^{\beta}\,\frac{\alpha\,\beta\,P}{C})} = -1$$

so that

$$\frac{rk}{E} + \frac{M}{C} + \frac{M^{\beta-1}\;(\frac{b\,\mu\,V}{t\,C})^{-\beta}}{\alpha\,\beta\,P} = 0 \tag{10''}$$

The solution for equation (10″) is an expression for the optimal court size M**.

EMPIRICAL RESULTS

Results can now be obtained by finding and substituting the appropriate parameters. The following section attempts to solve equations (7′) and (10″) and some further relationships. The jurisdiction that is investigated is the District of Columbia; the crimes considered are five of the seven FBI index crimes. (Murder and forcible rape are omitted because of their special nature and because of their small number relative to total crime; they do not lend themselves to an elasticity-based analysis. Court capacity for these cases must be based on different considerations.)

The parameter r is the adjustment factors for unreported crime. The share of unreported crime in Washington was estimated from a recent victimization survey of 9,541 households, 18,353 residents, and 1,528 businesses.[6] The weighted average of actual index crime as a proportion of reported index crime is r = 1.87.

k is the direct economic loss to society caused by an average felony. Its estimation presents some conceptual and practical problems. The figures used are those found by a presidential commission.[7] The weighted average for the five index crimes, in terms of 1978 dollars, is k = $331.

E, the cost of a judgeship, was calculated by the Administrative Office of U.S. Courts as E = $196,000.[8]

β, the determinants of the crime rates, are from an estimation by I. Ehrlich.[9] The weighted average elasticity is β = -.65, and α = .83366.

From census figures, P= 763956.

t, the ration of cases λ to the crime rate C, has been, on the average during the past five years, t = .067.[10]

λ , the felony case inflow, is for 1976 λ = 3737.[11]

μ is the average trial capacity per judge per year. The average number of trials per judge for the federal court system was forty-seven in 1972.[12] Because this figure includes civil cases, proper consideration of the respective time averages[13] results in an estimated criminal trial capacity of $\mu = 59$ per judgeship per year.

The existence of the relationship

$$\frac{W}{V} = \frac{bM\mu}{\lambda} \tag{5'}$$

was confirmed by estimating a regression across federal district courts with a heavy criminal case load.[14] The equation used was

$$\frac{W}{V} = b\frac{M\mu}{\lambda} + aS.$$ [15]

Values for W (average sentence for trial and guilty plea disposition) and for V (average sentence for trial disposition) were obtained from data of the Administrative Office of the United States Courts.[16] These records contain all federal criminal cases for the year 1973. Data for the court case load and trial capacity are also from the Administrative Office of the United States Courts.[17] Details of the estimation are described in a different paper.[18]

The results show the strong explanatory power of the hypothesis with $R^2 = .9824$; the coefficient that is found is $b = 2.15$ at a significance level of 95 percent.

The remaining parameters are as follows:

The reported index felony crime rate for the District of Columbia in 1975 was $C = 55{,}158$.[19] The weighted average trial sentence V for the available years 1967–1971 is $V = 81.2$.[20]

After determining these parameters, we can calculate the optimal court size. Substituting, we find as results for

$$M^* = \left(\frac{rk\,\alpha\,\beta P}{E}\right)^{1/1-\beta} \left(\frac{b\,\mu\,V}{\lambda}\right)^{\beta/1-\beta} \tag{7'}$$

the optimal court size as $M^* = 51.83$.

When allowance is made for the impact of the changing crime rate on the case load, we have, from equation (10″)

$$\frac{rk}{E} + \frac{M}{c} + \frac{M^{1-\beta}\left(\frac{b\mu V}{tc}\right)^{-\beta}}{\alpha\beta P} = 0 \qquad (10''\,')$$

and the optimal court size is $M^{**} = 61.2$.

It is interesting to contrast these results with the actual number of criminal judgeships. In 1976 a total of forty-four trial level judgeships existed in Washington[21] to handle criminal as well as civil, family, juvenile, small claims, and other cases. It is not easy, in the absence of better data, to identify the fraction of time attributable to criminal cases. Forty percent of all cases in the court system were criminal.[22] Assuming generously that trials are allocated in a similar proportion and considering that civil cases take, on the average, somewhat longer,[23] criminal case capacity is comprised of roughly the equivalent of M = 15.6 full-time judgeships.

As can be seen, the calculated optimal size of the court is about three times as large as the actual size. This result suggests that a serious underinvestment in the court system exists.

FURTHER FINDINGS

The suboptimal capacity of the criminal courts can also be observed by looking at the marginal benefit of investment in the present court. Since

$$\frac{dZ}{dB} = \frac{rkP\alpha\beta}{E}\left[\frac{b\mu V}{\lambda}\right]^{\beta} M^{\beta-1}$$

the benefit of the marginal dollar spent is

$$\frac{dZ}{dB} = \$9.06$$

This is a very high-return of nine dollars of benefits for one dollar of investment in the criminal court system.

It is also interesting to express the optimal numbers of judgeships as a function of the crime rate, so that, for example, court needs can be anticipated from a projected crime rate. From equations (7′) and (6′)

$$M^* = f(C) = \left[\frac{rkP\alpha\beta}{E}\right]^{1/1-\beta} \left[\frac{b\,\mu\,V}{t}\right]^{\beta/1-\beta} C^{-\beta/1-\beta}$$

which solves fairly exactly into the simple relationship

$$M^* = .7C^{.4}$$

The marginal requirement for judgeships is $\frac{dM^*}{dC} = .286^{-.6}$. For the present crime rate C this becomes $\frac{dM^*}{dC} = .0004$, or one additional full-time *criminal* judgeship for an increase of 4.5 percent in crime rate.

Other interesting results can be found by differentiating optimal court size M* with respect to other variables. For example, if the "efficiency" of judges increases, the optimal court capacity will change according to

$$\frac{\partial M^*}{\partial \mu} = \left(\frac{rkP\alpha\beta}{E}\right)^{1/1-\beta} \left(\frac{bV}{\lambda}\right)^{\beta/1-\beta} \left(\frac{\beta}{1-\beta}\right)\mu^{\left(\frac{2\beta-1}{1-\beta}\right)} = -.3816$$

Therefore, an increase of one case per year per criminal trial judgeship equivalent will reduce required optimal resources by nearly $75,000.

If the cost per judgeship increases, optimal court capacity is reduced according to

$$\frac{\partial M^*}{\partial E} = \left(\frac{-b\mu V}{\lambda}\right)^{\beta/1-\beta} (rkP\alpha\beta)^{1/1-\beta} \left(\frac{-1}{1-\beta}\right) E^{\left(\frac{\beta-2}{\beta-1}\right)} = -.00038.$$

Finally, an increase in the case load should lead to a change of the court size according to

$$\frac{\partial M^*}{\partial \lambda} = \left(\frac{-rkP\alpha\beta}{E}\right)^{1/1-\beta} (b\,\mu V)^{\beta/1-\beta} \left(\frac{\beta}{1-\beta}\right) \lambda^{\left(\frac{-1}{1-\beta}\right)} = .006.$$

This results in one additional judgeship for each 164 additional criminal cases, a figure that may be contrasted with the much higher current unofficial standard of 400 cases per new judgeship in the federal court system.[24]

SUMMARY

This paper is an attempt to determine the resource requirements of the court system. In contrast to the usual *ad hoc* approach of calculating the required number of judgeships on the basis of current court overload, this analysis tries to find an optimal level of the social investment in the court system. A seven-equation model is defined. It traces the effect of additional court capacity and permits a new way of analyzing costs and benefits in the courts. Optimal court size can then be expressed as a function of several factors, such as the crime rate, the case load, the cost of a judgeship and its capacity to try cases, economic losses caused by crime, the effects of sentences, and so on. These equations can be applied to analyze the resource needs of most jurisdictions.

The empirical part of the paper concentrates on the District of Columbia. Optimal criminal court capacity is found to be about three times its present size. For the relationship of optimal court size to the crime rate, the result is given by the simple relation $M = .7C^{.4}$. The model suggests that there should be an additional criminal judgeship for evey 164 additional cases per year, as contrasted with the present unofficial guideline of 400 in the federal system. The need for additional judgeships is also suggested by the high marginal benefits that are found in the courts. An additional dollar spent of expanding the criminal court results in at least nine dollars worth of crime reduction — a cost-benefit ratio that is impressive in an absolute sense and considerably higher than the one usually found for the police.

The benefits of the criminai court that were investigated were those associated with crime reduction. There are other benefits to be gained from court expansion, for example, improvements in the speed and quality of the disposition of justice.

Thus the magnitudes found in this paper represent only a lower boundary. Where values beyond efficiency are considered, the optimal size of the court will be even larger.

NOTES

1. Special thanks go to James E. McCafferty of the Administrative Office of U. S. Courts. Advice by Martin Feldstein and research assistance by Scott Alvarez are gratefully acknowledged. All responsibility remains with the author.

2. Ohio Rev. Code Ann. 1907.041.

3. Iowa Code, 604.8 (1971).

4. Arthur Young and Co., *Judicial Weighted Case Load System Project,* Final Report, prepared for the Judicial Council of California, 1977.

5. U. S. Senate, Committee on the Judiciary, Report 95-117, Omnibus Judgeship Bill, 95th Congress, 1st Session, March 28, 1977, p.10. The Committee was helped by a sophisticated forecast of cases for each district. See Battelle Pacific Northwest Laboratories, *District Court Case load Forecasting.* October 1975: Executive Summary Federal Judicial Center 75-7, and four volumes.

6. U.S. Department of Justice, LEAA, National Criminal Justice Information Service; *Criminal Surveys in Washington, D.C.. A National Crime Survey Report,* No. SD-NCS-C-19, July 1977, Tables 40-74.

7. President's, Commission on Law Enforcement and the Administration of Justice. *Assessment Task Force Report,* p. 42. Values for aggravated assault were extrapolated using the Wolfgang-Sellin Index.

8. U.S. Senate, Committee on the Judiciary, Omnibus Judgeship Bill, *Report* 9S-117, p. 53. May 3, 1977.

9. I. Ehrlich, "The Deterrent Effect of Criminal Law Enforcement," *Journal of Legal Studies* 1, (1972): 259. Found by substitution of demographic variable for Washington, D.C.

10. Using data by the Administrative Office of U. S. Courts, *Offenders in the Federal Courts,* and the FBI, *Uniform Crime Reports.*

11. District of Columbia, *1976 Annual Report of the District of Columbia Courts,* p. 49.

12. U. S. Senate, Committee on the Judiciary, *op. cit.,* p. 9.

13. Federal Judicial Center, *The 1969-1970 Federal District Court Time Study,* p. 45.

14. Defined as those courts with 300 or more criminal trials per year; the Middle District of Florida was omitted because of problems with its data.

15. S is a dummy variable for southern courts, because of regional variation.

16. Administrative Office of U.S. Courts, James A. McCafferty, Chief, Statistical Analysis and Reports Branch. Part of the computation of the data was done at the Criminal Justice Research Center in Albany.

17. Administrative Office of U.S. Courts, *Management Statistics for U.S. Courts,* 1973.

18. E. Noam, Court Congestion and Plea Bargaining, Discussion Paper, Columbia University, Graduate School of Business, 1978.

19. District of Columbia, Criminal Division, Clerk's Office, communication.

20. From weighted average sentences for the District of Columbia; tables supplied by the Administrative Office of U.S. Courts, Norma Stern.

21. District of Columbia, *1976 Annual Report of the District of Columbia Courts,* p. 33.

22. *Ibid.,* p. 45.

23. Federal Judicial Center, *op. cit.,* p. 45.

24. U.S. Senate, Committee on the Judiciary, *op. cit.,* p. 9.

REFERENCES

Administrative Office of the U. S. Courts. *Judicial Work load Statistics, July-December 1976.*

Batelle Pacific Northwest Laboratories, Forecasts of Case Filing Volumes in the Federal District Courts. A Research Report for the Federal Judicial Center, 1975. Executive Summary and four volumes.

Federal Judicial Center. *Priorities in the Handling of Litigation in the U. S. District Courts,* April 1976.

The 1969-1970 Federal District Court Time Study, June 1971.

Robert W. Gillespie, "Measuring the Demand for Court Services: A Critique of the Federal District Courts Case Weights," *Journal of the American Statistical Association* (Applications *Section*), March 1974, volume 69, pp. 38-43.

Jerry Goldman, *Measuring a Rate of Appeal,* Federal Judicial Center, March 1973.

J. Woodford Howard, Jr. *The Flow of Litigation in the U.S. Courts of Appeals for the 2nd, 5th, and DC Circuits,* Federal Judicial Center, 1976.

Judicial Council of California, *Annual Report of the Administrative Office of California Courts,* 1974.

James A. McCafferty, "Statistical Measurements Used by the Administrative Office of the Unived Stated Courts," *American Statistical Association Proceedings,* 1965 (Social Statistics Section', pp. 14-28.

Federal Judicial Center, North American Rockwell Information Systems Company, *A Management and System Survey of the U. S. Courts; An Overview Study of the Five Court of Appeals and the District Courts, October 1969.*

Christopher A. Manning , *Judgeships Criteria: Standards for Evaluating the Need for Additional Judgeships,* American Judicature Society, Research Study, 1973.

U. S. Department of Justice, LEAA, National Criminal Justice Information and Statistics Service, *Criminal Victimization Surveys in Washington, D.C.,* 1977.

U. S. Senate, Committee on the Judiciary of Congress, *Omnibus Judgeship Bill,* Report to Accompany S11, March 1977. Also *Report,* September 24, 1975.

Charles Vagner, *Study of the Disposition Time of Civil Cases in the U. S. District Court for the Northern District of Illinois,* Federal Judicial Center, Washington, D. C., 1971.

A. Young and Company, *Judicial Weighted Case Load System Project,* Final Report Prepared for the Judicial Council of California, 1974

Comments on "The Optimal Size of the Criminal Court System"

MALCOLM GALATIN*

Professor Noam's formulation is essentially of the following kind: Z is total losses caused by crime, B is the budget cost of the court system, hence, the total cost caused by crime is

$$\text{(i)}\quad TC = Z+B\ .$$

Then, given that Z and B are functions of M, the number of judgeships, the problem is to determine what value of M minimizes TC. Differentiating (i) with respect to M, and setting this differential equal to zero, the first order condition for a minimum of TC is

$$\text{(ii)}\quad \frac{dZ}{dM} + \frac{dB}{dM} = 0$$

that is, $dZ/dB = -1$. Of course, intervening variables make Noam's analysis somewhat more complex.

My comments on some points in Noam's paper are as follows:

(a) Noam's measures of costs are strictly in money terms. No attempt is made to measure the variables in utility terms or to use utility (distributional) weights. Thus $100 of property loss by a poor family is given exactly the same weight as $100 of

*Dept. of Economics. The City College of The City University of New York.

property loss by a wealthy family, or \$100 of taxes paid by a wealthy family to finance the court system.

Imagine that U_1 is the average (and marginal) utility of \$1 lost by a victim of crime, and U_2 is the average (and marginal) utility of \$1 to the payer of taxes financing the court system. Let $U_1 \neq U_2$. Then

$$\text{(iii)}\quad TC = U_1Z + U_2B$$

and the condition for TC minimization now becomes

$$\text{(iv)}\quad U_1 \frac{dZ}{dM} + U_2 \frac{dB}{dM} = 0$$

that is, $(U_1/U_2)\dfrac{dZ}{dM} = -1.$

This formulation will alter the results, derived by Noam, for the optimal size of the court system.

(b) The measure Z employed by Noam is "total losses due to crime," and k is its average measure. Both of these variables measure only the direct economic loss to society as a result of criminal activity. Noam makes no attempt to measure, or to incorporate into his analysis the indirect costs associated with crime: bolts, bars, locks, security guards, alarm systems, and so on. Surely, in order to offer policy conclusions about the optimal size of the criminal court system, the indirect costs of crime somehow have to be included in the analysis.

Also, something should be said about Noam's exclusion of murder and forcible rape in the empirical part of his paper. Those crimes were omitted by Noam "because of their small number relative to total crime." However, the *costs* of those crimes may be very large, and their omission may seriously bias the results of the paper.

(c) Noam's analysis proceeds in a strictly static framework, that is, his cost minimization procedure is in terms of a single period. However, the analysis of crime would seem to demand an intertermporal or dynamic analysis: As laymen, the most strident question involving crime that we hear is how the handling of criminals today will affect their behavior (and the behavior of others) tomorrow. How will the certainty and the severity of sentences for crimes committed today affect the nature of crime committed tomorrow? There is no way of answering this question by Noam's analysis — the optimal court size from a strict single period analysis may differ substantially from the optimal court size in a fuller, dynamic, analysis. For example, fewer judgeships may save on costs today but give rise to more criminal activity tomorrow.

Hence, a more detailed attempt to establish the optimal size of the criminal court system would have to consider the intertemporal costs of the court system and of criminal activity. Further, the costs of other elements of the criminal justice system, for example, police, prosecutors, and their effect on crime, would have to be incorporated into a more complete analysis.

Rent Seeking

Gordon Tullock*

Rent seeking is a comparatively new subject, and its relevance to the law may not be immediately apparent. As a matter of fact, the amount of rent seeking in any society is greatly influenced by the complexity of the laws and the degree to which administrative actions are depended on for government activity. Thus a society that has relatively simple legal codes and nothing in the way of administrative discretion would have very little rent seeking.[1] The point of this paper is to discuss in some detail the cost of elaborate law codes and elaborate administrative structures, subjects that normally have been ignored.

Rent seeking is a relatively new term, and many may not be familiar with it. I shall begin by explaining the term and its application.

I have just sold one house and bought another. The transaction was completed very quickly, taking less than seventy-two hours; and during that time the realtor who managed both of these transactions spent something under four hours talking to me, to the person who bought my old house, and showing us around. For this rather short period of time, he collected commissions totaling about $5,000. If we regard this as a return on the time that he spent on this specific transaction, it represents $1,250 an hour, which gives him an hourly rate well ahead of the president of General Motors.

Obviously, this is not the proper way to explain his income. In addition to the actual sales effort, he has many other expenses. He maintains a well equipped office, complete with a radio beeper that makes it possible for him to be reached anywhere within fifteen miles of Blacksburg. He is very well informed about the local real estate market; indeed, it was this very fine information — together with his ability to discern people's needs for housing from rather brief conversations — that led to the extreme speed with which this transaction was completed. There are also advertising costs, time involved in creating the impression on his clients of great efficiency and helpfulness (he has given me a good deal of assistance since the transaction was completed), and simple "waiting" time involved in his business.

If we consider all of these factors, it is doubtful that he makes an excessively high return on his investments. Note, however, that the bulk of his costs occur before and are not directly related to any given individual transaction. He invests over a long period of time in acquiring information, specialized abilities to deal with clients, and a good reputation; the payoff comes in the form of relatively rare but lucrative commission payments.

To take one (probably fairly small) example, I have seen him and his partner selling to farmers, a group of hippies, and to university professors. They must maintain a sizable wardrobe in the office to change clothes between these various activities because they certainly look like farmers, college professors, and hippies at the appropriate time. This investment is perfectly normal, and I presume that all of us would agree that the realtor is probably earning only a normal return on these resources, counting his personal talents among them.

There is, however, one more preliminary investment in the sale of real estate that I have not mentioned: It is necessary for him to take an examination before he can become a realtor at all. Although the subjects covered in the examination are not irrelevant to his business, they are not so closely connected that the resources that he invests in studying for the examination can be said to have a direct return at the same rate as those shown above. He earns a return on his complicated wardrobe by using it continuously. He earns a return on the resources that he invested in passing the examination because the existence of the examination means that the real estate business is not quite as competitive as it otherwise would be.[2] Hence his income is slightly higher.

For the purposes of this paper, I am going to call income derived from *this* kind of resource investment a *rent,* and *rent seeking* is the effort to obtain such income. Thus an individual who invests in something that will not actually improve his productivity or will improve it less than would other investments but does raise his income because it gives him some special position or monopoly power is rent seeking, and the rent is the income derived from the search. Note that this is different from the normal economic meaning of rent seeking but not so radically different that we must seek a new word.

Let us now turn to a somewhat similar situation. In Imperial China the highest status and wealth positions, other than those of the Imperial Family, were occupied by high officials in the bureaucracy. Entrance into the bureaucracy was by way of a very difficult competitive examination. Its difficulty can be gleaned from the fact that only about 100 people a year in China passed. Further, of those who passed the examination, only a minority — those who finished very near the top — had much chance of high government office.

The returns to those people who *did* rise to high positions by becoming a grand secretary, a viceroy, and so on, were very great indeed. The Imperial government did not believe in saving money on the compensation of its high-level executives, although a good deal of this compensation came in the form of fees for specific services rather than as salaries.

These returns were not only high by the standards of the world at that time, they were high by the standards of China. There was substantially no other occupation in China that could lead to anywhere near the same amount of income, power, and prestige possessed by the high official. It is fairly certain that Chinese of equivalent talent could have been hired at lower salaries if some other method had existed for determining their suitability.

As a result of this institution, there were immense investments of resources all over China in preparation for the examinations. The examinations had a bad press because they contained sections on poetry and good handwriting. Nevertheless, to a considerable extent they were devoted to the kinds of problems that could affect governmental performance. An understanding of hydraulic engineering, a critical view of history, and knowledge of the basic philosophy that was supposed to guide the Chinese government were clearly important in passing the examination.

The return was to a large extent a return on talents and work that had been invested long before individuals became public officials. Further, there was an immense gamble involved. The number of people who spent a great deal of time and energy in preparation for the examination was a very high multiple of those who finally reached the top rank. Of those who did invest large amounts of time in an attempt to pass the examinations, the overwhelming majority was eliminated in the first stage, which meant that they actually got no return at all on their educational effort, except insofar as there might have been a direct consumption return. The remainder, although they received some return from their investment, received a relatively small return, except for those few who became very high-ranking officials.[3]

Presumably, the individuals who invested resources in the preparation (or, more commonly, in the preparation of their children) for the examination invested these resources only to the point where the marginal expected return matched that on other possible resource investments. In practice, it was like a lottery in which a large number of people buy tickets and only a few win. Of course, in this case the winners were not selected by luck — or at least not primarily by luck. There is, I take it, little doubt that the people who passed the examination with high scores were in fact genuises. But when the formal education of a child who was preparing for the examination began, no one could tell whether he was going to pass; hence the initial investment was made under conditions of stochastic risk.

The situation, looked at economically, is unusual. Individuals were entering into a high-risk activity and investing resources in a way that discounted both the probability of failure and the extremely high rate of return if success were achieved. Nevertheless, it is hard to avoid the impression that the system was economically wasteful. The education given to the students preparing for the exam was of little or no use in any walk of life other than government. Further, most of the people who passed the examination and received minor government jobs made only rather modest use of their highly intensive and expensive educational backgrounds. It was not necessary that a Hsien magistrate at the bottom of the official system be learned in Chinese philosophy and history and be well into what psychologists would call the "genius" category. In the old days of the British Empire, the district commissioners who held somewhat similar jobs were selected essentially for personality traits rather than for learning and high intelligence. They seem to have done about as good a job as the Chinese Hsien magistrates.

Even at higher levels, it is not obvious that China gained a great deal from the extremely high qualifications of its senior officials. They might have invested the bulk of their superior knowledge and intelligence in maneuvers and intrigue rather than in improving governmental efficiency. Nevertheless, most visitors to China before about 1800, when the system was functioning well, admired it.

It will be seen that this system raised the same problems that modern education does with respect to the capital investment-screening problem. It is not clear whether the examination impelled people to acquire valuable capital or simply screened out the inherently brightest people. Probably it did both. In any event, it is clear that the majority of the people who participated in the process did not gain from it, regardless of its social effect. They entered into a gambling game, and they lost.

Looked at from the standpoint of individual parties, it is not clear whether this game is a positive-sum, zero-sum, or negative-sum game. Indeed, I am preparing another, somewhat mathematical paper in which I make a preliminary investigation of the theory of the nature of this game. To anticipate that argument and to put simply what is really quite a complicated line of reasoning, the game can be positive, zero-sum, or negative-sum from the individual's standpoint, depending on certain parameters. Unfortunately, the empirical work necessary to determine the real-world parameters has not been done and will be extremely difficult.

From the social standpoint, however, it is clear that this was a negative-sum game. Assuming, as I think we can assume, that the very large amount of learning undertaken by the candidates for the examination was partially screening and partially capital investment, the capital investment failed for those people who did not complete the examination. It is clear that the total social cost must have been much greater than the social benefit, regardless of the rationality or irrationality of the individual resource investment.

The problem is that the individual invests resources in a form in which they cannot readily be transferrable to other uses. If, for example, the Imperial Chinese government had sold government positions at auction, it would have obtained quite a different type of candidate; but the funds invested would have been useful for something else. When the individual candidate invested the same amount of resources in learning to write Tang dynasty poetry of a somewhat stuffy nature, it was just as rational from his standpoint; but society lost those resources, except insofar as having one more producer of rather stuffy Tang dynasty poetry might have had a positive value.[4]

Thus there was a straightforward waste of resources that would not have occured if the investment had taken the form of paying a fee that might have been used. The same reasoning applies if it is invested in some resource — human or otherwise — that pays a positive and a continuing return at whatever is the existing marginal rate of interest. A student who had invested a great deal of time and effort in preparing for the Imperial examination and failed had invested a great deal of resources and produced no personal or social gain. Similarly, those very numerous people in India, Kenya, and so on, who go to the local equivalent of a university and then remain "unemployed" while they maneuver for government jobs for many years are making large investments that may yield no return at all. The situation resembles the potlatches of the Pacific Northwest, in which prestige and power were obtained by destroying valuable objects. The one who destroyed the most in the way of valuable products "won" the game and increased his prestige and influence.[5]

The situation can be contrasted with the custom of buying government jobs for cash, a custom common on the Continent until recently. The French government is a particularly good example. Most of the jobs held by French civil servants under the old regime were obtained by purchase. It should be emphasized that it was not true that anyone could purchase a job. It was true that after one had purchased a job, he was subject to a good deal of control and supervision (mainly by people who had purchased supervisory jobs); but the fact remains that the job seeker had to put up a large sum of money for the job. This money was regarded as ordinary government income and was spent accordingly. Once again, the person who bought the right to collect a particular tax in Orleans made an investment in much the same way that a restaurant proprietor does. In this case, although he created no capital assets, the money he paid was at least used for government expenditures, such as extending Versailles.

Another outstanding example of a somewhat similar institution was the officer corps of the British Army prior to about 1860. Almost all of the officers of the rank of colonel or below had purchased their commissions and then purchased their promotions. They were compelled to spend time in each rank (at least one day), but they could buy a lieutenant's commission, spend a day as a lieutenant, sell that commission, buy a captain's commission, and so on. Many wealthy men who wanted to be colonels went through precisely that process. Generals, however, were not appointed through that method.

It is a notable fact that although this system was criticized very widely, there does not seem to be any evidence that it worked badly. The British Army undeniably had the best infantry in Europe. Further, it was noted for its very long record of military success. Essentially, these "purchasing" officers appear to have been superb trainers and leaders of men. Why this was so, I do not know.

Turning to the French example, although many people criticized the *ancient regime,* the fact remains that during the 200-year period before the French Revolution (the period in which this system operated), France was generally considered the most powerful and progressive state on the Continent. Certainly it would be hard to argue that its government was worse than others of the same time.

William Niskanen has offered an argument for this kind of government, an argument that is not intended to be conclusive but does have some interest. If you bought an office and later were found guilty of bad performance, you could be removed from the office and the purchase price would *not* be refunded. Thus, in essence, every individual posted a large bond for good performance. Bad performance led to forfeiture of the bond, but good performance meant that he could eventually sell the job to someone else — like a British Army officer's commission — leave it to his heirs, or, as a third possibility, it would terminate with his death. In the latter case, of course, the price paid for the office was actuarially discounted for the life span of the individual who was to hold it. Further, in the latter case the amount forfeited in case of bad behavior fell progressively as the incumbent aged.

Thus we have several different kinds of "investment" that will produce rent. In the first, an ordinary capitalist investment is made with the objective of obtaining rent in the future. Granted that there is a speculative element; it is quite possible that the rent will not be obtained. However, real assets are created by the investment, and therefore society is better off — although perhaps not as well off as it would have been had the investment been successful. The second type is the case in which the rent is obtained by purchasing the right to collect it, as in the case of the young man who purchased the job of lieutenant in the Light Brigade in 1853. In this case no social assets were produced, but at least there was no waste because the payment went to someone who gained from it. It is a pure transfer operation.

People who object to the second kind of rent seeking characteristically object only if the income source that is purchased is some kind of government employment. If I purchase an income stream by buying government bonds, they do not object. But if I buy the right to be a customs inspector, they do. The objection to my purchase of the right to be a customs inspector is apparently based on two distinct arguments. The first is that the person who can afford to buy the job may not be the best qualified person for it. In a perfect capital market, of course, this would not be true; but capital markets are not perfect, and the Fourteenth Amendment makes them especially imperfect in the United States.

Leaving this argument aside, the second objection is that the individual will use his job to repay himself for his "investment" and obtain gains if he can. Whether this is an objection depends entirely upon the type of supervision that the individual faces. If the supervision is adequate so that he maximizes his return by efficient service, then the argument cannot stand. Presumably, in most cases the performance is not *that* well supervised. Nevertheless, it is not obvious that supervision in such cases would be worse than supervision exercised over people who obtained jobs in other ways. Hence it is not obvious that this system would lead to poorer performances that those produced by other systems. The question of good or bad performance depends on rewards and penalties that are administered during the course of the job, not on how the job was obtained.[6] If supervision is known to be good, one would anticipate that the amount bid for the job, or the rent of the job, would be lower than if supervision of the job were bad and it was possible to steal.

Our final case, and the one to which this paper is primarily devoted, concerns obtaining a rent by competition in what we may call a potlatch — in wasting resources. This situation obtains when a job is given to one of a group of people, all of whom have invested a great many resources in seeking the job, none of which can be used for any other purpose. There is, therefore, a loss to society on those resources that are invested by the unsuccessful job seekers and a good deal of loss on those resources invested by the successful job seekers as well if the resource investment does not improve their efficiency in the jobs that they have obtained.

As we shall see below, the "rent-seeking economy" leads to further waste, but let us temporarily consider only this one particular waste — the waste of resources used in obtaining employment. Anne Krueger looked into the issue of the returns to those engaged in organizing foreign exchange regulations in India and Turkey. She showed that the gain obtained by those people was about 7 percent of the GNP in one case and about 15 percent in the other.[7] If we assume that the people who obtained those jobs were not simply selected at random — that they had maneuvered for the jobs — and that the people maneuvering for each customs inspectorship invested resources that totaled about the current value of that inspectorship, this would mean that a capital value, perhaps 70–150 percent of GNP, had been dissipated in obtaining those jobs.

Note that the fact that individual customs inspectors may be compelled to kick back to their superiors does not change this conclusion. Superiors had to maneuver for their jobs, and their superiors. . . . What happens is that a very large number of resources is transferred from the productive sector to an activity that pays off for the individual participant but does not increase the consumer surplus for other citizens. Indeed, looking at my own experience in Asia, it seems to me that this cost is one of the basic reasons for Asia's backwardness. Asian countries have been doing this for a very long time.

It should be noted in this connection that Kreuger's numbers apply to only one aspect of the centralized economic control maintained in both India and Turkey. When we consider that there is very much more in the way of such rent-seeking activity, it is clear that the economic waste must be extremely high.

So far in discussing our formal models, we have been discussing what we could call a mature system of government rent seeking, one that has been in existence a long time, with the result that resources have adjusted to their long-run best use. In practice, probably most rent-seeking economies in the world today generate many large incomes that are windfalls rather than the results of investment.[8]

This windfall income arises because many of these

governments are newly established, and it seems very doubtful that anyone anticipated that these large gains would become available at the time that the young intellectual first turned his attention to political matters. For example, presumably many of the district commissioners in Ghana actually made quite modest investments in political maneuvering in the British colonial period, and then, when the Nkrumah dictatorship was established, they found themselves in very high-paying jobs. In general, this situation characterized the former colonial world. The previous colonial governments were not completely free of bribery, corruption, and so on, but there was less than has developed since then. Furthermore, the people who collected those payments are now gone, and the new holders of sinecures (in the technical sense of the word) generally got them much more easily than their successors will.

In another context, we may contrast the career of Thomas Corcoran (Tommy the Cork) with that of a present-day graduate of Harvard Law School who is considering entrance into the Washington legal business. It seems dubious that Corcoran, when he was going though law school, or even when, in the early Depression years, he was recommended for a job in Washington by one of his former professors, thought seriously about a permanent career in negotiations with government agencies, most of which did not even exist at that time. He got in early, however, and through great natural talents, application, and good connections became an extremely wealthy man.

The present-day lawyer coming out of Harvard has thought about a career in Washington for a long time. He works to get into Harvard Law School (which in Corcoran's day was fairly easy), and then he quite deliberately takes a job in Washington at comparatively low pay for the purpose of developing the appropriate capital. Furthermore, because he faces much competition in Washington, it is very unlikely that he will be able to achieve the kind of position that Corcoran achieved so easily.

This is not an example of rent seeking but of rent avoidance (to be discussed below); however, the time structure is the same as in many existing governments in which rent seeking is important. The resource cost of the high income of the present district commissioner in Ghana did not occur at the time he was maneuvering for the position because in those days it was a relatively low-cost operation. It occurs now because many citizens in Ghana, observing his success and large income, are devoting themselves to the attempt to get such jobs in the future.

We shall consider a few additional costs of the rent-seeking economy. Note that these costs will depend to a considerable extent on the assumption that the rent is obtained by soliciting bribes for the performance or the nonperformance of duties. I think that this is normal in most of the countries that we think of as rent seeking, although when I turn to American applications, this particular problem will be relatively small.

Suppose that an individual wants to start a factory in Ghana. First, he must obtain the necessary customs license to import his equipment. The license may or may not involve foreign exchange controls as well, depending on whether the applicant is a foreigner who is making a commitment in Ghana or is someone who is using funds that have been generated in Ghana at some time in the past. Once the equipment is in the country, he must move it to the investment site and begin construction. This action will involve him with a set of officials who are not the same administrators who approved the entry of the equipment. Furthermore, the district commissioner in the area where he is establishing his plant will assume continuing jurisdiction over it, and hence he must be pacified.

Other officials may also be involved. There may be lawsuits, in which case if they do not go to the district commissioners' courts, the regular judge will be involved. The use of public utilities may require special side payments, and so on.

The problem with these very large series of payments is that they are not coordinated. The fee to the government that would maximize government revenue would be a single fee on the whole transaction. The fee to the customs inspector that will maximize his revenue, plus the fee to whoever arranges transportation, plus the fee to the district commissioner, and so on, will probably amount to much more than would the revenue-maximizing fee paid to the government as a whole. The reason for this discrepancy can be derived from the usual rule that when there are a number of stages in production and a monopoly exists on each one, the output (unless all monopolies can reach an agreement) is apt to be low and the monopoly payments per unit are likely to be high.

Such a monopoly situation usually characterizes this kind of government activity. The result is that the total fees are markedly larger than those that would optimize the revenue of the government, even assuming the government had no other objective. In consequence, the investments that are made pay very high fees, but a great many investments that would be desirable are not made at all.

One may ask why the government itself does not aim at mazimixing its income and deal with this matter by extablishing a single payment. The explanation appears to be mostly simple inefficiency, in that the government does not realize the extent of the payments involved; but in part it is characteristic of the use of illegal payment. These illegal payments are, almost of necessity, not recorded, and therefore no one knows what the total is. Furthermore, it is not necessarily obvious to a high-level official whether some particular delay that he observes at a lower level is genuinely technical (as his inferior tells him) or reflects an effort to hold out for additional payments.

Inefficiency is complicated by the fact that normally all of the different agencies dealt with by a person who is attempting to establish a new factory are not even parts of the same ministry; hence coordination is very difficult. The result is a series of payments that are markedly higher than would be desirable, even if we assume that the government's sole objective is to maximize its own revenue. The rate of growth, living standards, and so on are markedly lower than they would be if a purely exploitative but efficient government were in charge of matters.

I have discussed rent seeking in terms of establishing a new manufacturing enterprise, but it is obvious that it fits many other situations. Simply living in a rent-seeking country may involve fairly high payments. This is particularly true if the person who is living in the country has a higher-than-average living standard. The officials are apt to follow a policy that Ludwig von Mises called egalitarianism, but I think should be described as private egalitarianism. They do not attempt to equalize incomes throughout society, for that would involve a reduction in their own incomes, but they do tend to equalize incomes in the private sector. It seems likely that the reason is not a desire for equality, although the officials may well rationalize it in that sense, but simply that this is the easiest way to collect their fees.

Plucking $10,000 from a wealthy man is much easier than plucking $100 apiece from 100 poor men. Thus people who operate in the private sector face what amounts to a very highly graduated income tax, one that may effectively penalize productive labor much more severely than does the type of progressive income tax with which we are familiar in Western countries. The wealthy man whose assets are relatively immobile and hard to conceal (for example, the builder of a steel plant) is an obvious target, whereas a wealthy man whose wealth was transferred to Switzerland, who lives moderately while he is in Ghana, and who spends large amounts only when he is elsewhere, is much harder to tax. Thus the system not only penalizes progress by lowering the incentives for hard work, intelligent investment, and so on, but in particular it penalizes those kinds of activities that tend to produce conspicuous assets.

This situation prevailed for many generations throughout China. One particular example may be informative. The first major all-Chinese steel mill was built in the 1930s in a well-chosen spot north of the Yangtze River. Coal, iron ore, and limestone were accessible, and there was good transportation available. The management largely consisted of foreign-trained engineers, who, I think we can agree, were technically competent.

The steel mill was driven into bankruptcy and eventually closed down. The primary cause was a particular and rather peculiar equalizing activity on the part of local officials. Individual workers stole pieces of iron and steel from the plant, taking about 10 pounds home every evening. Local officials took the view that because the plant owners were wealthy and the workers were poor, they should not complain about small losses. From the standpoint of the individual worker, of course, the amount that he stole was indeed very small, and there was no reason why he should minimize the theft; but the sum total was more than the plant could afford to lose. Thus this highly important industrial installation was eliminated.

There is another and very large cost imposed by the rent-seeking society of the kind that we are discussing. This cost is becoming important in the United States, too, although I think that the previous costs that I have mentioned are not yet significant. Let me begin by telling a story about Korea. In the years after the Korean War, President Rhee drove around the streets of Seoul in an old Packard that had originally been shipped to Korea as the personal car of the American ambassador; it was sold when the American ambassador got a newer car. The most important single businessman in Korea visited the United States and returned to Korea not by airplane or by passenger ship, but on a freighter. The freighter docked at Inchon, about twenty miles from Seoul, and there were on the deck of the freighter two Buicks, one green and one blue. Also in the hold of the freighter there were large quantities of various things that the businessman wanted to bring into Korea. When he arrived at Inchon, the customs inspectors promptly informed him that substantially everything that he had with him could not be imported legally. They expected payments, of course.

The businessman was a very good businessman. He had planned for this contingency in advance. There was no reason why *he* could not land, and he went from the ship directly to the Kyung Mu Dai (the Korean White House). There he told President Rhee that because he was concerned that the president of Korea was driving around in an old car, he had brought back a Buick for the president. In fact, he said that he had brought back two Buicks so that the preisdent could choose between them; he would use whichever one the president did not want. President Rhee was pleased and asked where the Buicks were. The businessman said, "Well, all of my personal effects are currently being held up in Customs in Inchon, but if you would like to see them immediately, I'm sure that you can arrange to get them released. "President Rhee accordingly ordered that the businessman's personal luggage, including large items, be released. The businessman arrived the following day at Kyung Mu Dai with two Buicks, and President Rhee chose the blue one.

Note that this very ingenious operation resulted in the businessman getting a very large amount of material into Korea for the payment of only about $5,000 or $6,000. If he had negotiated with the individual customs inspectors, the cost would have been on the order of $75,000 to $100,000. This incident illustrates what I call rent-avoidance activity, and it is a major source of inefficiency in rent-seeking economies.

In these societies a major cost, and a cost that varies a good deal from enterprise to enterprise, is government interference.

In most of the rent-seeking societies government officials want bribes, but in the United States the government makes specific administrative rules. Minimizing the cost of these bribes or regulations is a major activity ot higher management and indeed may become the *sole* activity. Some friends of mine who were visiting a factory on the outskirts of Seoul began their visit by talking to the president of the company. They asked, in the course of conversation, whether his equipment was mainly Japanese (which would have seemed likely, granted the product that he was making) or imported from Europe. He replied that it was mostly imported from Europe. They went to visit the plant and discovered that almost every machine was in fact Japanese.

This issue is unimportant in substance; there was no reason why the plant should have one kind of machinery rather than another, although it was true that the visit occured during Rhee's tenure as president, and President Rhee was anti-Japanese. The impressive fact, however, is that the president of the company did not know enough about his own capital stock to know where it had originated. He could not have engaged in a deliberate lie because he knew that the visitors were going to go look at the machinery. He had to have spoken from ignorance.

This lack of knowledge does not imply in any sense that he was inefficient. He had been devoting his time and attention to the area in which he enjoyed the highest comparative advantage and that generated the highest payoff — greasing the wheels of government. He was asked a question about what was, from his standpoint, a minor aspect of the company (production), and he answered to the best of his ability, which was not very high. He left production decisions to inferiors, who probably did at least a moderately good job, just as most American corporate presidents pay very little attention to the janitorial staff in their factories.

The activity to which the Korean corporate president

devoted himself is what I call rent avoidance. He was atempting to minimize the total rents that would be imposed on his company by the payment of bribes solicited by higher officials and/or unfortunate administrative decisions. The job is a difficult one. From the cost-benefit standpoint, is it better to invite the provincial governor to an elaborated dinner with *kisang* girls than to make a direct payment to the local magistrate? Perhaps the corporate president should visit the capital and spend several months there in general socializing.[9]

Many of these decisions are long-term investments. The careful cultivation over a period of years of individual officials develops human capital in the form of friendly relations that can be used. In the American context, Tommy the Cork, Clark Clifford, and Abe Fortas are all examples of people whose main stock-in-trade is this kind of connection.

No doubt such people are invaluable to their companies or, their branches of government if a government enterprise is involved. In a socialist economy a person who has good contacts in the planning bureau is probably of more use to his enterprise than is a good engineer. Probably also his personal income is a good deal higher than that of a good engineer.

Although it is efficient from the standpoint of individual enterprises, the problem of cost avoidance relates to the fact that it involves a tremendous waste from the standpoint of the society as a whole. Large resources of human capacity are diverted to the rent-seeking part of the government and to rent-avoiding activity in the private sector. In a way, the two activities tend to cancel each other and produce no net social gain. In rent-seeking societies — such as traditional (or Communist) China, Korea, India, and so on, — those activities are in a real sense the major sources of income and wealth. In a way, there exists a vast negative-sum game in which people with high natural talents who are willing to work hard can get very large returns without generating any social benefit at all.

This activity illustrates a very old point in economics. Competition is not always a good thing. In a well-organized market individuals who aim solely at benefiting themselves end up benefiting other people. In a badly organized market, and the market I am now describing is an example, they simply generate waste. Further, in most rent-seeking societies the sum of the activities of the rent seekers and the specialists in rent avoidence is not zero-sum. They do not merely waste their own talents; in the course of their maneuvering, they impose costs on the rest of society that retard development.

The provincial governor who promulgates a new regulation with the intent of increasing the number of fees that he gets for permitting people to avoid it not only increases his own income and the potential income of the specialists in rent avoidance, but he also imposes a real burden on society in that the regulation, in at least some areas, will be enforced. Further, as a result of concentrating on this kind of activity, he might have been distracted from such necessary functions of government as maintaining public order. He may not be supervising his junior officials, with the result that the kind of multiple exactions that I have described above occurs. One would expect poverty from this system, and if we turn to those places where it is dominant, that is what we see.

If we examine the United States and most modern European countries, we find relatively little direct solicitation and payment of bribes on the part of government officials. Note that I say relatively little, not zero. I should also add that in my opinion the amount is increasing; unless changes are made, it will become quite a large amount in a generation or so. Thus in a direct sense the phenomenon of rent seeking does not exist.

In a indirect sense rent seeking does exist to some extent, and bureaucrats tend to be paid a good deal more than is actually necessary for the performance of their services, although the very highest officials are normally paid less than would be needed to attract people capable of managing these immense organizations. The conflict between fairly high pay for the lower officials and fairly low pay for the higher officials may be one of the reasons why in most Western countries the lower level bureaucracy tends not to be controlled from the top. For the salaries that are offered to the upper administrators, people who have the ability necessary to control such a large apparatus cannot be attracted.[10]

Bureaucrats and other government officials, if they do not do very much in the way of soliciting bribes, do in fact issue a very large number of regulations and laws that have direct effects on many businessmen. Further, the administration of these laws is invariably subject to a good deal of discretion. The highest level of discretion of this sort is in fact exercised not by what we think of as bureaucrats but by an older bureaucracy, this is, the courts. Judges are far more likely to make decisions on their own, without being deeply bound by the law, than are regular bureaucrats. This mode of decision making is concealed from view to some extent by the fact that judge's decision is defined as the law. We seldom notice how little a decision is controlled by the law that existed before he pronounced it.

Leaving this matter aside, what we observe is the development of very large-scale rent-avoidance activities. The DuPont Corporation was headed for many generations by chemical engineers. In the early days, these engineers were members of the DuPont family. But after two generations of being headed by a president who had married the daughter of the previous president, rather than a DuPont, the company slipped into the control of people who were not members of the family. It is notable that the current president, Mr. Shapiro, is not a chemical engineer but an attorney who is a specialist on public relations and government influence. I do not wish to criticize DuPont for this decision, which I think was very sensible, and I certainly do not wish to criticize Shapiro, who I think, is extremely competent, intelligent, and well-motivated. However, I do criticize the social order that made it necessary for this company to switch to manipulation as the criterion for selecting its chief executive. Surely our medicines, plastics, and so on, will be poorer than they would have been had the company continued to concentrate on essentially technological matters.

Note that all of these developments reflect a sharp change in emphasis, not an absolute change in the nature of the world. Businessmen engage in a good deal of rent seeking and rent avoidance, too, but it is a relatively minor factor. As a bachelor, I usually spend Christmas with my sister and brother-in-law. About nine years ago my brother-in-law went to a small town in Iowa to take over the management of a very small company that had been founded by his father. It had been operated until that time by a very pleasant man who was essentially a salesman who had little interest in the formal details of management.

I well remember his first Christmas in Iowa and the deluge of expensive gifts that my brother-in-law received from the suppliers of various raw materials used by the company. My brother-in-law was intensely interested in the quality and the price of the products that he bought and less interested in personal relations with the companies that generated them. As a result, although the company purchases something like ten times as many raw materials as it purchased nine years ago he gets Christmas cards instead of expensive presents.

It is apparent that the sales vice-presidents of the various companies with which he deals made the same kinds of calculations to which I have been referring in my discussion of rent avoidance. When my brother-in-law replaced his predecessor, the relative cost-benefit calculations of an expensive gift changed compared to the very slight reduction in price. Therefore, these vice-presidents switched their approaches. This kind of behavior is a characteristic of the market. Salesmen, like the one from whom I bought my house, do cultivate the personal arts that characterize the rent-avoidance expert in a rent-seeking economy. There is a payoff, to it, but it is relatively modest payoff this particular kind of personality and type of activity yield a reasonable but not a gigantic return.

As we move to more and more government activity, however, and as government activity becomes more and more a matter that various individual officials can change at their discretion, we move to higher and higher investments in rent avoidance on the part of private individuals and companies. This activity is not inefficient from their standpoints. They are indeed behaving in an appropriate manner. From the standpoint of society as a whole, however, this activity represents almost total waste. Today the small company of which my brother-in-law is president invests a fair amount of executive time in worrying about, and in some cases attempting to influence, government regulations. When he assumed direction of the company this activity was pursued on a very small scale. Now it is quite significant. Surely this use of time means (a) that the executive staff is larger than it was before, and (b) that the executive staff devotes less attention to problems of production, product design, and distribution. The economy as a whole is less efficient, even though the adjustment by this little company to reality is an efficient one.

When I went into the diplomatic service, a classmate from the University of Chicago Law School entered at the same time. I ran into him again about twenty years later. Like myself, he had left the diplomatic service, but in his case he had gone into writing novels and rent avoidance. He was vice-president of the Bank of America in Washington, although the Bank of America at that time had no branches east of the Mississippi. His job, which left him enough leisure so that he could write novels, involved serving on several government commissions, representing some of the international banking organizations that had headquarters in Washington, and, of course, developing friends. He was also very interested in public relations activities and apparently approved almost all press releases issued by the Bank of America, although I am not sure that that was the case. I am sure that the Bank of America was getting its money's worth from his activities, but it is very doubtful that the United States was.

He was only one member of a very widespread fraternity. Indeed Mobil is involved in the process of moving its headquarters to the outskirts of Washington, apparently realizing that merely having a specialized vice-president in Washington is not enough. I anticipate that with time the problems of New York will be complicated by the movement of more and more companies to Washington. As the principal economic activity of high officials becomes more and more concentrated on rent avoidance, we can anticipate the growth of the Virginia and Maryland suburbs of Washington.

Note that in the United States rent avoidance is not the only thing that absorbs resources. Private companies may be interested in influencing the government not for the purpose of reducing their costs but to increase the costs of their competitors or perhaps to organize a government-sponsored cartel, a case of rent seeking by government activity. Further, civil servants frequently believe that promotion can be achieved through expanding the scope of their bureaus, another instance of rent seeking. It is likely, however, that under present circumstances in the United States and in most Western European countries rent seeking is of much lower importance than is the activity of the rent avoidance. I doubt that this will continue to be true.

Thus the problem in the United States, although real and growing, is very modest compared to that in the developing parts of the world. It seems to me that this difference is to a large extent, the backwardness of these areas or, perhaps more accurately, the advance of the West. The situation in which there was a relatively open economy and governments that had relatively little influence over the details of economic life was historically highly exceptional. The rent-seeking economy combined with rent avoiding was the historic norm and is today the world norm. In a way, what is happening in the United States and in Europe is the return to the usual form of government from an extraordinarily unusual form. This normal form of government apparently coexists with that condition that has been normal in the past and characterizes the world today — poverty.

If we look around the world, the United States still seems to be a rather favorable place in which to live, both from the standpoint of existing capital assets and the prospect of producing more of them. Perhaps the Common Market, the individual governments of which are highly interventionist but are limited in their power because freedom of trade is the economic rationale of the Common Market, may surpass the United States in real wealth. Nevertheless, we are well off. We have far less rent seeking and rent avoidance than do most countries. But we have far more rent seeking and rent avoidance than we had 100 years ago, and I fear that in another 100 years we will be a relatively normal country in this regard.

NOTES

1. There would still be some rent seeking because in the private sector the generation of monopoly is an example of rent seeking.

2. The exam is actually fairly easy, and hence the effect is small; but it does go in this direction.

3. All of this is to some extent an oversimplification, but I think it is basically correct. For a more detailed account, see almost any history of China.

4. Most of the writers on this subject seem to think that this actually had a negative value, but I think that this is an extreme conclusion.

5. I have always been doubtful about the anthropological discussion of these potlatches, and hence I would not like to certify the statement above as true. Nevertheless, this is what anthropologists say happened.

6. Discarding temporarily our previous comment about the quality of the job seeker.

7. Anne O. Krueger, "The Political Economy of the Rent-Seeking Society," *American Economic Review* 64 (June 1974): 291-303.

8. See Donald L. Huddle, "An Estimate of Import Surplus under a Disequilibrium System," *Public Choice* 5 (Fall 1968): 113-20.

9. The refugees from Communist China sometimes include reasonably high-level officials. One of them revealed that the governor of the province of Shantung characteristically spends nine of the twelve months of the year in Peking rather than in Shantung. This allocation of time is no doubt sensible from his standpoint and may even be sensible from the standpoint of Shantung, but it surely does not lead to what Niskanen would call process efficiency in the Shantung government.

10. This assumes that there are people who possess this kind of ability. No private company is anywhere near as large as, let us say, Health, Education, and Welfare.

Comments On "Rent Seeking"

GERALD SIRKIN*

Professor Tullock has opened the subject of rent seeking for analysis as a general economic and political ailment, and he has provided memorable illustrations in his best style. It is now time for the taxonomists to refine the concept, classify the species, and label them.

Rent arises when the demand curve intersects the supply curve in a segment of the supply curve that has zero price elasticity. Rent seeking occurs when the seeker uses factors of production in order to obtain rent.

Thus if government jobs offer rewards in excess of the rewards for similar private jobs, a rent is available. If the jobs are auctioned by government, the rent is collected by government. No factors of production are used by rent seekers. The rent is a pure transfer. Similarly, if a private party sells the job (for example, a congressman taking "kickbacks" from members of his staff), the seller collects the rent by a transfer, and there are no rent-seeking costs. If, on the other hand, the pursuit of the job requires the use of resources in passing tests or in getting degrees, rent seeking occurs.

Rents can be classified into two types. Some are by-products of an efficient economic process; allowing the owner of a property to receive the rents in these cases contributes to

*Professor of Economics, The City College of the The City University of New York

economic efficiency. For example, a patent may create a temporary rent as part of a procedure by which a potential external benefit is internalized, thus improving the allocation of inputs. Rent on a factor fixed in total supply is a price that serves to allocate the factor among alternative users.

The second type of rent serves no useful function. It arises from an inefficiency introduced into the system, usually for the purpose of creating the rent. A simple case is the hoodlum who collects for providing "protection," protection from the threat created by the hoodlum. More sophisticated examples are the rents created through restrictions on supply by occupational licensing, import licensing, and other barriers to entry.

When rents are created by threats, restrictions, and regulations, four kinds of costs may be incurred. First, there is the cost of creating the rent; the threats, restrictions, and regulations must be established and administered. Second, there is the cost to society of the misallocation of resources that results from restrictions on the free movement of resources and from the inefficiency of allocative decisions made by rent seekers compared to decisions made by a competitive market. Third, there is the cost of rent avoidance, that is, the cost of resources used by rent payers in an effort to reduce their rent payments. Fourth, there is the cost of rent seeking.

Economists concerned with non-market decisions have concentrated almost entirely on the second of these costs — the misallocation and inefficiencies of non-market economic administration. No doubt those costs vastly exceed the more obvious costs of rent creating, rent seeking, and rent avoidance, like the costs of administering regulations and the costs of passing tests and getting degrees. However, there is a cost of rent seeking and rent avoidance that is not obvious but may loom very large among the social costs of moving from a market toward a non-market economy.

A rent-seeking society rewards unproductive activity at the expense of productive activity. The structure of rewards is distorted to provide the greatest inducement to efforts and talents that have nothing to do with innovation, cost saving, allocative efficiency, or any other aspect of productive success. The growth of rent seeking, by twisting the structure of rewards, turns the steering wheel of society in a most costly direction.

This development is not new. Throughout much of history, banditry, extortion, restriction, regulation, and other methods of skimming off the cream of production have been more rewarding than production itself. We are only witnessing a return to that system of rewards and the condition of economic stagnation that always accompanies it.

A possible solution to the rent-seeking problem implied by Professor Tullock's illustrations is to have rent-receiving opportunities sold in a competitive market. If government jobs, import permits, and licenses of all kinds were sold by auction, rent seeking and rent avoidance in those fields would disappear. But we have no reason to expect that solution to be adopted. The same elements of the public choice process that led to market interventions that created rent opportunities will block the use of markets to handle rent opportunities.

We have before us examples of rent seeking and rent avoidance that arise from laws (regulations and restrictions) and others that arise from lawlessness (the "protection" racket, the thefts from steel mills that are winked at by the authorities, the purchasing agent who cheats his employer and collects from the sellers). This parallel is not a paradox. Laws that violate the rule of law, that cannot be applied impartially but must be administered, that impose the rule of men rather than the rule of law, are a form of lawlessness.

Thus government in the economy generates rent seeking that could not exist in a free market. There is also a second difference between rent seeking in government and in the market. Although opportunitites to cheat are present in both, market institutions are self-policing. Within a business there are people who have property interests in detecting and stopping theft. Within a government institution, no one has a property interest in preventing theft, and so the institution lacks motivation for self-policing.[1]

Rent seeking and rent avoidance, the decay of the rule of law, and the growth of corruption are then part of the total costs, material and spiritual, of the movement from the market to the non-market economy.

NOTES

1. George J. Stigler, "The Economics of Conflict of Interest," *Journal of Political Economy,* February 1967.

The Toehold Acquisition Doctrine: Economic Theory and Judicial Application

ROBIN CAREY*

Theoretical and legal issues posed by toehold acquisitions under Section 7 of the Clayton Act remain to be clarified by economists and by the courts.* In some circumstances a toehold acquisition is held to be permissible under the law when another acquisition or merger would not be permissible. The evolving toehold merger doctrine is an offshoot of potential competition doctrine, which is itself evolving and receiving judicial interpretation, not the least with respect to its toehold offshoot. As we shall see, two lower court decisions in 1976 and 1977, *U.S.* v. *Black & Decker and McCulloch*[1] and *BOC International Ltd.* v. *FTC,*[2] suggest that the attitude of the courts will not necessarily be consistent with the best uses to which the economist would put the toehold doctrine. Although the potential competition doctrine itself may be accused of skirting paradox and causing confusion, it will be contended in this paper that the toehold doctrine when rightly understood resolves seeming paradoxes and cuts through confusion.

At first glance, questioning a merger on grounds of harm to potential, in contrast to actual, competition may appear to be

*Associate Professor of Economics The College of Staten Island Of The City University of New York.

preventing, not promoting, competition. We find this argument strongly expressed in some judicial decisions. For example,

In fact, in so far as competitive benefits are concerned, the Government is in the anamolous position of opposing a geographic market extension merger that will introduce a third full service banking organization into the Spokane market, where only two are now operating, in reliance on alternate means that appear unlikely to have any significant procompetitive effects.[3]
Introducing a bull into a china shop is a good way to break through the central vices of oligopoly.[4]

The National Bank of Commercc, which wished to enter the somewhat concentrated — highly concentrated, according to the FDIC — Spokane, Washington, area through merger with a $96 million bank, and Cargill Company, which wished to buy the Missouri-Portland Cement Company, may well serve as invading bulls in an oligopoly china shop. Yet in opposition to the merger, it was argued, in the bank case by the Justice Department and in the cement case by the owners of the company to be acquired, that less anticompetitive mergers, that is, toehold mergers, would be feasible and preferable. In any event, the courts did not find these particular mergers illegal. The potential competition doctrine does not, however, intend to rule out entry into a market by strong competitors; it is not intended to preserve the oligopolistic china shop from the competitive bulls.

The potential competition doctrine means many things to many people. It perhaps can be introduced by pointing out what it does not involve; it does not involve the merger of firms engaging in direct competition in the same market; that is, the merger of two firms trying to sell the same product to the same customers at the same time. Instead, potential competition refers to the proposed merger of two firms that are not competing with each other but a merger that may have implications for the structural and behavioral aspects of competition. Purely conglomerate mergers all may affect competition in the broadest meaning of the word.

Where to draw the line between horizontal mergers, which do involve direct competition, and product extension or market extension mergers, which do not, is of course not easy to decide. It is a question of the delineation of the most relevant market. It is not unusual for firms to have some customers who are more far-flung geographically than most customers, or who use a product for a wider range of purposes than most customers. These customers may even have become customers as a result of the pricing and other behavior of firms possessing some degree of monopoly power, which when exercised broadened their markets by changing latent competition into direct competition.[5] Thus the existence of some direct competition may not render potential competition issues irrelevent.

Furthermore, in banking and to some extent in many other industries, markets exist in layers, depending on the economic scale of the customer. In, *Philadelphia National Bank,* Justice Brennan called for

> some fair intermediate delineation which avoids the indefensible extremes of drawing the market either so expansively as to have the effect of the merger seem insignificant, because only the very largest bank customers are taken into account in defining the market, or so narrowly as to place appellees in different markets because only the smallest customers are taken into account.[6]

However, difficulties over delineating markets are not crucial to potential competition theory. If two firms are essentially operating in the same market, and therefore direct competition, not potential competition, is the issue, then the proposed merger is a horizontal one, subject to the stringent interpretation of Section 7 laid down in *Von's Grocery,*[7] in which two small grocery chains with a combined 7½ percent of the Los Angeles markets were not allowed to merge. Indeed a by-product of a carefully stated and widely accepted potential competition doctrine would be that less reliance in Section 7 cases needs to be placed on the problematical delineations of relevant markets.[8] We do not invite antitrust authorities to subsitute for gerrymandered market definitions unproved assertions that whatever the market may be, entry through merger must injure either direct or potential competition; we only suggest that it should be plain that under clearly conceptualized conditions mergers not involving direct horizontal elements are within the reach of Section 7.

Potential competition doctrine, if it serves to prevent the lessening of competition, is clearly consistent with the purpose of antitrust. Economists argue that underlying antitrust legislation, including Section 7 of the Clayton Act, is the notion that competition compels an allocation of resources optimal for the consumers; monopoly prevents this allocation.

> The objective of antitrust law is to assure a competitive economy, based upon the belief that through competition consumer wants will be satisfied at the lowest possible price with the sacrifice of the least amount of scarce resources.[9]

Furthermore, it has been assumed that valued political and economic institutions go together. As Justice Black expressed it,

> the unrestrained interaction of competitive forces will yield the best allocation of our economic resources, the lowest prices, the highest quality and greatest material progress, while at the same time providing an environment conducive to the preservation of our democratic political and social institutions.[10]

Competitive results may indeed be compelled by competitive structure, but pure competition with its numerous firms in each market and its absolute ease of entry is rare, and what is sought is a technologically feasible structure competitive enough to approximate competitive results.[11]

It is important to recognize that there is no single measure of the degree of competition. Competition is a process in which there are many elements. Therefore, it is not often a simple matter to ascertain whether a merger substantially lessens competition and thus violates Section 7. Similarily, it is not often a simple matter to ascertain whether a merger tends to create a monopoly, which also would render the merger illegal under Section 7, for the creation of monopoly power is also a complex process. However, it was the clear intent of Congress to arrest the creation of monopoly power in its incipiency.[12]

Hence the courts are mandated to practice preventive antitrust. A proposed merger must not tend to lessen competition substantially; it is also illegal if it tends to promote monopoly. Of course, the burden is on the government (or other plaintiff) to prove that the defendant is actually doing one or the other or both. In assessing actual situations the economist is forced to consider structure, processes and outcomes, and a host of somewhat loose connections among the three. The courts, unlike economists, consider the structural and behavioral matters that are the subject of legislation, and they must by and large leave outcomes to the causal mechanisms that are in fact at work. The courts and other enforcers of the law have less responsibility than do economists to consider the validity of assumptions on which received theory rests and the implications of whatever missing ingredients there may be. The courts must start from the basis that existing laws are to be enforced, although interpreting the laws, of course, pushes the courts, too, into some measure of economic analysis.

In this study the question of toehold *versus* larger acquisitions will be considered as the Clayton Act requires, that is, with the idea in mind that acquisitions that substantially lessen competition and those that tend to create monopoly are illegal. The underlying rationale of the Clayton Act provision will not be ignored, and indeed it may provide guidance for toehold acquisition policy.

THE TWO STRANDS IN POTENTIAL COMPETITION DOCTRINE

Potential competition theory consists of two distinct strands that must be sorted out before the significance of toehold acquisitions can be considered. (See Table, page 202.) The first strand, with its emphasis on present behavior, behavior that may influence future structure, can be called the potential entry theory; the second strand, with its emphasis on change in structure, structural change that may influence future behavior, can be called the theory of probable future competition. Potential entry focuses on obtaining the behavioral results of entry without the entry actually occurring; probable future competition focuses on the occurrence of some type of entry and the way the structural changes effected by the entry will affect competition. This distinction has been recently insisted upon and elaborated by Rhoades:

> According to the theory of potential competition [potential entry above], the mere existence of a potential entrant, posing a threat of entry to established sellers, may influence the present conduct of firms in the market. In contrast, the concept of future competition is based on the expectation of a change in market structure (and competitive conditions) due to actual entry or expansion by the potential competitor.[13]

Both the behavioral and structural elements can be further divided into their immediate aspects and their contingent aspects. The latter will come into play only if the proposed merger were to occur. Contingent potential competition is relevant both to the relevant market and to the wider area in which the firms involved operate.

It should be recognized that if there are causal links running from structure to behavior, as is recognized in the structural probable future competition theory, and from behavior to structure, as the behavioral theory of potential entry suggests, the theories will inevitably become interrelated.

POTENTIAL ENTRY THEORY

The potential entry theory rests on the assumption that what attracts entry is profits; the more profits; the more easily entry can be accomplished, and that firms are likely to behave in an entry-discouraging mannner, for the firms already in a market may not welcome additional strong competitors in the market.[14] They may wish to increase or at least protect their market shares against the inroads of their present rivals. Increasing or even maintaining their shares will be more difficult if they face the efforts of an additional rival to attract customers. If they have the ability to do so — for example, some power to set prices — they will avoid actions that would invite the potential rival to enter. Both high profits and profits that could be higher because the present level of output could be produced at a lower unit cost serve as lures to entry. Firms will keep prices down and even if demand rises, they will delay delivery and increase their own capacity rather than raise prices.

If entry into the industry is not difficult, an entry-limiting pricing and production strategy would keep industry performance at all times close to the long-run competitive outcome. Were the industry purely competitive and were the firms price takers, resources would be pulled into the industry by existing firms and by newly established firms whenever increasing demand raised prices and thus profits. Then as short-run supply curves shift outward, prices fall to the original level (assuming a constant cost industry). The entry-limiting oligopoly model suggests that prices will be held down under conditions of increasing demand and that oligopoly may produce a short-cut of the process by which consumers tend to receive desired output at lowest prices. Thus although it explains competitive results, the potential entry theory, that is, the fear of potential entry, is relevant to the situation in which minimum optimum scale is so large that the number of firms

Potential Competition Doctrine

Behavioral Strand		*Structural Strand*
Possible Potential Entry	*Declared Potential Entry*	*Probable Future Competition*
Firms satisfy customers' needs without earning the entry–attracting profits that would be possible.	An outside firm has declared an interest in entering the industry through the acquisition most attractive to it. If this acquisition is barred, existing firms will behave in a way to keep profits low enough so that less attractive acquisitions will not be undertaken by the declared potential entrant.	Competition is increased when a firm enters *de novo* or through a toehold acquisition.
	If the proposed merger were to occur	
Contingent Potential Entry		*Contingent Probable Future Competition*
Additional potential entry perceived as feasible causes firms to satisfy customers' needs without entry-attracting profits.		Competition is further increased if additional firms enter *de novo* or through toehold acquisitions.

necessary for pure competition cannot operate in the same industry.

Lest the entry-limiting oligopoly model seem to suggest the existence of a sort of ideal substitute for the generally unfeasible state of pure competition, it should be mentioned that the costs of carrying on nonprice competition may be substantial and, furthermore, may enhance the desirability of the products of the present firms enough to give them the ability to keep prices higher than those of any new entrant. Then there are other barriers to entry, such as the need to enter with a large level of output in order to achieve minimum optimum scale, and the possession of advantages in production, for example, patent rights, and advantages in raw material supplies, such as favorable long-term leases. The height of the barriers to entry serves, of course, to determine the rate of supernormal profit that may be earned without attracting entry.[15]

In banking and several other industries the barriers to entry also come from regulation. Permission to charter a new bank or a new branch of an existing bank must be given by the appropriate agencies. In addition, present law for all practical purposes limits the branching of United States banks to a single state, and in some states branches are not permitted at all or they are restricted by such laws as Connecticut's Home Office Protection Law.

There has not been much evidence that firms actually do practice entry-limiting strategies.[16] Firms may choose to sacrifice moderate long-term profits for high short-term profits.[17] But if the potential entry theory is to have relevance for antitrust policy, what we should be able to observe is entry occurring when profits are above the entry-inhibiting level.[18] At first glance then, it would appear that entry should never be impeded by the courts. If entry into industries with above normal profits did not occur, potential entry would not affect the pricing and other behavior of the firms in such way as to encourage them to keep prices low so that supernormal profits and unnecessarily high costs are prevented. Just as unions cannot expect their power to call strikes to influence negotiations if strikes are never called, entry by some means must occur when there are high profits to be made if potential entry is to be any force on firm behavior. It does seem odd then that in the name of potential competition entry by any means should ever be questioned. But the situation that can be observed is not that simple. Once a firm does decide to enter an industry, the relevance of potential entry theory to antitrust policy must be closely examined. If a possible potential entrant has taken steps that indicate that it will actually enter, that is, a firm has become a declared potential entrant, it is a sign that an entry-limiting pricing strategy, for whatever reason, has not been used in the industry or at least that it has not been used in a way that brought maximum benefits to consumers, for that strategy would have prevented entry-attracting supernormal profits. Potential entry theory should not be used in Section 7 cases in the expectation that forbidding entry through merger will bring about entry-limiting behavior when it was the entry-inducing behavior that made the firm want to enter. Therefore, we have not yet established the relevance of potential entry theory when a declaration of intended entry has occurred.

On the other hand, if two firms engage in a joint entry into a new field, as did Pennsalt Chemicals Company and Olin Mathieson Corporation, which planned to produce sodium chlorate in a joint venture in the southeastern part of the United States one of them will not be "waiting in the wings," ready to enter in order to share in any excess profits in sodium chlorate; and on the grounds of the potential entry theory, such a joint venture can be held to violate Section 7.[19] The potential entry theory is clearly relevant, for the behavior to be influenced has not yet taken place.

Also we should note that there will exist an array of entry

possibilities (Bain's General Condition of Entry)[20] These possibilities range upward from that mode of entry that produces minimum average cost for an entrant. Now if markets for existing capital stock were to operate perfectly, the prices for acquiring existing firms in an industry would tend to push the cost involved in all the modes of entry toward equality, and entry through merger with a substantial existing firm would have no cost advantage over entry through acquisition of a small firm, that is, a toehold acquisition, or indeed over *de novo* (also refered to an unilateral) entry. Yet frequent testimony is given in support of the existence of significant cost differentials among the different ways of entry.

For example, in *Missouri-Portland,*[21] Cargill testified that each barrel of cement would cost $3 to $4 if it were permitted to acquire Missouri-Portland, whereas *de novo* entry or entry through the acquisition of a smaller firm would mean costs of $20 to $30 a barrel. This difference has inspired the courts to prevent firms from making a proposed merger and so keep them "in the wings," as declared potential entrants. The purpose is to encourage firms in the target industry to keep prices low enough so that the more expensive modes of entry do not become attractive, even though they were not so low to discourage entry entirely. This declared potential entry reasoning (Perceived Potential Entry to the courts), should be recognized as a distinct part of the behavioral element in potential competition, but it will be relevant only if the possibility of potential entry has failed to produce entry-inhibiting behavior, that is, behavior most beneficial to the consumer.

There is a more important reason than a progressive condition of entry that the possibility of entry through conglomerate acquisition of a leading firm is not the essential ingredient to potential entry doctrine that it first appeared to be. If entry is to be viewed as undesirable by existing firms, it should erode the profitable situations of established firms. But if entry is likely to be accomplished through the acquisition of a firm established in the market, it is not clear that the shares of the other firms will be threatened. Granted, the merger may provide assistance over whatever entry barriers there may be. But the profits that attracted the entry through merger are available and require no effort to enlarge the acquired firm's market share in order to get them. Thus it is not impossible that the acquiring firm will do nothing more than change the name on the door, continuing the pricing and other policies of the acquiring firm exactly, neither threatening the profits of the other firms, nor benefiting the consumers. (Whether this scenario can properly be described as a merger that "would leave competition in the marketplace exactly as it was, neither hurt nor helped"[22] is a question to which we shall return.) Of course, existing firms are not guaranteed that firms entering in that manner will behave that way. But the more likely the prospect of entry through merger with a substantial existing firm, the less of a behavior-affecting threat it is likely to be to the firms already in the industry. Expectation of entry through merger with a large established firm is unlikely to be effective in producing entry-limiting pricing behavior with its concomitant benefits to the consumer. Unilateral entry, or entry through a toehold acquisition, may be relatively costly to accomplish; as a mode of entry, however, it is likely to ensure a competitive scramble for shares.

Before the topic of declared potential entry is left behind, another possible implication of a declaration of intent to enter should be mentioned, a somewhat more sinister implication. Suppose the firms in an industry had been following an entry-limiting pricing strategy and an outside firm perceived that the industry was thus foregoing short-run profits. Thereupon the outside firm decided to enter the industry to do what it could to reap at least some part of the profits that short-run industry profit maximizing could produce. It would have little chance of success unless it could enter as a substantial and financially powerful competitor. In any event, the potential entry theory has been reversed: Entry is to undo rather than to produce the beneficial effects of potential entry. Thus it is not a situation in which the potential entry theory is relevant.

To reassert our argument at this point in the analysis, potential entry theory is not seen to call for entry to be as unimpeded as possible in all cases by Section 7. It is not correct to say that Section 7 should never serve as an impediment to entry; rather, Section 7 should not serve as an impediment to entry that is likely to threaten established firms.

PROBABLE FUTURE COMPETITION

The theory of probable future competition is the structural element in the potential competition doctrine. The important structural outcome of a proposed merger is the fact that the acquiring firm will not enter the market through any other means. If it enters by acquiring a substantial firm, then it ipso facto will not enter unilaterally or through the acquisition of a toehold. Had it taken the latter course, there would be competition between itself and the substantial firm that it did in actuality acquire. Future competition between the acquiring and the acquired firm has thus been eliminated, and if both firms are substantial, competition is substantially less than it might have been had the proposed merger not been permitted. The takeover of a substantial firm, as noted in the discussion of potential entry, may merely perpetuate the pattern of behavior that attracted the entry. Behavior is relatively unlikely to change if structure in the market is not changed.

In his very thorough study of mergers, Steiner suggests that in assessing this possibility the degree to which the present price is above a competitive price should be considered.[23] The nearer the price is to a shared monopoly level, he suggests, the more likely an acquisition of a major firm by an outsider is to improve competitive conditions by upsetting a tight oligopoly; whereas the closer the price is to the competitive level, the more likely it is that an acquisition will produce harm to consumers because the new entrant may serve as a focal point for transforming the market behavior in an anticompetitive direction. It is impossible to disagree with Steiner on the dangers of the acquisition of a significantly sized firm when the existing price level is relatively low. Indeed this situation is the one that we noted before as the exact reverse of what is called for in the potential entry theory.

But when the price level is relatively high and a major firm is being acquired, there is every reason to suppose a *a priori* that the situation is likely to invite behavior that will continue the profit stream, and there is scant loss in disallowing the proposed merger and holding out for one that is more likely to achieve a desired result.

If conditions are attractive to entry, the firm, a declared potential entrant, may indeed pursue entry even if it is forced to use a less attractive means of entry. It is a question of how attractive the entry is vis-à-vis the additional costs of other means. In commercial banking,despite the need for entry to be approved by regulators, in a substantial proportion of cases in which a proposed merger was not allowed, entry did occur *de novo* or by the acquisition of smaller banks.[24] These are cases of probable future competition being realized in the form of *de novo* entry or toehold acquisition that the proposed merger would have prevented.

Thus the theory of probable future competition carries a message for antitrust policy not dissimilar to that of the theory of potential entry. The structure of an industry can be rendered more competitive through entry by disallowing mergers with leading firms but encouraging entry through toehold acquisitions.

As we consider contingent effects of proposed mergers, the same distinction as to modes of entry allowable under Section 7 appears to be appropriate.

CONTINGENT COMPETITIVE EFFECTS

Contingent on a proposed merger are other possible changes in market structure and changes in firm behavior that the merger may influence, hence contingent probable future competition must be considered. If the proposed merger does occur, it introduces a second generation, one could say, of influences on future behavior and structure. These second-generation effects can be considered under the heading of contingent potential entry and contingent future competition, for their emergence is contingent on the occurrence of the proposed merger.

Just as probable future competition theory and potential entry should be kept distinct, so is it necessary to draw a distinction between contingent probable future competition and contingent potential entry. Contingent probable future competition asks: If the proposed merger is allowed, what are the implications for actual future entry beyond the fact that this firm, the declared potential entrant, will not actually enter in any other way? Contingent potential entry asks: What is the implication of the proposed merger for future behavior of firms in the market; if it occurs, will firms be more or less likely to price in such a fashion that consumers are benefited and further entry is discouraged? We can start to answer these questions by noting that a merger means all of the following: (1) The combined firm has replaced the acquired firm in the market. (2) No other firm may enter the market by acquiring the acquired firm. (3) The acquiring firm has strengthened itself through the merger in the totality of its operations in this field and the others in which it operates. (4) The acquired firm no longer exists as an independent force to sell output or to buy inputs.

The fact that the acquired firm is no longer available for acquisition may have implications for future structural changes. To the extent that its acquisition eased the passage over the entry barriers, such help will not be available in the future. This fact does not matter if there are a lot of similar firms to be acquired. If there are not, future entry into the industry is inhibited. Probable future competition, contingent on entry prospects after the proposed merger, will have been lessened.

Even if there are a lot of firms available for acquisition, the entry of a large and powerful firm, regardless of the mode of entry, may lessen contingent future competition as it may be perceived to be in a position to fight off new rivals. The new firm in the market is inevitably somewhat larger and stronger than the acquired firm.

If the market is highly concentrated, contingent probable future competition of a deconcentrating sort will have been thwarted. If the market is not highly concentrated and the concern is more for preventing an increase in concentration, there is still a lessening of the probability of future entry for any given level of future profits.

PROBABLE FUTURE COMPETITION OUTSIDE THE IMMEDIATE MARKET

Probable future competition will be affected in wider areas than the immediate market. The acquiring firm (and possibly also the acquired firm) is operating in one or more additional markets.

Shull poins to what he terms a flaw in the banking structure that is arising in some states. In these states there are several large banks that have offices in many towns so that the same competitors face each other in many markets. This situation is referred to as linked oligopoly. It has been argued that linked oligopolies are conducive to parallel pricing and lessen the likelihood of entry and contingent probable future competition.[25] The condition of linked oligopoly develops when small independent banks are merged in district after district by one or another of the same set of large competitors.

Apart from linked oligopoly, if the now stronger acquiring firm uses profits from the merger to strengthen its position in other markets in which it operates, probable future competition in other markets has been lessened.

The proposed merger may produce vertical aspects that are likely to affect future competition. Either the acquired or the acquiring firm may have a large distribution system that will be less open to the output of other firms. On the other side of the coin, the distribution outlet or any downstream activity will have a more assured source of supply. In banking, as Austin and Solomon point out, correspondent balances and correspondent services may be at stake.[26] There is always the possibility, too, of a pricing squeeze by vertically integrated firms agains nonintegrated firms. The increase in vertical integration thus may serve to lessen future entry or even to hasten the exit of the weaker firms in the market and must be considered an element in contingent future competition.

WIDER CONTINGENT ASPECTS

All of these considerations are important in assessing the probability of additional entry after the merger, the contingent future competition element. They are thus important in assessing the operation of contingent potential entry as an influence on the behavior of the firms after the merger. The more protected from additional entry the firms feel themselves to be, the less will their behavior be entry inhibiting and the farther from the competitive norm will the results be.

Contingent potential entry necessarily involves competition by firms of which at least one is operating in more than one market; with linked oligopoly there will be many such multimarket firms. Adams makes the important point that multimarket operation obscures the degree of profitability of operating in each of the markets, and so high profits in a particular market may not attract entry.[27] (The reluctance of large firms to provide the FTC with data by product lines provides suggestive evidence on this point.)

Contingent potential entry that is made less effective and contingent probable future competition that is made less likely because the firm entering the industry is efficient and sets its prices to keep the profits of all the firms in the industry low are obviously not something to worry about even if the number of firms in the market eventually shrinks. It is the competitive process, not individual competitor firms, that is to be safeguarded.

TOEHOLD DOCTRINE AND SECTION 7

All of the foregoing comments seem to imply that the cause of competition can be served by making sure that the mode of entry of an established firm into a new (for it) industry is within the reach of Section 7. Both the structural and the behavioral aspects of potential competition seem to call for entry *de novo* or through a toehold acquisition rather than through merger with a substantial established firm. Have judicial decisions been consistent with this assertion? A brief review of the leading cases is in order before we consider the two recent lower court cases that provide two examples of judicial obstacles to the toehold doctrine.

Bendix-Fram [29]

The first antitrust decision hinging specifically on the probability of a toehold acquisition as an alternative to a contested mergeer was the Bendix-Fram case.[30] The commissioner of the FTC found that Bendix was both able and likely to enter the passenger car filter market through toehold acquisition rather than through acquisition of Fram, the third largest manufacturer, with 12 percent of the overall market and 37 percent of the passenger car replacement market.

Falstaff

A review of the views of the Supreme Court on the toehold theory can begin with *Falstaff.*[31] The Supreme Court addressed itself explicitly to potential competition in *Falstaff.* It restricted its consideration to the declared potential entry aspect, remanding the case to the district court. Falstaff had acquired Narragansett, a New England brewery, in an attempt to penetrate the New England market. The district court had found that the merger did not violate Section 7. Justice White ruled that the district court had erred in giving no separate consideration to whether there would be beneficial effects on competition exerted by Falstaff's position at the edge of the market were its merger with Narragansett to be ruled illegal. Justice White explicitly deferred a ruling on the probable future competition element, as he put it, "on a merger that would leave competition in the market place exactly as it was, neither hurt nor helped, and that is challengable under Section 7 only on grounds that the company could but did not enter de novo or through 'toehold' acquisitions. . . .[31] Justice White saw that competition not at the immediate time and not in the immediate market place could be affected by the proposed merger. Thus he considered "competition in the market place" something distinct from contingent potential entry and contingent future competition, as well as distinct from probable future competition.

His order of remand was intended to test whether the declared potential entry did affect competition in the market place. It could do that if more costly modes of entry were preceived both as feasible and as threatening to the present behavior of the brewing industry. In reconsidering the case on remand, Judge Day found that the removal of Falstaff from the edge of the market had had no anticompetitive effect,[32] and the case did not come before the Supreme Court again.

Marine[33]

A case in which the Supreme Court might have considered

the question reserved in Falstaff occurred in 1974. Marine Bancorporation owned National Bank of Commerce,Seattle, a $3.1 billion bank which had received permission from the controller to merge with Washington Trust Bank, the third largest in Spokane, with deposits of $96 million. National was second largest in the state. The two largest Washington banks held 52 percent of the deposits between them, and it was agreed that banking in the Spokane area was highly concentrated. Justice Powell held that the relevant geographic market was the Spokane area, the area in which the acquired firm competed directly with others.

Justice Powell argued that the potential competition doctrine was not irrelevant to banking, but that regulatory barriers to entry meant potential competition had to be considered in a special way.[34] There was insufficient evidence, Justice Powell held, that *de novo* or toehold entry provided an alternative. Washington law prohibited *de novo* branching, and so National Bancorporation would at best have been able to sponsor a new bank and acquire it years later. It had been argued by the banks that such a procedure violated the spirit of the law and would be unlikely to be approved. Justice White, however, pointed out in his dissent that sponsorship had been used in Washington, by National itself among others.[35] Toehold acquisitions were not considered feasible by Justice Powell. A branch of another bank (were one for sale) was not considered a possibility, for banks not in downtown Spokane, of course, could not branch there, and one small bank that was there could not be acquired until 1975, four years after the decision to merge Washington Trust Bank had been approved. Because the Justice Department had provided no indication that procompetitive effects could have resulted from alternative methods of entry, the question of the legality of the merger, if there were a reasonable probability of such effects were the merger barred, was not addressed.

Three other cases on which the Supreme Court might have

acted should be noted before two recent, and to some observers, dismaying, descendents of *Marine* are discussed. In *Missouri-Portland*[36] the Court's denial of certiorari boded ill for toehold doctrine, but in *Kennecott*[37] and *Phillips Petroleum,*[38] the respective denial of certiorari and the affirmation of the judgment of the lower court suggested that potential competition doctrine may yet figure in Supreme Court decisions.[39]

Kennecott Copper

The FTC had challenged the merger of Kennecott Copper Company, number one in the field, with Peabody, the largest coal producer. This challenge was affirmed by Judge Doyle who stated that all mergers are in reach of Section 7. Kennecott had previously acquired Knight, a small coal company (a true toehold), and was considered a probable entrant into the coal industry. The judge found that it had thus had an effect on the behavior in the coal industry. Issues other than declared potential entry were not treated.

The case was appealed to the Supreme Court, but certiorari was denied in April 1974. Because only Justice Stewart would have granted certiorari, this denial suggested that a majority of the Supreme Court was willing to accept the declared potential entry theory of potential competition.

Missouri-Portland

Cargill, a privately owned corporation that with one other firm, accounts for a substantial percentage of grain dealing in the United States, was attempting to acquire Missouri-Portland Cement. The district court had enjoined its solicitation of tender of Missouri-Portland shares. Cargill appealed to the court of appeals. Circuit Judge Friendly reversed this decision.

Cement is a classic example of a locally produced commodity. Missouri-Portland was the leading cement producer in several local areas:

30 percent-St. Louis metropolitan market area
30 percent-Kansas City metropolitan market area
30 percent-Memphis metropolitan market area
21 percent-Omaha metropolitan market area.

Judge Friendly found that entry *de novo* was unlikely and that converting a small plant into a big one would be as costly as a *de novo* entry. He stated that because there was no evidence that it would not enter by a toehold entry was no indication that it would. Eager to let the bull into the china shop of the local cement market, Judge Friendly found the merger legal under Section 7. The Supreme Court denied certiorari in July 1974.

Phillips Petroleum

Toehold acquisitions were considered in the Phillips Petroleum case in 1973, after *Falstaff,* by Judge Ferguson. He found that Tidewater, with 6 percent of the California gasoline market, could not be acquired by Phillips Petroleum as a toehold market extension acquisition. He defined a toehold acquisition as

> one which is sufficient to assist the potential entrant over the entry barriers and into the market, but not so large that the entrant merely replaces the acquired company; the acquiring company must have a substantial need to build upon the acquisition. Such a foothold acquisition is fully consistent with the concept of unilateral entry, since both envision a significant market-penetration effort by the entering company quite apart from whatever assets or market position have been acquired. In contrast to an independent unilateral entry, however, the foothold acquisition normally entails the elimination of a significant independent factor in the market. For this reason, the foothold acquisition cannot be looked upon with favor unless it is not only a foothold from which to achieve a substantial market entry, but is also necessary to such market entry — that is, unless the potential entrant could not have achieved a substantial market entry on a unilateral basis, perhaps supplemented only by incidental acquisitions of a *de minimis* nature.[40]

Significantly, Judge Ferguson commented that the fact that Phillips used Tidewater's assets as a major element of its entry, rather than building on them in a substantial way, indicated that Tidewater was not a toehold acquisition. The judgment in Phillips Petroleum was affirmed by the Supreme Court in July 1974.

U.S. v. Black and Decker and McCulloch: Heads — The Merging Companies Win; Tails — The Antitrust Division Loses

The Black and Decker/McCulloch merger decision,[41] handed down by district Judge Blair in August 1976, may further weaken the potential competition doctrine as a potentially effective Section 7 weapon, a trend marked by the Supreme Court's 1974 decision in *Marine*. The decision comes perilously close to inviting merging companies to demonstrate either that a certain set of conditions is likely to develop, in which case the potential competition doctrine does not render the merger illegal, or that the same set of conditions is not likely to develop, in which case the potential competition doctrine does not render the merger illegal. Furthermore, this invitation follows closely the approach of the Supreme Court in *Marine*.

Black and Decker, the acquiring firm, is a manufacturer primarily of portable electric tools and accessories. Its sales in 1973 were $427 million, and it ranked number 372 in total sales in the Fortune 500 top firms for that year. It acquired McCulloch Corporation, a manufacturer of gasoline-powered chain saws, with net sales in 1972 of $60 million (85 percent of which were gasoline-powered chain saws).[42] Judge Blair identified McCulloch as "one of the largest chain saw manufacturers."[43]

The rank and the share of McCulloch in gasoline-powered chain saws in its market and submarket have been deleted from the published text of the decision as confidential data.[44] It seems likely, though, that it was one of the top two gasoline-powered chain saw manufacturers. (Judge Blair stated that the largest manufacturers, including McCulloch, lost in market shares, and that the top two lost in market shares from 1970–1974,[45] while the top four manufacturers grew in market shares).[46] McCulloch was one of the three largest firms in the field in 1977.[47] The two largest firms had slightly less that 50 percent of the gasoline-powered chain saw market in 1974.[48]

Judge Blair determined the relevant product market to be the manufacture and the sale of gasoline-powered chain saws. Also on the basis of its distinct class of customers, distinct prices, and specialized retailers, Judge Blair recognized a submarket, the manufacture and the sale of gasoline-powered chain saw retailing for less than $200, which he labeled the "occasional user gasoline-powered chain saw market" in contrast to the larger market that includes the models bought for large-scale lumber operations.[49]

Citing *Marine,* Judge Blair stated that because the government charged that the merger involved the loss of potential competition, the relevant market must be shown to be concentrated "since in a competitive market, potential competition will not influence market behavior."[50] According to *Marine,* Judge Blair stated, concentration ratios provide a prima facie case for the noncompetitive nature of the market; the merging firms may, however, attempt to show that the concentration ratios fail to reflect the reality of the competitive situation.[51] Then, Judge Blair continued, *Marine* requires the demonstration of two preconditions for the application of potential competition doctrine: (1) that the acquiring firm have feasible alternative means of entering the relevant market other than by acquisition of the target company; and (2) that those alternative means "offer a substantial likelihood of ultimately producing deconcentration of that market or other significant procompetitive effects."[52]

Judge Blair stated that in 1972 the two largest of the gasoline-powered chain saw manufacturers accounted for 54.3 percent of the units sold; the top four, 77.5 percent; the top eight, 93.5 percent. In the relevant submarket in 1972 the top two accounted for 51.9 percent of the units sold; the top four, 79.4 percent; the top eight, 93.6 percent, which sufficed "to evidence a heavily concentrated market and submarket, requiring a potential competition analysis," unless the defendents proved the contrary.[53]

The defendents did attempt to offer such evidence. There had been a threefold growth in gasoline-powered chain saw sales from 1970 to 1974 and a substantial number of new entrants, of which six were named. The top two had found their market share of the submarket (in units) reduced from 53.9 percent to 50.3 percent.[54] Judge Blair found, though, no trend toward deconcentration to have emerged. He explained the absence of such a trend by noting the existence of technological barriers to entry in that "the design and sales of a gasoline-powered chain saw entails subtle calculations of two cycle engine design and demands considerable technical manufacturing expertise." The need to obtain marketing outlets and a service network and, to a lesser extent, advertising also served as entry barriers.[55] Judge Blair noted that there had been in gasoline-powered chain saws considerable product innovation and a decline in average prices, but he attributed the latter largely to the shift of sales to the occasional user segment of the market where smaller machines are desired, that is, the lower price submarket had expanded relative to the entire market for gasoline-powered chain saws. Thus he concluded:

> [g]iven the lack of any trend to deconcentration, the high levels of concentration that characterized both the gasoline-powered chain saw market and the occasional user submarket, the relatively significant entry barriers and the lack of clear price competitiveness, the court believes that defendents have failed to meet their burden to establish that the concentration ratios and structional analysis "did not accurately depict the economic characteristics of the market."[56]

From this conclusion, Judge Blair considered whether there were feasible alternative means for Black and Decker to enter, and, if so, whether substantial deconcentration or other procompetitive effects were likely to ensue. As noted previously, he had explained *Marine* explicitly required these two preconditions to be considered in the application of the actual potential entrant aspect of the potential competition doctrine, and he noted that in *Marine* the court had also suggested that these same preconditions were relevant to the perceived potential entrant doctrine.[57]

Judge Blair was persuaded by the evidence that Black and Decker had ample incentive to enter the market.[58] But *de novo* entry was not likely; even though Black and Decker had had a history of diversification through *de novo* entry, this possibility was effectively foreclosed for entry into gasoline-powered chain saws. The reasons for this foreclosure included its lack of expertise in gasoline engine technology — Black and Decker purchased the gas engine for its power generator from an outside company — and the intricate and changing technological problems of two-cycle gasoline chain saw engine design.[59] He mentioned the process of chromium plating as a specific example.[60] Marketing and service provided additional obstacles.[61] As for advertising, Judge Blair did find that the Black and Decker name would help in *de novo* entry,[62] but on balance he found *de novo* entre not feasible.[63]

Judge Blair also concluded that a toehold acquisition was not a feasible mode of entry. Either the small firms mentioned by the government were not available, or would not supply an adequate technological base, or they possessed too great a market share to be considered toeholds.[64] Furthermore, Judge Blair concluded that

> [e]ven if viable toehold candidates had existed, there appears little likelihood they could have satisfied *Marine Bancorporation's* second precondition by precipitating deconcentration or other significant procompetitive effects in the gas chain saw market in this case.

He referred to the continuing oligopolistic structure of the industry despite entry and the lack of any expertise on the part of Black and Decker that would enhance the expertise of the toehold firm.[65]

Judge Blair then considered the perceived potential entrant claim, quoting the remand by the Supreme Court of *Falstaff.*

> The District Court erred as a matter of law. The error lay in the assumption that because Falstaff, as a matter of fact, would never have entered the market *de novo*, it could in no sense be considered a potential competitor. More specifically,the District Court failed to give separate consideration to whether Falstaff was potential competitor in the sense that it was so positioned on the edge of the market that it exerted beneficial influence on the competitive conditions in the market.[66]

Judge Blair also stated that in *Marine,* the court

> appears to have engrafted the two preconditions to actual potential competition onto the perceived potential competition doctrine. In other words, the Court now apparently requires that the firms in the relevant market not only perceived that the entering firm will enter the market but also that the avenue of entry be perceived as possessing the capability of precipitating procompetitive effects.[67]

The evidence, he concluded, indicated that Black and Decker was not positioned at the edge of the market as a perceived potential entrant largely because *de novo* entry had not been successful unless the entering firm had possessed knowledge of gasoline engine technology.[68]

Judge Blair also rejected the notion that the merger would entrench Black and Decker/McCulloch in the gasoline-powered chain saw industry, noting that earlier portions of his opinion had largely taken care of the possibility. He cited the lack of complementarity in engineering, marketing, and servicing; although Black and Decker's advertising could enhance McCulloch's sales, the result would not be entrenchment because product design and engineering, about which Black and Decker lacked expertise, would be more crucial.[69]

Thus there is a certain cohesiveness to Judge Blair's view of the gasoline-powered chain saw industry. Expertise in gas technology is rare, difficult to acquire, and impossible to develop from within. Therefore, there has been no effective deconcentration despite new entry, nor is such deconcentration likely even if a giant firm lacking such expertise were to enter *de novo* or through a toehold acquisition. Futhermore, this lack of expertise would prevent entrenchment if a giant were to acquire one of the largest manufacturers of gasoline-powered chain saws.

What is disturbing about this view is that in essence if the defendants failed to show that the industry was heading toward deconcentration and was more competitive than concentration measures suggested, thus removing the merger from the reach of Section 7, they have ipso facto shown that *de novo* entry or entry by toehold acquisition would not produce procompetitive results, and the merger is again removed from the reach of Section 7. Black and Decker had tried to prove that the industry was so competitive that Section 7 did not apply. Judge Blair did not accept this argument because of what he perceived to be a crucial need for expertise in gas technology. But the need for expertise in gas technology also meant that even if an alternative mode of entry were feasible, it would fail to produce sufficient procompetitive results. By the same token, the acquisition by a giant of one of the largest firms in the target market would not entrench that market. How could the Antitrust Division fail to lose its case?

Consider the obverse. Were it likely that Black and Decker could have entered the market without acquiring McCulloch and in so doing could have brought about substantial procompetitive changes, then the barriers to entry that Judge Blair accepted as indicating that the market was not only concentrated but also would remain concentrated would in effect have been paltry barriers indeed, and the industry would have been on its way toward deconcentration; hence the merger would not have been in the reach of Section 7, and neither alternative modes of entry nor the possibility of entrenchment would need to be considered by the court.

Yet, as Judge Blair noted, Justice Powell in *Marine* laid down the analysis that Judge Blair held was relevant to *Black and Decker/McCulloch.* The market must be shown to be not competitive, and then as preconditions to applying potential competition analysis, means of entry other than the proposed merger must be shown to be feasible, and the alternative means must "offer a substantial likelihood of ultimately producing deconcentration of that market or other significant procompetitive effects." In *Marine* the concentrated nature of the market was established.[70] The court found that the second precondition had not been demonstrated, for in 1964 a large bank holding company had entered the Spokane area by acquiring a foothold bank with two offices, and in eight years it had grown to only 2.2 percent of the Spokane market, an insignificant increase.[71] Yet if the bank that had been acquired in 1964 had grown substantially, the Spokane market would have been less concentrated by the time of the Marine Bancorporation case so that, one may suggest, the market might not have been viewed as sufficiently uncompetitive for potential competition doctrine to apply. Although Judge Blair can hardly be faulted for following this model, surely the toehold doctrine need not be squeezed into oblivion in this fashion. Yes, some degree of concentration is necessary in the industry for Section 7 to be relevant. If competition were atomistic, the firm acquired would *ipso facto* be a toehold, and barring special circumstances, questioning the acquisition of one of them by an outside firm, no matter how large and powerful, is close to a *per se* barring of expansion through acquisition, at least for certain classes of firms. But in a somewhat uncompetitive industry, if the toehold doctrine is applied and the entry of an outside firm is feasible and is accomplished not through a merger with a large firm in the target industry but through a toehold, competition, at least in one respect, has been augmented, and the second (numbered) precondition of *Marine* has been met. Recall that the *Falstaff* reserved question referred to a merger "challengeable under Section 7 only on grounds that the company could, but did not, enter de novo or through 'toehold acquisition' and *that there is less competition than there would have been had entry been in such a manner.'*[72] The insistence in *Marine* on "a substantial likelihood of ultimately producing deconcentration or other procompetitive effects"[73] should mean no more than that. Thus we should expect a very wide zone of competitive conditions in which there is enough concentration so that Section 7 would apply and in which procompetitive effects can be expected if it is applied.

There seems then to be no reason that the case should not have been considered on the basis of the toehold doctrine. Before we consider what the decision might and should have been — the reader no doubt has an inkling of our prediliction — we should consider a 1977 case that provides another way in which the toehold doctrine can be derailed by the *Marine* preconditions.

BOC International v. Federal Trade Commission: "Uncabined Speculation" as Good Evidence as "Precisely Calibrated Plans"?

The next judicial test of the toehold doctrine was in a case lost by the FTC in May 1977. The second circuit court of appeals found in favor of the petitioner. BOC had appealed the FTC order directing it to divest itself of Airco.[74] The toehold doctrine itself was not reached. Judge Oakes held that the FTC had not established that the preconditions set forth in *Marine* had been met, and therefore it was not necessary to consider whether the availability of a toehold acquisition as an alternative to the acquisition of a large firm in an oligopolistic market would render such an acquisition illegal.[75]

The case involved two very large corporations. BOC (formerly British Oxygen Company), the acquiring firm, a British company not operating in the United States, had acquired 35 percent of Airco's common stock in December 1973, after Airco management had reached an agreement with

BOC to provide an alternative to a public tender offer for Airco stock by Curtis-Wright.[76] The BOC-Airco combination was to be substantially larger than any other gas producer in the world.[77] The FTC administrative law judge, after an initial complaint in February 1974, concluded in March 1974 that charges that the merger was in violation of Section 7 had been sustained. On appeal from BOC, the FTC issued an opinion which sustained the administrative law judge insofar as he held that there existed a reasonable probability that BOC would have entered the United States industrial gases market by internal expansion or by toehold acquisition if barred from acquiring Airco[78] and that entry of a firm such as BOC by internal growth or expansion of a toehold firm would not only add a new competitor but, judging from experience, would also be likely to set competitive pressures in motion. Thus Section 7 had been violated.[79]

BOC is a multinational corporation, the largest producer of industrial gases in the world.[80] Industrial gases include, but are not limited to, oxygen, nitrogen, hydrogen, argon, helium, acetylene, carbon dioxide, carbon monoxide, nitrous oxide, and various mixtures. (BOC also produces medical gases, medical and cryogenic equipment, and other items. A separate issue of actual competition between BOC and Airco in the three product lines of medical inhalation anesthetic equipment was remanded to the FTC and is not considered here.)[81] In 1973, the year of the acquisition, BOC had sales of approximately $766 million.[82]

Airco, the acquired firm, at the time of the acquisition was the third largest producer of industrial gases in the United States and the fifth largest in the world. Its sales, including other industrial products, were $584 million in 1973.[83] The FTC held from census data that in 1972 Airco had 15.9 percent of the shipment by United States domestic plants of industrial gases and that the four-firm concentration ration was 70 percent, the eight-firm, 86 percent.

Judge Oakes dismissed the contention that Airco itself was a toehold acquisition as the British government had argued in its *amicus curiae* brief, the British government being concerned "that unless toehold analyses were made in cases involving the acquisition of American firms, foreign entry into United States markets would be severely impeded."[84] He did not, however, consider explicitly Airco's market share and the challenge to the FTC figures presented in the Brief for Petitioner.

Industrial gases are marketed in two ways.[85] Tonnage plants supply a single customer, often a steel company that uses oxygen, from a plant convenient to the customer's location. Merchant plants sell gases in smaller quantities, shipped in liquid or gaseous form to the customer. Merchant prices are eight to nine times higher than tonnage prices. Tonnage plants often have excess capacity relative to their tonnage demands and sell the excess in the merchant market.[86]

The decision by Judge Oakes hinged on a negative answer to the question, "Would the firm in question enter de novo or by toehold acquisition if not permitted to enter by acquiring a large company?"[87] He was following the familiar preconditions from Marine:

> (1) that in fact [The acquiring firm] has available feasible means for entering the [target market] other than by acquiring [the acquired firm]; and (2) that those means offer substantial likelihood of ultimately producing deconcentration of that market or other significant procompetitive effects.[88]

Judge Oakes accepted the challenge of BOC to the standard that the FTC had used in testing the first precondition. He stated that the FTC standard, "reasonable probability of eventual entry — place[d] a lighter burden on the FTC than is justified by Section 7 and the purposes of the potential entrant doctrine,"[89] and thus he did not consider whether the record supported the decision of the FTC on its own standard.[90] The FTC had said in its divestiture order, "We conclude that as of December 1973 there was a 'reasonable probability' that BOC would have eventually entered the U.S. gases market by internal expansion, or its [toehold] equivalent."[91] The opinion continued, "In view of the trends in the market existing at the time of the hearings in 1974, and attested to by witnesses, the probability that BOC would enter the U.S. market in the future, if divestiture if ordered, has even increased."[92]

Judge Oakes took care not to challenge the "reasonable probability" test, but he did not accept the reference to eventual entry, stating that there was nowhere in the FTC opinion a spelling out of what eventual entry meant and how long a time period would be involved, that in fact "decades" might pass.[93] Although Judge Oakes would not require "any exact, precisely calibrated assessment of time of entry," he held some reasonable temporal estimate to be essential,[94] that "the uncabined speculation of the FTC could not be the basis of a finding that Section 7 had been violated. . . . It seems necessary under Section 7 that the finding of probable entry at least contain some reasonable temporal estimate related to the near future, with near 'defined' in terms of entry barriers and lead time necessary for entry in the particular industry, and that the finding be supported by substantial evidence in the record."[95]

It seems that evidence for this type of temporal estimate would in both cases, including *BOC International/Airco,* be difficult to find. Negative kinds of evidence, for example, as in *Marine,* statutes requiring a certain number of years to elapse before new banks can legally open branches,[96] may well be available, but the existence of convincing positive evidence is most unlikely.

It is not merely a question of subjective versus objective evidence.[97] An acquiring firm will be reluctant to provide evidence of how it could proceed with the next best solution when it is making every effort to be permitted to undertake the best solution from its own viewpoint and when the existence of a feasible second best alternative would render the preferred solution legally suspect. The problem goes deeper then the natural lack of desire to hang oneself. It involves the way in which decisions are made in corporations. A considerable body of literature devoted to the behavioral study of the firm has appeared. Although a review of that literature will not be attempted here, it must be pointed out that the decision-making process in firms is not one in which every conceivable action receives continuous scrutiny by an omniscient decider. Few projects will be considered, and of them, the alternatives, not chosen, will not have been recorded as having been perceived as attractive.[98] Decisions are very neatly implicit in the estimates made of the relevant characteristics of very few alternatives. Perception is very close to being a function of preference, rather than the other way around.[99] Furthermore, it is usually not just a case of organizations looking for alternatives; "alternatives are also looking for organizations,"[100] as did Airco when its management did not want a takeover by Curtis-Wright. The gloomy attitude of BOC toward concrete proposals to enter the United States became irrelevant when the Airco opportunity presented itself. (Fortunately or unfortunately, history cannot provide irrefutable data on what might have happened had different decisions been made; it can illuminate only what did happen, and we can never be sure whether better results might have been obtained even for firms that appear well managed.)

What evidence could we expect, given BOC's professed interest in entering the United States market? What information on additional feasible modes of entry would be available? The evidence is likely to support the lack of feasibility of anything but the mode decided on. What might have happened to change BOC's view of alternative modes of entry if it were barred from acquiring Airco? We might as well ask what made Bethlehem Steel rethink the feasibility of building an integrated steel plant in the Chicago area when it was not permitted to merge with Youngstown.[101]

It is necessary to resort to economic forecasts for profitability and growth of the industry. The FTC supplied evidence of "supply lagging behind demand" until the 1974 recession and argue that *de novo* or toehold entry was feasible. For example, a tonnage plant cost $7–8 million to construct; several could have been build and expanded for less than the $82.8 million Airco purchase.[102] The FTC expected demand for industrial gases to rise, partly as a result of the rise of the prices of petroleum products; industrial gases are used in synthetic natural gas and gas produced from coal and oxygen, in generating chemical feedstock for manufacturing fertilizers and methanol, in nitrogen food freezing, and in sewage treatment.[103]

L'Aire Liquide, number 5 in the United States in 1972, had entered the United States via the purchase of a toehold in 1968. The FTC argued persuasively:

> We have difficulty in perceiving why this international firm (which was the world's largest industrial gases firm before BOC acquired Airco) was able to enter on such a modest scale, yet BOC could not. The record indicates the existence of many small companies which could presumably be purchased in similar fashion.[104]

Ironically, the argument by BOC that the possibility of upstream integration by industrial users limits the ability of the industrial gas industry to raise prices[105] — a contention not accepted by the FTC[106] — suggested that BOC did not need Airco to enter. If a medium sized steel company can build a tonnage plant, why could BOC not do so?

Another point about the BOC decision is that the position taken by Judge Oakes may deter firms from even beginning to consider alternative modes of entry. It is not only a question of a company's viewing as feasible only those modes of entry that are immediately attractive, but also of discouraging investigation of the other modes of entry. As Areeda asks in his basic textbook on antitrust law, if a defendant can be shown to have investigated independent entry, the government can use this evidence against a merger — "but might this have the ironic consequence of paralyzing and thus discouraging firms from exploring the independent entry we prefer?"[107] The same question applies, of course, to toehold acquisitions.

No subjective timetable, precisely calibrated or not, should be sought by the courts nor by those charged with upholding the antitrust laws.[108] If Section 7 is to serve the purpose of preventive antitrust, should not "a reasonable probability of eventual entry" in a manner more conducive to competition than the takeover of the third largest United States firm in the industry by the world leader more than suffice to disallow the takeover?

THE TOEHOLD DOCTRINE AND THE RESERVED QUESTION

We have seen that these two recent decisions, far from giving evidence of the role that the toehold doctrine can play in making coherent the potential entry theory and the probable future competition theory, suggest that the doctrine is foundering on the preconditions set forth in *Marine,* preconditions that must be met before the question reserved in *Falstaff* is reached. But this outcome is not necessary.

In fact it is difficult to quarrel with the essential notions of the preconditions. If a merger does leave competition in the market place entirely unchanged, then the *Marine* preconditions are not illogical. Even though firms have no constitutional right to merge,[109] why should the enforcement provisions of Section 7 prevent them from merging unless the prohibition of the merger will produce some economic benefit or prevent some economic harm?

(1) The acquiring firm should have available means of entering the target market other than the questioned merger. But the existence of formidable barriers in *Marine* by reason of state banking laws implies nothing about the situation in unregulated industries.[110] If a firm wants to enter an industry by any means, this desire suggests on the face of it — though the suggestion should be rebuttable — that entry is possible by

other means. (2) The other means of entry should indeed offer a substantial likelihood of ultimately aiding competition. But the more need to build *de novo* or to expand a toehold acquisition is in itself an augmentation of competition. As a precedent, *Marine* should be handled with care so that the preconditions do not become greater stumbling blocks than *Falstaff* implies.

What remains then is the reserved question from *Falstaff*. The question was posed to focus the attention of the lower court on the perceived potential entry doctrine (our declared potential entry), which the lower court had not addressed. Is a merger that would leave competition in the market place exactly as it was, neither hurt nor helped, within the reach of Section 7 if the merging company could have entered *de novo* or through a toehold? Potential competition theory offers a clear answer to the reserved question. Yes, such a merger if it existed would be within the reach of Section 7, and, yes although Section 7 should serve as an impediment to entry that is unlikely to threaten established firms, at the same time it is precisely entry that will threaten established firms that Section 7 should facilitate.

Having answered the reserved question affirmatively, we must question the relevance of the question even though in so doing we disagree with authorities, including Justice White, who agree to view mergers such as those considered here as having no effect on competition in the market place. The reserved question implies nothing more than a change of a name on a door; that company one has been replaced by company two. If it is certain that competition is being left exactly as it was, company two must be identical to company one. But is not company two almost inevitably someting different from company one that it replaced? Yes, the resources of the acquiring firm, its goals, especially as evidenced by its past behavior in other markets, its history with respect to pricing and product improvement, various horizontal and vertical relationships with other firms, its financial resources — all must be compared with the same aspects of the acquired company.[111] Nor are all of them subsumed under the consideration of the possibility of entrenchment, which Judge Blair was careful to consider in *Black and Decker/McCulloch.* Questions of goals, behavior, resources, potential entry, probably future competition, contingent potential entry, and contingent future competition are analytically distinct. But when they have been analyzed in all the manifestations relevant to a contested merger, what is left of the reserved question? A merger that leaves the market place exactly as it was turns out to be a hollow shell. As such it should hardly bemuse the courts.[112]

A merger will have many effects on competition. Under Section 7 it must be determined what they are and whether the anticompetive effects outweigh the procompetitive effects. A merger will not be illegal under Section 7 merely because it does not augment competition, but it will be illegal if the potential anticompetitive effects substantially outweigh any procompetive effects. A merger that produces no effects on competition is not an illegal merger; it is a merger that we are not likely to encounter in the real world.

There remain the question of what constitutes substantial effects on competition of a toehold merger versus another merger and the question of what kind of acquisition is small enough to be considered a toehold. The answer to the first question must refer to the basic question of the potential competition doctrine. If the acquiring firm is large enough to take over (in contrast to being taken over) a major firm in the target industry, then its entry into the industry unilaterally or through a toehold would create a presumption of substantial procompetitive effects. An initial answer to the second question is to be found in Judge Ferguson's definition in *Phillips Petroleum.* A toehold acquistion is one that requires addition to capacity to implement the entry; that is, the acquired firm must be smaller than minimum optimum scale.

Guidelines for a three-way classification — presumed legal/questionable/presumed illegal (the first and third presumptions being rebuttable — such as Steiner suggests[113] — would be appropriate for this approach. Mergers in which the acquired firms are clearly smaller than the minimum optimum scale would be presumed legal, mergers in which larger firms are entering by acquiring existing major firms would be presumed illegal. There no doubt would be many cases that are neither obviously legal nor obviously illegal, cases in which careful analyses of all the effects of the proposed merger and its alternatives would have to be made.[114]

Black and Decker/McCulloch and BOC International/Airco almost certainly belong in the first category. It is unfortunate that the special features of the regulated banking industry in *Marine* led to decisions in which major firms in target industries were taken over when alternatives more favorable to competition appear to have available.

Demsetz urges that economists exercise caution in advocating antitrust policy, as

> unlike most regulatory agencies, the Antitrust Division and the Federal Trade Commission are likely to take our suggestions seriously. Partly this is because the theoretical vacuum encourages these regulatory agencies to rely more heavily than other agencies on any help they can find, and partly this reflects the fact that these agencies, since they do not work persistently on the task of regulating a particular industry, are less likely to be "captured" by those they oversee. This combination of unsatisfactory theory and absence of "captors" encourages them to be overly influenced by the scribblings of academics.[115]

Fear of influence on policy makers should not silence economists. Leaving the structure of United States industry to "natural forces" is itself a policy even if advocated by not advocating anything else.

If the overall concentration of the United States economy proceeds apace, it will not be because the toehold element in potential competition doctrine has been proved useless or inconsistent. Indeed toehold doctrine resolves an apparent conflict between the theory of potential entry theory and the theory of probable future competition and should play a major role in economic and legal approaches to antitrust.

NOTES

*The author would like to thank Benjamin Klebaner, professor of economics, City College, for many helpful comments. She also wishes to thank Jacqueline Carey for editorial assistance.

1. *U.S.* v. *Black and Decker Manufacturing Co.* and *McCulloch Corp.* U.S. District Court D. Md. (1976) CCH Trade Regulation Report, Para. 61,035, pp. 69, 566-69, 607.
2. *BOC International Ltd.* v. *Federal Trade Commission,* U.S. Court of Appeals, Second Circuit (1977).
3. *U.S.* v. *Marine Bancorporation,* 418 U.S. 602, 639.
4. *Missouri-Portland Cement Co.* v. *Cargill, Inc.,* 498 F. 22d 851, 860.
5. *Cf.* Shull (1968).
6. *U.S.* v. *Philadelphia National Bank,* 374 U.S. 321 (1963) 399.
7. *U.S.* v. *Von's Grocery Co.* et al., 384 U.S. 270 (1956).
8. Cf. Asch, p. 313. Asch is uncomfortable with the Supreme Court's apparent holding in *Pabst (U.S.* v. *Pabst Brewing Co.* et al., 384 U.S. 547 1966) that is "any market definition exists under which evidence of reduced competition can be shown, it does not matter whether that market definition is theoretically 'good' in economic terms."
9. Gellhorn, p. 1.
10. *U.S.* v. *Northern Pacific Railways,* 356 U.S. (1958) 4.
11. "Second best" issues are beyond the scope of this paper.
12. Senate Report, p. 1, cited by Scherer, p. 474.
13. Rhoades, p. 35.
14. See Bain, 1949, 1956, and Sylos-Labini for the early development of the concept.
15. See Bain, 1956.
16. Koch, pp. 285. *f.*
17. See Stigler, Ch. 13.
18. See Scherer, pp. 219-234.
19. See *U.S* v. *Penn Olin Chemical Co.* et al., 378 E.S. 158, 1964.
20. Bain, 1956. *Cf.* Steiner, pp. 259 ff.
21. *Missouri-Portland* v. *Cargill,* U.S. Ct. Appeals 2nd Cir 1090 (1973).

22. The phrase is from the reserved question in *U.S.* v. *Flastaff Brewing Co.,* 410 U.S. 526 (1973).
23. Steiner, p. 263.
24. See Rhoades and Yeats, Kohn and Carlo.
25. See Shull, 1974; *cf.* Solomon, 1972.
26. Austin and Solomon, p. 306.
27. Adams, p. 1286, note 48.
28. Docket No. 8739 (1970), 1970 Trade Cases, 19,288, in Stelzer, pp. 192-203.
29. Stelzer, pp. 179 f.
30. *U.S.* v. *Falstaff Brewing Co.,* 410 U.S. 526 (1973).
31. *Ibid.,* 537.
32. *Falstaff Brewing Co.* v. *U.S.,* 332 F. Supp 970 (1974).
33. *U.S.* v. *Marine Bancorporation,* 418 U.S. 602 (1974).
34. See Klebaner for a thorough discussion of the relevance of entry barriers to this case.
35. *Cf.* Fox, 1975, p. 419.
36. *Missouri-Portland Cement Co.* v. *Cargill, Inc.* 498 F. 2nd 861 Certiorari denied 95 Sct. 150 (1974).
37. *Kennecott Copper Corp.* v. *FTC* 467 F2d 67 10th Cir (1972) (Affirming FTC 1971) Certiorari denied 95S.Ct. 3210 (1974).
38. *Phillips Petroleum* 367 F. Supp. 1226, D.c. Calif. (1973) affirmed 94 S Ct. 3199 (1974).
39. *Cf.* Fox, 1975.
40. p. 1258.
41. *U.S.* v. *Black and Decker Manufacturing Co.,* U.S. District Court, District of Maryland, Civ. No. 73-964-B. *Commerce Clearing House Trade Regulation Reporter,* para. 61,033, pp. 69,563-69,607.
42. *Ibid.,* pp. 69,566 f.
43. *Ibid.,* p. 69,567.
44. *Ibid.,* p. 69,567.
45. *Ibid.,* p. 69,581.
46. *Ibid.,* p. 69,577.
47. Richard W. Dempster, President of McCulloch Corporation, stated in a letter to the writer that "it would be accurate to say that McCulloch is one of the three largest firms in the market and submarket." (February 8, 1977).
48. *Ibid.,* p. 69,577.
49. *Ibid.,* p. 69, 467 ff.
50. *ibid.,* p. 69,572. *Cf. Marine,* 418 U.S. 630.
51. *Ibid.,* p. 69,574.
52. *Ibid.,* p. 69,574. Quotation is from *Marine,* 418 U.S. at 633.
53. *Ibid.,* p. 69,579 and note 43.
54. *Ibid.,* p. 69, 578 f.
55. *Ibid.,* p. 69, 580 f.

56. *Ibid.*, p. 69, 583, citing *Marine,* 418 U.S. 602, 631.
57. *Ibidl.*, p. 69, 574, citing *Marine,* 418 U.S. 639-40.
58. *Ibid.*, p. 69 583 ff.
59. *Ibid.*, p. 69, 585 ff.
60. *Ibid.*, p. 69, 589.
61. *Ibid.*, p. 69, 590f.
62. *Ibid.*, p. 69, 591.
63. *Ibid.*, p. 69, 592.
64. *Ibid.*, p. 69, 592ff.
65. *Ibid.*, p. 69, 594 f.
66. *Ibid.*, p. 69, 595, quoting *United States* v. *Falstaff Brewing Corp.*, 410 U.S. 526, 532 (1973).
67. *Ibid.*, p. 69, 596, note 76. *Cf. ibid.*, p. 69, 574.
68. *Ibid.*, p. 69, 595 ff.
69. *Ibid.*, p. 69, 599 f.
70. *U.S.* v. *Marine Bancorporation,* 418 U.S. at 631.
71. 418 U.S. at 638.
72. 410 U.S. 526 at 537. (Emphasis added)
73. 418 U.S. at 633.
74. *BOC International, Ltd.* v. *Federal Trade Commission,* U.S. Court of Appeals 2nd Cir. 3669 (1977) DKT 76-4044.
75. *BOC International* v. *FTC.* p. 3671.
76. FTC Brief p. 11, and FTC Opinion, p. 4.
77. FTC Brief, p. 12.
78. FTC Brief, p. 5.
79. FTC Opinion, p. 3.
80. Brief for Petitioner, p. 5.
81. *BOC International* v. *FTC,* p. 3681.
82. Brief for Petitioner, p. 9.
83. *Ibid.*, p. 5.
84. U.K. Brief, p. 22.
85. Brief for Petitioner, p. 93.
86. FTC Opinion, p. 6.
87. Brief for Petitioners, p. 100, p. 111.
88. *BOC International* v. *FTC,* 3674 f.
89. 418 U.S. 630.
90. *BOC International* v. *FTC,* p. 3677.
91. *Ibid.*, same page; FTC Opinion, p. 27.
92. FTC Opinion, p. 27.
93. *BOC International* v. *FTC.* p. 3678 f., citing as a reference for "decades" the transcript of the oral argument.
94. *BOC International* v. *FTC,* p. 3680.
95. *BOC International* v. *FTC,* p. 3679, p. 3680.
96. *cf.* Klebaner.
97. *Cf. U.S.* v. *Falstaff Brewing Corp.*, 410 U.S. 426, 564-569, Concurring Opinion by Justice marshall.

98. Cyert and March, p. 64 ff.

99. The Perham-Greenfield study made in 1961 for BOC and the slightly later Arthur D. Little study can be interpreted as rationalizations of the attitude that at that time the attractive United States market was not being entered.

100. Cyert and March, p. 80.

101. *U.S.* v. *Bethlehem Steel,* 168 F. Supp 576 SDNY1958.

102. Respondent's Brief, p. 39 f., p. 22 f.

103. FTC Opinion, p. 25.

104. FTC Opinion, p. 25.

105. Petitioner's Brief, pp. 94 ff.

106. FTC Opinion, p. 37.

107. Areeda, p. 518 f.

108. Justice Marshall's concurring opinion in *Falstaff* supports this reasoning. In order to make a prima facie case, the Government need only show that objective measurable market data favor a de novo entry and that the alleged potential entrant has the economic ability to make such entry... Where objectively measurable market forces make clear that it is in a firm's economic self-interest to make a de novo entry and that a firm had the economic capability to do so, I would hold it in error... to conclude that the firm is not an actual potential entrant on the basis of testimony by company officials as the firm's future intent. (526 U.S. 506).

109. Cf. Justice Douglas's dissent to the granting of a motion to vacate the stay of the Missouri-Portland/Cargill merger, 44 S.C.T. 3210 (1974)

110. It is significant that Justice White, who wrote the court's opinion in *Falstaff,* dissented in *Marine.* He stated in his dissent that the court was raising barriers to the application of the potential competition doctrine not only in the banking business but in other lines of commerce. (418 U.S. at 654)

111. A dramatic if curious suggestion of the change in competitive ability that a merger may cause is to be found in the British government's *amicus curiae* brief in which it is suggested that a thriving Airco would be reduced by the merger to the state of a rather helpless foreigner, unfamiliar with laws and mores!

112. The idea that competition can be masured by noting the number and size distribution of the firms in the market flows from the structural approach to competition. The incompleteness of this approach is revealed in that the replacement of one firm by another may have important implications for the structure of the industry, to say nothing of behavior. A simple structural approach would, ironically enough, give an affirmative answer to the reserved *Falstaff* questions.

113. Steiner,pp. 329 f.

114. Cf. Benston who argues that mergers that do not substantially eliminate competition are in the public interest, given relatively unrestricted entry (Benston, p. 233). We would turn this around; it may be that mergers

that would be illegal if entry were unrestricted would be permissable if entry were restricted, as in commercial banking in some states.

115. Demsetz, p. 383.

CASES

Bendix Corporation v. *F.T.C.* FTC Docket no. 8739 (1970), 1970 Trade Cases, Para. 19,288, 450 F., 2d 534, 6th cir 1971.

Black and Decker Manufacturing Co. and McCulloch Corp., U. S. v. U. S. District Court, District of Maryland, Cov. no. 73-964-B (1976), Commerce Clearing House Trade Regulation Reporter. Para. 61,033, pp.69,566-69, 607.

BOC International Ltd., f/k/a The British Oxygen Co., Ltd., BOC Financial Corp. *BOC Holdings, Ltd., and British Oxygen Investments, Ltd.,* v. *Federal Trade Commission, U.S. Court of Appeals for Second Circuit* Nos. 173, 175, September Term 1976, Docket nos. 76, 4044, 76, 4045.

Falstaff Brewing Co., U.S. v., 410 U.S. 526 (1973).

Falstaff Brewing Co., U.S. v., 332 F. Supp 970 (1974).

Kennecott Copper Corporation v. *F.T.C.* 467 F., 2d 67 10th Cir., 1972 (affirming F.T.C., 1971). Certiorari denied, 94 S. Ct. 1617 (1974).

Marine Bancorporation, U.S. v., 418 U.S. 602.

Missouri-Portland Cement Co. v. *Cargill, Inc.* 498 F., 2nd 851; U.S. Ct. Appeals, 2nd Cir., 190 (1973), Motion to vacate stay granted 44 S. Ct. (1974). Certiorari denied 95 S. Ct. 150 (1974).

Northern Pacific Railway, U.S. v., 356 U.S. 1 (1958).

Pabst Brewing Co., U.S. v., 384 U.S. 547 (1966).

Penn Olin Chemical Co. et al., U.S. v., 378 U.S. 158 (1964).

Philadelphia National Bank, U.S. v., 374 U.S. 321 (1963).

Phillips Petroleum, U.S. v., 367 F., Supp. 1226, D.C. Calif. (1973). affirmed 94 S. Ct. 3199 (1974).

Von's Grocery Co. et al., U.S. v., 384 U.S. 270 (1966).

REFERENCES

Adams, W. J., "Market Structure and Corporate Power," *Columbia Law Review,* November 1974, pp. 1276-1297.

Areeda, Phillip, *Antitrust Analysis,* Boston: Little Brown &Co., 1967.

Asch, Peter, *Economic Theory and the Antitrust Dilemma,* N.Y.: John Wiley and Sons, c. 1970.

Austin A. D. and Solomon, E. H., "New Antitrust Problem: Vertical Integration in Correspondent Banking." *University of Pennsylvania Law Review,* December 1973, pp. 366-412.

Bain, Joe S., *Battiers to New Competition: Their Character and Consequences in Manufacturing Industries,* Cambridge, Mass.: Harvard University Press, 1956.

"A Note on Pricing in Monopoly and Oligopoly," *American Economic Review,* vol. 59, March 1949, pp.448-464.

Benston, G., "The Optimal Banking Structure: Theory and Evidence *Journal of Bank Research,* vol. III, Winter 1973, pp. 220-257.

Demsetz, Harold, "Economics as a Guide to Antitrust Regulation," *Journal of Law and Economics,* vol. 19, no. 2, August 1976, pp. 371-384.

"Economic Evaluation of Merger and Holding Company Cases," in *Proceedings of a Conference on Bank Structure and Competition.* Federal Reserve Bank of Chicago, 1968, pp. 20-36.

Fox, Eleanor M., "Antitrust Mergers, and the Supreme Court: The Politics of Section 7 of the Clayton Act," *Mercer Law Review,* vol. 26, no. 2, Winter 1975, pp. 389-425.

Gellhorn "Introduction to Antitrust Economics," *Duke Law Journal,* March 1975, pp. 1-43.

Klebaner, Benjamin, "Potential Competition in Banking and the Supreme Court," *Banking Law Journal,* vol. 92, no. 6, June-July 1975, pp. 545-604.

Koch, James V., *Industrial Organization and Prices,* Englewood Cliffs, N.J.: Prentice-Hall, c. 1974.

Kohn, E., and C.J. Carlo, *Potential Competition: Unfounded Faith or Pragmatic Foresight?,* Albany: New York State Banking Department, 1970.

"Merger Guidelines of the Department of Justice," Commerce Clearing House, Trade Regulation Reporter, 4510, p. 6681/ff.

Rhoades, Stephen A., "A Clarification of the Potential Competition Doctrine in Bank Merger Analysis," *Journal of Bank Research,* vol. III, Spring 1975, pp. 35-42.

Rhoades, Stephen A., and A.J. Yeats, "An Analysis of Entry and Expansion Predictions in Bank Acquisition and Merger Cases," *Western Economic Journal,* September 1972, pp. 337-345.

Scherer, F. M., *Industrial Market Structure and Economic Performance.* Chicago: Rand McNally & Co., 1971.

Senate Report no. 698 Accompany H.R. 15,657, 63rd Congress, 2d Session, 1914.

Shull, Bernard, "Bank Expansion: The New Competition and the Old Predatory Practices," *Banking Law Journal,* vol. 91 (1974), pp. 726-747.

Solomon, E. H., "Bank Merger Policy and Problems: A Linkage Theory of Oligopoly," *Banking Law Journal,* vol. 89 (1972), p. 116.

Steiner, Peter O: *Mergers, Motives, Effects, Policies,* Ann Arbors University of Michigan Press, C: 1975.

Stelzer, Irwin M., *Selected Antitrust Cases: Landmark Decisions*, Homewood, III.: Richard D. Irwin, Inc., 1976.

Stigler, George, *The Theory of Price*, New York: the MacMillan Co., 1952.

Sylos-Labini, Paolo, *Ologopoly and Technical Progress:*, Cambridge, Mass.: Harvard University Press, 1962.

"Toehold Acquisitions, Potential Toehold Acquisitions and Section 7 of the Clayton Act," *Antitrust Law Journal*, vol. 42, no. 3, 1972-73, pp. 573-586.

Comments on "The Toehold Acquisition Doctrine"

BENJAMIN J. KLEBANER*

Toehold (or foothold) acquisitions in potential competition antitrust cases represent an area "on the frontiers of antitrust law."[1] The Carey paper discusses several toehold mergers in the industrial area; my comments include some actual examples of toeholds in the entry-regulated sector of banking in which the Antitrust Division has filed a substantial number of suits.

POTENTIAL ENTRY THEORY

Professor Carey urges an affirmative answer to the reserved questions in *Falstaff* in the name of potential entry theory. However, evidence thus far accumulated is insufficient to make the theory the basis for a "legal presumption regarding competitive impact."[2] A reasonable doubt remains that as formulated for the purposes of use by the courts, it could be supported empirically.[3]

Entry theory suggests a variety of possible outcomes,

*Professor of Economics, The City College of the City University of New York.

Research on banking potential competition has been made possible by CUNY Grant R F 1393. The author is also regional economist, Second Nation Bank Region. The opinions expressed in this paper are those of the author and should in no way be construed to represent those of the Office of the Comptroller of Currency.

depending on the model's initial assumptions. The theory predicting the effects of entry conditions on market conduct and performance is unusually complex, as Professor Joe S. Bain has pointed out. The economist who is mainly responsible for our analytical understanding of entry also noted that "the variety of predictable influences [is] correspondingly great."[4]

Behavior of potential entrants depends on their expectation of how established firms will react to entry. The latter's behavior depends on how they think potential entrants expect them to react to entry.[5] These matters remain to be investigated empirically.

Professor Carey appears to identify entry-inhibiting behavior with "behavior most beneficial to the consumer." Certain forms of nonprice competition, however, may serve as very effective barriers to entry, without enhancing consumer welfare. Further, the fact that a firm may wish to enter is not *necessarily* an indication that limit-pricing strategy has not been used in a way that maximizes consumer benefits. Demand in this industry may be expanding rapidly, or the entrant may be introducing new production techniques or a somewhat differentiated product, to cite some alternative possibilities.

We read that an acquiring firm "has strengthened itself through the merger," but is this outcome inevitable? When a substantial established firm is acquired, the profits that attracted entry via merger are said to be "available and require no effort to enlarge the market share in order to get them." Does this not depend on the price paid for the acquired firm? Similarly, Carey argues that a now stronger acquiring firm "uses profits from the merger to strengthen its position elsewhere," thereby lessening probable future competition in those other markets. What if there are no supernormal profits?

TIME FRAME

In *Continental Can* (1964) the Supreme Court stressed that the potential competition must be "sufficiently probable and imminent."[6] Yet a decade later the Justice Department argued before the court that we are "dealing here with very long-term trends."[7] A period of up to a decade or so for potential competition to evolve was deemed reasonable by an economist testifying for the Antitrust Division in the *Marine Bancorporation* case.[8] The Justice Department did not believe that the test of probability under Section 7 should be placed in a time frame. As long as a firm's presence on the edge of a market makes it a competitive force, the government should not have to demonstrate the likelihood of actual entry within a certain span of time.[9]

In *Marine* the government was convinced that the bank holding company exerted a procompetitive effect by standing in the wings. In *BOC,* however, no claim was made that the British firm exerted such an effect. FTC counsel conceded that decades might have to elapse under the commission's "reasonable probability of eventual entry" standard. The circuit court's request for an estimate of when in the future competition would increase if BOC were to divest its acquisition does not appear to be unreasonable, given the absence of a wings effect in this case.

Carey doubts that convincing positive evidence is available. Some clues may be found in the experience of recent entrants in the same or related fields: How long did it take them to build similar plants and establish not insubstantial market positions?

Areeda's argument that all alternative modes of entry may not be investigated for fear of providing the governmnent with detrimental evidence is doubtful in case of well-managed acquiring firms. A poorly-run firm, on the other hand, is unlikely to maintain its market share in the long run, and thus may not be a substantial threat under the potential competition doctrine.

In a dynamic economy a time frame of several decades is too speculative for antitrust policy purposes. Potential entry that is projected for many years into the obscure future is a very weak competitive force; it may be nonexistent unless the wings effect can be shown to be operative in the particular case.

ENTRENCHMENT IN BANKING CASES

Entrenchment, an issue carefully considered in the *Black and Decker* opinion, has been defined by the Supreme Court as a merger producing an "enterprise likely to dominate the target market."[10] The Justice Department 1968 merger guidelines refer to a situation in which "an acquisition of a leading firm in a relatively concentrated or rapidly concentrating market may serve to entrench or increase the market power of that firm or raise barriers to entry in that market."[11] The Supreme Court in *Marine* and the district court in *Black and Decker* were careful to point out that the challenged mergers would not lead to entrenchment.

In the *Greeley* banking case the government argued that First National Bancorporation's acquisition would entrench the high concentration existing in that market and would eliminate the possibility of "spreading competitive power a little more evenly."[12] However, the share of Weld County deposits held by the acquired bank declined from 26.4 percent to 22.1 percent between mid-1969 and 1979, while that of the three largest went from 79.4 percent to 61.6 percent.[13]

In *Marine* the district court rejected the government's argument that Old National Bank would be entrenched after Washington Trust Bank had been acquired and could no longer compete for branch sites in the Spokane area.[14] As the holding company was precluded by Washington law from operating additional branches, the Comptroller of the

Currency saw the law as enabling lesser Spokane-based banks "to grow and acquire competitive muscle."[15]

The evidence in Washington and Colorado does not support the broad entrenchment argument. Despite high concentration, forty-seven new banks were established in Washington from September 1960 to May 1972; four of these opened in Seattle, headquarters city of the two largest banking organizations in the state, and another nine in their county.[16] In ten of the eighteen markets in which the Marine-owned bank, National Bank of Commerce (NBC) competed, its share declined from 1965 to 1970.[17] NBC's market share dropped in fourteen of sixteen communities where it had branches, and a competing bank was established after 1957.[18]

Neither did experience support the government's allegation that would-be entrants might be frightened off by the prospect of having to compete with the three largest banking organizations in Colorado. Thus twenty-four, new banks opened in the seven markets where Western Bancorporation and United Bankshares had acquired banks at least five years before.[19] Of the twenty-four, seventeen were in Denver.[20] In three of the seven markets, the holding company subsidiary's share had fallen markedly.[21]

A comprehensive study of 146 acquisitions throughout the nation during the 1947–1969 period found little evidence of superior subsequent deposit growth after a bank became a subsidiary of a registered bank holding company. A subsequent investigation of 71 banks acquired by holding companies in states that do not permit branching showed no significant changes in the market shares of the acquired banks after an average of almost four years had elapsed.[22] For that matter, a study of product extension and other conglomerate mergers in manufacturing and mining in which the acquired firm had at least $10 million in assets, showed no measured change in concentration ratios between 1954/1958 and 1963.[23]

Toeholds in Banking

Some of the practical issues that arise in connection with the toehold doctrine are illustrated by the three banking potential competition cases appealed to the Supreme Court as well as by several others lost by the government in the district court.

Washington's inflexible limitations on *de novo* bank expansion were noted in *Marine.* Nevertneless, the Justice Department was of the view that NBC might have entered Spokane other than by acquiring the third largest bank.[24] Even small-scale entry by an important banking organization was said to inject a significant new competitive force.[25]

Had NBC sponsored a new bank or made a foothold acquisition, competition in the concentrated Spokane market might have been enhanced. NBC had earlier negotiated for the purchase of the Farmers and Merchants Bank of Rockford, including two branches, one in a suburban shopping center six miles east of downtown Spokane.[26] American Commercial Bank, another possibility mentioned by the Antitrust Division, had downtown Spokane headquarters as well as four branches.[27] Under Washington law it would not be eligible for puchase until 1975, four years after the Washington Trust Bank (WTB) acquisition had been approved.[28] As of 1971, officers of American had no interest in selling.[29]

An existing Spokane branch was another possibility suggested. However, the president of NBC had never heard of a branch for sale anywhere in the state; he was sure that one would not be worthwhile buying even if available.[30] The Regional Administrator of National Banks had a dim view of a bank that might sell a branch; he, too, knew of no bank that wished to do so.[31] The district court concluded that other than WTB, there was no bank or branch available for purchase at the time or "in the reasonably forseeable future."[32]

NBC sought to get into a market in "a meaningful way;" "there is no use buying peanuts."[33] In a metropolitan area like Spokane, foothold entry was incompatible with "prudent business practice,"[34] In the view of the district court, in order to be competitive, a substantial downtown office was required.[35]

In the Connecticut case, the Connecticut National Bank of Bridgeport (CNB) had received permission to acquire the First New Haven National Bank (FNH). The government mentioned two city banks and one suburban bank as toehold possibilities for FNH in the Bridgeport metropolitan area. The district court disagreed; the premium that might be exacted would tend to discourage FNH's merger with any of the three.[36] Not a single New Haven bank was small enough to qwualify as a toehold for CNB. The Antitrust Division mentioned five suburban banks in the metropolitan area,[37] arguing that "core city offices are not indispensable to effective market penetration... of metropolitan banking markets."[38] However, the district court correctly understood the need for a downtown location from which to serve certain important business customers.[39] Effective competition with FNH would call for a CNB office in the city of New Haven, the former's primary market.[40] The government did not identify any banks as actually for sale then or in "the foreseeable future," hence the government did not satisfy the district court that either challenged bank could expand by toehold acquisition.[41]

In the Colorado case the government named as foothold candidates for First National Bancorporation the State Bank of Greeley as well as banks in two neighboring towns.[42] State Bank's owners were reported to be unwilling to relinquish active management even if they sold out to a holding company; the district court did not consider that bank a "likely possibility."[43]

In a defeat that the Antitrust Division did not appeal, the court found that First National Bank of Maryland aimed to provide "city-type services on a countywide basis." There was no one major town in Harford County, hence the bank needed offices in five areas. Other smaller banks did not have enough locations in the county. The judge added that to permit the bank to merge with the second rather than with the largest bank "is to draw lines and to create shades of distinction which cannot be justified in as elusive and delicate a process as is posed by the scanning of the Harford County banking event, horizon in search of objective clues for the foreseeable future."[44]

In a Virginia case, Prince William County had no toehold bank at the time of the merger application. The availability of a new bank in the process of opening was considered by the court a matter of "sheer speculation"; there was no evidence that it was for sale.[45] The holding company would not contemplate such an unusual acquisition in any event, and had not previously gone the *de novo* route.[46]

In all five banking cases, then, the courts set aside the toehold acquisitions proposed by the government as unsuitable, unavailable, or not likely to make a difference.

What Is a Toehold?

Whether a particular bank qualified as a toehold acquisition was decided against the Antitrust Division in a 1974 case involving Deposit Guaranty National Bank, the largest in Mississippi. This bank had settled a previous potential competition merger challenge by agreeing not to acquire any bank for a decade without the Attorney General's approval. The Antitrust Division would not consent to the acquisition of the Leflore Bank of Greenwood, third largest with 18 percent of the county's deposits. The bank had declined from second place because of the age and infirmities of the top management. As even the smallest had 17.1 percent of deposits, in the Justice Department's view no Greenwood bank qualified as a toehold. The district court disagreed,[47] and the merger took place. Here was a county with an 11 percent population decline during the 1960's and with a buying level only three-fourths of the low Mississippi average. Grenwood already had one banking office for every 2,240 people; *de novo* hardly appeared plausible under such circumstances. The Comptroller of the Currency deemed the number of banks to be "adequate."[48]

The 1968 merger guidelines of the Antitrust Division drew the line for considering a prospective acquisition as a toehold at 10 percent of the market. Professor Brodley has suggested 5 percent for market-and 10 percent for product-extension acquisitions by very substantial firms.[49] Any such limitations, however, should be subject to rebuttal evidence (of the kind offered in the Mississippi bank case) in the interest of a rational approach.

Alternative Mergers In Banking

When a particular banking merger was blocked either by the Antitrust Division or by the federal supervisory agencies, would-be sellers generally found other buyers. In a dozen instances from 1968 to 1971, horizontal combinations were replaced by out-of-territory acquiring banks.[50]

In the case of would-be-buyers, seven out of twenty-two state member banks found less anticompetitive acquisitions or entered *de novo* after their original proposals had been turned down (1960–1969). The average time that elapsed was two years.[51]

When the then largest banking organization in Colorado was blocked from acquiring the third largest Colorado Springs bank, the holding company proceeded to buy the smallest of the four downtown banks. About a year earlier it had not been available for sale.[52]

Even more notable was the alternative course taken by First National Bancorporation. The holding company called off the plan to acquire the second largest bank in Colorado Springs (a downtown, "wholesale" bank), when challenged by the Justice Department.[53] Instead, a year later, it acquired a small ($9.2 million deposit) bank three miles from downtown Colorado Springs.[54]

Alternatives *are* often available and feasible. The basic issue remains, though, whether in a given case compelling the would-be acquirer to choose a different partner makes a not insubstantial difference in competitive impact.

How Much Deconcentration?

A currently unresolved potential competition issue is the amount of deconcentration that would satisfy the Supreme Court's *Marine*, criterion of "significant. . . . procompetitive effects." If the share of the four largest in a given industry is the concentration measure used, then a toehold acquisition may result in little (if any) decrease, except possibly after a lapsc of many years.

In *Marine* the Supreme Court had as an example the Pacific National Bank of Washington, Seattle-based subsidiary of the giant Western Bancorporation, that acquired the two-office Spokane National Bank in September 1964. At the end of 1966 Pacific's offices had 1.5 percent of total deposits in the Spokane standard metropolitan statistical area (SMSA) and 2.2 percent by mid-1972. Justice Powell considered this increase in share "insignificant,"[55] echoing the district court's position that Pacific's branches had not exerted any significant procompetitive effect.[56]

Foothold acquisitions by bank holding companies from 1966 to 1972 did *not* result in a decline in the three-firm concentration ratio in the 112 SMSAs involved. Perhaps a substantially longer interval would produce different results. In New York and Virginia the market share of acquired large banks declined, whereas that of foothold acquisitions rose.[57]

In any event, the Justice Department has recognized that "there is no guarantee that the entrant, in the face of renewed [sic] competition from the market leaders, will in fact enlarge its market share, nor does this matter for Section 7 purposes: the antitrust laws protect. . . . competition.[58]

This is a sound position, but it has implications for merger cases that may not altogether please the Justice Department. Although deconcentration is often cited as the goal of potential competition policy, the ultimate goal of more competitive performance may be attained without deconcentration taking place. Logically this means that potential competition cases cannot be decided entirely on the basis of concentration ratios; conduct and performance must also be considered.

Professor Carey's Paradox

Black and Decker does not involve us in the paradox cited by Professor Carey. The fact than an industry is *not* moving toward deconcentration (and hence more competitive than concentration ratios could lead us to believe) is *not "ipso facto"*[59] the same as showing that *de novo* or toehold entry would not produce procompetitive results. The complexity of gasoline engine technology cited by the court was the counterpart of Washington's restrictive branching laws in *Marine.* In both cases the courts reasoned from these constraints that alternative entry via a lesser firm would not serve to enhance competition. In other fact situations, the courts may find a substantial procompetitive impact from a toehold.

The Toehold Standard

Professor Carey recommends that the Supreme Court's requirement of "a substantial likelihood of procompetitive effects" should mean that there is less competition than if a *de novo* or a toehold had been acquired instead. Where feasible, toehold acquisitions should be the only acceptable ones for (presumably) substantial well-established firms. Thereby Section 7 would achieve procompetitive effects. However, I doubt that the Burger Supreme Court will find a merger illegal merely "if the potential anticompetitive effects substantially outweigh any procompetitive effects."[60] For a merger to run afoul of the amended Clayton Act, the *net* potential anticompetitive effects would have to be substantial by themselves.

The critique of the BOC case does not deal explicitly with the court's observation that all parties were agreed that if the acquisitions had not been blocked, competition in industrial gases would have been "neither hurt no helped" (in the phrase from *Falstaff)*.[61] Carey does observe that in the real world we are not likely to encounter a merger with literally no effects on competition. However, we are likely to encounter mergers whose impact on potential competition is very unclear. Economists cannot yet claim to have the knowledge that would support simplified rules for judging potential competition issues. Indeed some argue that it is impossible to develop workable rules in this area.[62]

It may be possible to find reliable postacquisition evidence in nonbanking merger cases, in which injunctions are not automatic. Thus in the industrial gases market we could analyze what has happened since the 1974 FTC complaint, on remand in the BOC case. An examination of the market conduct and performance after the challenged merger has taken place may contribute significantly to the court's understanding of its competitive impact.

NOTES

1. *BOC International Ltd.* v. *FTC,* 1977-1 Trade Cases 71677.
2. Thomas W. Dunfee and Louis W. Stern, "Potential Competition Theory as an Antimerger Tool Under Section 7 of the Clayton Act: A Decision Model," 69 *Northwestern University Law Review* (1975), 852; Carey Paper, p. 11.
3. Dunfee and Stern, *loc. cit.,* p. 851.
4. A recent effort with a probabilistic model is offered by David P. Baron, "Limit Pricing, Potential Entry and Barriers to Entry," *American Economic Review* 63 (1973), 666-674. Joe S. Bain, *Industrial Organization* 2d. ed. (New York, 1968), p. 269.
5. Douglas Needham, *Economic Analysis and Industrial Structure* (New York, 1969), p. 109.

6. *United States* v. *Continental Can Co. et al.* 378 U.S. 458 (1964).

7. Oral Argument in Supreme Court, April 23, 1974, at 28 (Friedman); the Antitrust Division preferred ten statewide banks in twenty-five years to three to five banks in five years. Conn. App., 1403 (Clark).

8. Marine App., 481 (Smith).

9. Transcript of Proceedings at 1314 (Antitrust Division Attorney Schepoke); Id. at 31; Brief for U.S. at 42, First Nt'l. speaks of "some future time" when the Comptroller of Currency's attitude toward chartering an additional bank in Greeley might change. See also Reply Brief for U.S. at 9, note 11, First Nat'l.

10. Marine at 623, note 23. Such an acquisition violates Section 7. *United States* v. *Falstaff Brewing Corp.* 410 U.S. 531 (1973) citing 386 U.S. 578-580 (1967).

11. "U.S. Department of Justice Merger Guidelines 1968," 1 Trade Reg. Rep. 4510, no. 20 (1974), at 688-689.

12. Plaintiff's Initial Proposed Findings of Fact, no 84, First Nat'l. (D.C.). Earlier the Antitrust Division argued that the proposed acquisition would "further entrench the highly concentrated Greeley banking structure." Plaintiff's Pretrial Brief at 30. The complaint nowhere uses the words *entrench* or *entrenchment.* First Nat'l. App., 8 ff. The expert economist for the government stated that the acquisition "can't help but entrench the FNB of Greeley and the existing concentrated structure." Id. at 79 (Prof. Richard Walsh). Greeley Transcript of Proceedings, p. 1336 (Schoepke).

13. Paul Schweitzer and Joshua Green, "Greeley in Perspective: What Really Happens When a Bank Holding Company Expands into a Local Market?" 95 *Banking Law Journal* (1978), 147. FDIC Summary of Deposits in All Commercial and Mutual Savings Banks, June 30, 1979.

14. Marine App., 374 (Plaintiff's Contentions and pretrial Order); Marine (D.C.), 94,246 (Find. 23) (erroneously numbered). The majority opinion incorrectly stated: "There is no allegation that the instant merger would produce entrenchment in the Spokane market." Marine at 623, note 23. Section 21 (f) of the complaint specifically alleges that NBC "and other dominant Washington banks will become entrenched in many local markets in eastern Washington." Marine App., 15.

15. 1971 Comptroller of the Currency Ann. Rep. 140. Dean Haywood likewise viewed this statutory restriction as arguing against NBC's entrenchment in Spokane. Marine App., 648.

16. Id. at 1204-1207 (XA-41).

17. Office of the Comptroller of the Currency, Hearing, July 27, 1971, at 114.

18. Marine App., 1908-1919 (D47). All local markets were tabulated for which there were deposit data for offices of competing banks. In Burien a new bank was opened in 1969, while NBC's share went from 18.1 to 19.0 percent. In Edmonds no branch breakdown was available for the 1971

calculation. Another tabulation of thirteen local markets showed that NBC's share declined in eleven markets. The exceptions were Kent, where NBC increased from 7.3 to 18.5 percent, and Walla Walla, where it rose from 5.9 to 6.5 percent. Id. at 1905-1907 (DX 46).

19. Plaintiff's Pretrial Brief at 31, First Nat'l. (D.C.); Brief for Appellees at 56-58, First Nat'l. Only ten of the sixty-five new banks that opened for business from 1961 through 1970 were organized by large holding companies. First Nat'l. App., 1371-1372 (DX 28).

20. Id. at 1345-1350.

21. Brief for Appellees at 58, First Nat'l. The decline in market shares in the cases cited by Bancorporation was said to show "that the acquisition of local market leaders by such large banking institutions is not likely to make the acquired bank a more aggressive competitor. . . ." Brief for U.S. at 39, note 42, First Nat'l. If so, the government cannot simultaneously argue entrenchment.

22. Piper, "Economics of Bank Acquisition by Registered Bank Holding Companies," Federal Reserve Bank of Boston Reseach Report 48, at 161 (1971); Lawrence G. Goldberg, "Bank Holding Company Acquisitions and Their Impact or Market Shares," *Journal of Money, Credit and Banking,* 8 (1976), 127.

23. Lawrence G. Goldberg, "Conglomerate Mergers and Concentration Ratios," *Review of Economics and Statistics* 56 (1974), p. 309.

24. The plaintiff listed three other methods: buying one or more existing offices; acquiring a small state bank whose main office is outside the Spokane metropolitan area, which would convert to a national charter and relocate its headquarters into the area; or branching *de novo* [sic], Marine App., 373. On appeal these methods were not discussed. Brief for U.S. at 16, Marine.

25. Brief for U.S. at 31, Marine; Brief for U.S. at 57, Conn.

26. Brief for U.S. ar 44, 52, Marine. Marine considered the asking price excessive and dropped negotiations. Answering Brief of Appellees at 25, Marine. See also Oral Argument in Supreme Court, April 23, 1974, at 37-38, Marine.

27. Brief for U.S. at 44, 52, Marine.

28. 1971 Comptroller of the Currency Ann. Rep. 139. As the condition of American Commercial Bank was satisfactory, the Washington Supervisor of Banking had no reason to make an exception. Intervenor's Exhibit L. Marine App., 1916 (McCarthy).

29. Intervenor's Exhibit 500(1), Marine, 1918 (letter from Supervisor of Banking McCarthy); id. at 1016 (Selby, testifying about a letter from McCarthy); *American Banker,* Oct. 26, 1971, p. 23.

30. Marine App., 973 (Farragher). The plaintiff's complaint had not mentioned this alternative, nor was it referred to in the Brief for U.S. at 52, Marine.

31. Marine App., 1012, 1019 (Selby).

32. Marine (D.C.(, 94.245 (Find. 191).
33. Marine App., 875 (Carlson, president, Marine Bancorp.).
34. Marine (D.C.), 94,245 (Find. 19A).
35. Marine App., 1140 (J. Goodwin).
36. Conn. (D.C.), 256-257. The suburban Bank of Stratford had not been mentioned during the trial or in the Jurisdictional Statement. Brief for the Comptroller of the Currency at 57, note 27, Conn.

Second New Haven, though smaller than FNH, was one of Connecticut's ten largest. Conn. (D.C.), 257 (Find. 125). The five suburban banks are named in Brief for U.S. at 50, note 60. Four of the banks cited during the trial (Conn. App. 217) are analyzed in Conn. (D. C.), 265 (Find. 186). The fifth, Orange National Bank, had no New Haven branches, but both CNB and FNH were already in Orange.

38. Brief for U.S. at 50, note 60, Conn.
39. Conn. (D.C.), 257 (Find. 122), 265 (Find. 189); *id.* (Find. 287); Brief for Comptroller of the Currency at 61, Conn. However, Peter Stassa, Jr., who headed the tiny Lafayette Bank in Bridgeport, named several suburban bankers who called on customers in Bridgeport and New Haven. Conn. App., 1356.
40. Brief for Appellees at 40, Conn.
41. Conn. (D.C.), 265 (Find. 193), 287.
42. Brief for U.S. at 44, First Nat'l. The banks in Eaton and LaSalle were not analyzed as possibilities during the trial, and the district court decision did not discuss them. Brief for Appellees at 12, note 23, First Nat'l. Brief for U. S. at 15, *id.*, cites as evidence a tabulation that merely includes the two banks in a listing of Greeley area banks.
43. First Nat'l. App., 298 (Trautwein). However, the witness was testifying about events in the 1950's; he left Greeley in 1959. First Nat'l. (D.C.), 1003, 1015. In proceedings to reopen the trial for additional evidence, J. Doyle insisted that Bancorporation would not enter Greeley on any foothold basis. First Nat'l App., 2007.
44. *United States* v. *First National Bank of Maryland,* 310 F. Supp. 183 (1970).
45. *United States* v. *United Virginia Bankshares,* 347 F. Supp. 891 (1972).
46. Transcript of Proceedings, p. 376.
47. *United States* v. *Deposit Guaranty National Bank of Jackson,* et *al.*, 373 F. Supp. 1241 (1974).
48. 1974 Comptroller of the Currency Annual Report 74; see also 1974 FDIC Annual Report, pp. 11-13 for Leflore County data.
49. Merger Guidelines, *loc. cit.;* Joseph F. Brodley, "Potential Competition Mergers: A Structural Synthesis," 87 *Yale Law Journal,* 83 (1977).
50. Donald I. Baker, "Banking Competition in the Age of the Computer," 90 *Banking Law Journal* 208-211; For the Bank of Fulton

County acquisition, see 1973 Board of Governors Annual Report 310.

51. S.A. Rhoades and A.J. Yeats, "An Analysis of Entry and Expansion Predictions in Bank Acquisition and Merger Cases," *Western Economic Journal* 10 (1972), 340.

52. *Federal Reserve Bulletin* 58 (1972), 59; Second Supplementary Application Denver U. S. Bancorporation, Colorado Springs National Bank, p. 10.

53. *Ibid.,* 57 (1971), p. 348. Civil Action #C-3077 U.S. D.C., D. Col., filed April 28, 1971.

54. *Federal Reserve Bulletin* 58 (1972), 493-494.

55. Marine, 638. The 1966 share is given in *id.* at 608, note 2. Pacific's share was at a peak of 5.1 percent at the end of 1968. Marine App., 1220. The Answering Brief of Appellees at 24 quotes Pacific's Spokane manager, Robert Hurni, who testified that Pacific had not been able to increase the share of the market that the predecessor Spokane National Bank had. Marine App. 1103. However,in mid-1964, Spokane National Bank had only 2 percent of the deposits in all of the Spokane banks.

56. Marine (D.C.), 94,246 (Find. 20).

57. S.A. Rhoades, "The Impact of Foothold Acquisitions on Bank Market Structure," *Antitrust Bulletin,* 22 (1977), 119-128; on N.Y. and Va. see Bernard Shull, in *Federal Reserve Bank of Chicago Conference on Bank Structure,* 1972, p. 39.

58. *U.S.* v. *Connecticut National Bank,* Brief for United States, p. 57; *BOC International* v. *FTC, loc. cit.,* 71679.

59. Carey paper, p. 33.

60. *Ibid.,* p. 50.

61. *BOC International* v. *FTC, loc. cit.,* p. 71678.

62. Richard A. Posner, *Antitrust Law: An Economic Perspective* (Chicago, 1976), p. 122. A seven-step procedure in potential competition cases is recommended by Dunfee and Stern, *loc. cit.,* p. 871.

Law as a Capital Good

SVETOZAR PEJOVICH *

I

Full implications of the mutual interdependence between law and economics are yet to be researched. However, some important works on the subject have already been published, and the literature is growing. The relationship of law and economics is undoubtedly quite strong. It is also a two-way relationship. Laws have demonstrable and predictable effects on the character of economic life, and are, in turn, developed and modified in response to economic change. The economic test of positive laws is whether they create incentives for value-maximizing behavior in the future. I firmly believe that the study of the relationship of law and economics will turn out to be one of the most significant scholarly undertakings.

The literature has demonstrated that economic analysis is capable of explaining both the development of new laws as well as the effects of the prevailing legal systems on social life. The purpose of this paper is to shed some additional light on the nature of collective decisions and their social implications. To accomplish this objective the paper treats the prevailing legal system as a *public capital good.*[1] The term *capital good* refers to an asset that is costly to produce and maintain but which yields a flow of benefits over a period of time. Relevant questions that the paper deals with are (1) what is to be gained

*Professor of Economics University of Dallas.

from the analysis of law as a capital good, and (2) is it possible to treat the legal system as a capital good?

Collective decisions are of two kinds. At one level, collective decisions pertain to the development, specification, and modifications of institutions by which the community seeks to resolve problems that have their source in economic scarcity (rules of the game). At another level, collective decisions pertain to choices within a given set of legal constraints. For example, the decision to switch to a voluntary army represented a change in the "rules of the game." A decision to raise (or reduce) expenditures for national defense is a choice within the prevailing rules of the game. The paper applies economic reasoning to the process of collective decision making at both levels.

II

The major function of law is to generate the *predictability* of behavior. The prevailing legal system specifies the rules of the game; it enhances the stability in interpersonal relationships. From the point of view of an individual, the prevailing legal system yields a flow of benefits, which is the predictability of other people's behavior. The source of this benefit is law abiding behavior on the part of others. The flow of benefits from law depends on its stability. As time goes by we all learn the rules of the game better. We learn how to adjust to the system, identify additional exchange opportunities, and exploit the most beneficial ones.

In addition, many exchange opportunities have long-run consequences. Investment in plant and equipment yields benefits over a period of time that could be quite long. The purchase of land might yield benefits (capital gain) only after a long period of time. A stable legal order encourages people to exploit beneficial exchange opportunities that have long-run consequences. A *stable* social order means that changes in the prevailing legal system occur infrequently and only in response to a unanimous consensus. To quote Buchanan:

> [A rule of unanimity implies] an explicit prejudice in favor of previously existing rights, not because this structure possesses some intrinsic ethical attributes, and not because change itself is undesirable, but for the much more elementary reason that only such a prejudice offers incentives for the emergence of voluntary negotiated settlements among the parties themselves . . . this prejudice guarantees that resort to the authority of the state is effectively minimized.[2]

Frequent and unpredictable changes in the legal system or expectations about frequent changes in the legal system reduce incentives to exploit exchange opportunities that have long-run consequences. Legal instability introduces a degree of uncertainty into the system. It raises the cost (risk) of exploiting exchange alternatives that have long-run consequences. The flow of benefits from law falls, and the community is worse off. For example, wealthy South Americans prefer bank deposits in the United States or in Switzerland (often at a very low rate of interest) to investment opportunities at home. Jewish people in Central Europe used to invest their funds in jewelry and other liquid assets that could be easily withdrawn — rather than in land and manufacturing plants. American investors in South America prefer investments that have relatively short payouts.

Laws and regulations are generally negative and restrictive. They tell us what we are not allowed to do. It follows that laws impose restrictions on each person's freedom of choice. From the point of view of an individual, law abiding by himself is the cost of law. More specifically, the cost is the satisfaction that the individual foregoes by not being able to engage in some specific activities. Of course, making an activity illegal does not necessarily prevent people from engaging in that activity. Penalties can only reduce the rate at which people violate laws and regulations.

My knowledge that other drivers will stop at a red light is my benefit from the law. The fact that I must observe the same law is the cost I bear. In general, if my benefits from a law exceed my costs, I will vote for that law to be passed; if my benefits from a law are less than the cost I bear, my inclination would to be to vote against that particular law.

Different people evaluate costs and benefits from laws differently. Thus, any collectively chosen quantity of law will make some people feel overregulated, whereas others will think that the legal system allows for too much liberty. The problem with a collective good is that an individual cannot adjust his consumption of that good in accordance with this own preferences. We all have to partake in producing and consuming a fixed supply of any collective good.

III

The flow of benefits from an asset, or what is the same thing, the value of that asset, depends on how well it is maintained. Thus to protect the capital-good–feature of law, the prevailing legal system must be maintained. Legal changes that are motivated by external (extralegal) criteria tend to undermine the stability of interpersonal relationships, add to uncertainties about future consequences of current decisions, and reduce the flow of benefits from the existing legal order. Buchanan wrote:

> The object of the never-ending search by loosely coordinated judges acting independently is to find "the law," to locate and to redefine the structure of individual rights, not *ab initio,* but in existing social-institutional arrangements. . . . Law . . . is a stabilizing institution which provides the necessary framework within which individuals can plan their own affairs predictably and with minimal external interferences.
>
> Precedent, custom, tradition, expected ways of doing things, predicted pattern of behavior — there intralegal criteria provide ample searching ground for the imaginative jurist even in hard cases.[3]

Law is a *public* capital good. It means that those who incur the cost of maintaining it confer benefits on others. The lack of ability to appropriate benefits reduces incentives for any person to maintain the prevailing legal system. In fact each person has incentives to seek to modify or change the existing set of rules in order to increase the flow of benefits to himself.

A change in the "rules of the game" that favors a person or an organized group represents, in effect, a redistribution of income in the community. Changes in the existing legal system in response to efforts by individuals and organized groups should then be recognized for what they are: conversion of a public capital asset into a source of private benefits.

Instability of the existing legal system erodes the capital-good feature of law, and the community as a whole is poorer. Individuals and organized groups have incentives to erode the existing legal order. They capture incremental benefits for themselves *via* special interest legislation, whereas the cost is borne by the community as a whole.

The political process is a *method* for maintaining — properly or improperly, adequately or inadequately — the capital-good feature of law. The relevant questions are then whether the institutions of government provide incentives to harness private purposes to public outcomes. Do they encourage a shift toward, instead of away from, society's efficiency surface? Do the institutions of government enforce the "rules of the game" and allow institutional changes to occur only in response to a unanimity rule? In other words, the analysis of political processes which affect, modify, and change the institutions of government should reveal whether the capital-good feature of law is being maintained.

The responsive political system maintains the existing legal structure, enforces "rules of the game," encourages voluntary negotiated (intralegal) settlements among the interacting individuals and has a strong conservative bias against institutional changes that are motivated by external (extralegal criteria) criteria (economic efficiency, social justice, etc.). The analysis of political processes which affect, modify and change the institutions of government, should then reveal whether the capital good feature of the law is maintained.

The responsive political system discourages resort to authority as a method for seeking institutional changes. The critical issue here is *not* the decision maker's character. The issue is whether collective decisions made by public officials differ from those that people themselves would negotiate voluntarily. Niskanen said that "Good men do not assure good government, high purpose does not assure good law, and good analysis does not assure good policy."[4] The problem with the conventional prescription of good government — which is to seek and elect good men and to give them the power to do what they think is right — is that a well-defined common good requires some specific collective policies that promise to yield the intended outcome. Whatever the facade of words (for example, social justice), those collective policies have to be coercive. An important underlying assumption behind the rule of men prescription for responsive government is that a person who assumes public office experiences a sudden transformation from a selfish private decision maker into a nonselfish public decision maker (whatever that means). The problem with this assumption is that it simply is not consistent with empirical reality and predictability. Public officials do not differ from the rest of us. They are neither more human nor less human than each of us. Like anyone else, public officials have their own values, preferences, and judgments. In the process of making public decisions, they are guided by their personal motivations and private ends. The government of good men does for us what the government decides that we need.

I conjecture that the "rule of law" is preferable to the "rule of men", for it tends to maintain the capital-good feature of law. The "rule of law' defines the procedure for collective decision making; it does not specify public outcome. The argument is that if the procedure is both stable and equitable (for example, right of ownership and freedom of contract), public outcome — unintended outcome, to be sure — must also be equitable. Under the rule of law the institutions of government are organized so that the public decision maker maximizes his own utility by maintaining the capital-good feature of the law.

IV

The American political system and the institutions of government of the United States have until recently protected the capital-good feature of law quite well, that is, they have done well in protecting the American people from the rule of men. Let me discuss two implicit but clearly respected rules that have made major contributions to strengthening the capital-good feature of law.[5] Both rules were broken in the 1960s.

Fiscal Rule. This rule imposed an important constraint on public officials. The rule, which was respected throughout most of American history, said that government spending should be equal to or slightly less than revenues. This rule imposed an external constraint on the public decision maker's preferences for public spending. Government spending is determined annually. On the other hand, the tax structure in the United States is quite rigid. It changes infrequently and only after long public hearings. Thus the fiscal rule imposed an effective ceiling on government spending.

In the mid-1960s the relationship between government spending and tax revenues was broken. Moreover, no other rule developed to constrain the propensity of public officials to increase the level of government spending. The results were as follows: from 1947 to 1965, the federal budget had a surplus in eleven years and a cumulative surplus over the period. From 1966 to 1976, the federal budget had a surplus in only one year and a huge cumulative deficit over the period.

Monetary Rule. For most of American history the government was constrained to maintain the value of the dollar. In recent years this was accomplished by the so-called fixed rate of exchange. That is, the government had to maintain the value of the dollar relative to foreign currencies. Clearly, an imperfect but an objective external criterion was imposed on the government's control over the supply of money. Any unwarranted increase in the supply of money reduced the value of the dollar relative to foreign currencies. The government was restrained from printing money to finance its spending. The rule was broken in 1971 when the dollar was floated. Floating exchange rates for the dollar freed the government from any objective constraint on maintaining the supply of money and the value of the dollar. The results were as follows: from 1947 to 1971, the average rate of inflation in the United States was about 2.5 percent. Since 1971, the average rate of inflation has been several times higher.

V

Within the rule of law, the American political system has established and maintained until recently a strong relationship between the personal interests of public officials and the preferences of the American people. That is, the system has done well in protecting the American people from collective decisions that reflect the personal motivations and preferences of public officials.

The major feature of the two political parties in the United States is that they have remained nonideological. The American political parties do not require their supporters to hold and support some specific political views. In fact American political parties do not have firmly established aims and objectives. Unlike political parties in Europe, the two American parties are heterogeneous, loosely organized, pragmatic, and nonideological. They have incentives to nominate candidates and select policies that *maximize votes.* American parties have incentives to identify the preferences of the population and to select policies consistent with those preferences. Since different people value public consequences differently, the preferences of the median voter are decisive. A party that selects policies that are closest to the preference of the median voter wins the election. This is a significant point. It suggests that public decision makers capture rewards not by making choices which they think the population needs, but by pursuing policies that the population wants within the constraints of law. In other words, the public decision maker maximizes his own rewards by pursuing policies that are consistent with the preferences of the median voter.

The system of two nonideological parties protects the voter against the benevolent despot. As long as both parties have incentives to satisfy the preferences of the median voter, the candidates that they nominate and the policies that they select tend to be quite similar. Predictably, elections will tend to be very close. However, this absence of any appreciable differences between candidates for office and policies on various issues is the major source of strength of the American system of government. It offers evidence that the political system is responsive to the preferences of the population. When the Republicans nominated Goldwater in 1964 and the Democrats nominated McGovern in 1972, they ignored the median voter and the election results showed the voters' reactions to those decisions. The necessary condition for the continuing responsiveness of the system to the median voter is that both parties must be nonideological. Otherwise, another major party would be likely to emerge.

Satisfying the preferences of the median voter, within the framework of law does not mean satisfying all the people. We all value different goods differently, including those produced by the government. In the market for private goods we can adjust our spending for various goods to our preferences for them. In the case of public goods, such an adjustment is usually impossible. For example, whatever amount of schooling that the government decides to produce, we all have to participate in purchasing it (*via* taxes) regardless of whether we as individuals think that the amount of schooling financed by the state is too much or to little. Thus to satisfy the preferences of the median voter means that some people will think that the government is doing to much, whereas others will think that it is doing too little. The advantage is that incentives to satisfy the median voter impose an external, objective criterion on the behavior of public decision makers. That is, it makes all of us less dependent on the personal, subjective motivations of the public decision maker.

In recent years we have failed to maintain a responsive two-party system in the United States. Several institutional changes in the system have weakened the relationship between the personal interests of public officials and the preferences of the American people. Those changes have reduced incentives for both major parties to pursue vote-maximizing policies. Government outcome reflects this growing independence of the public decision maker from the median voter. Let me enumerate two of these institutional changes that have been advertised as "good" governmental reforms.[6]

Presidential Primaries. Presidential primaries are held in about one-half of the states. Those primaries are supposed to replace the party bosses in the selection of candidates. The candidate is, we are told, chosen by the rank and file rather than in "smoke-filled rooms."

Unfortunately, it is not so. The reason is rather simple. The preferences of the median voter in any primary election are not necessarily consistent with the preferences of the median voter in that state or in the country as a whole (unless those who vote in the election are precisely those who voted in the primaries). On the other hand, party bosses operating in smoke-filled rooms seek candidates and public policies that are consistent with the preferences of the median voter.

Patronage. A successful candidate can and does reward his supporters and friends by appointing them to government positions. To capture the rewards of office the candidate's associates, friends, and cronies must get him elected. Precinct captains, county chairmen, and party bosses at all levels find it in their self-interest to choose a candidate and select policies that maximize votes. The major consequence of patronage is to strengthen the relationship between the private interests of party leaders and their candidates, on the one hand, and the preferences of the American people, on the other. Nowadays the number of government jobs filled by civil servants is growing at the expense of the number of jobs that candidates can promise in the event that they win. The point is that civil servants are more concerned with the level of government spending than with the preferences of the American population. A decline in the relative importance of patronage means a reduction in incentives to select policies that reflect the preferences of the median voter.

NOTES

1. See J. Buchanan, *The Limits of Liberty,* Chicago: University of Chicago Press, 1975, Chapter 7.
2. J. Buchanan, *Freedom in Constitutional Contract,* College Station: Texas A & M Press, 1978, p.109.
3. *Ibid.,* pp. 46-47.
4. W. Niskanen, "Public Policy and the Political Process," in *Governmental Controls and the Free Market,* (Ed. S. Pejovich), College Station: Texas A & M University Press, 1976, p. 76.
5. For a detailed analysis, see W. Niskanen, *Ibid.*
6. *Ibid.*

Comments on "Law as a Capital Good"

MORRIS SILVER*

The quality of a legal system is a function of several inputs, including not only the predictability of behavior, but the substantive content of the laws, the degree of law enforcement, public respect for law. . . . It is reasonable to expect that the legal good can be maintained while substituting one input for another. Having made the general point, let me hasten to add that I share Pejovich's perspective that our society is being debilitated by unprecedented legal instability as well as by the dissolution of the rule of law. Because Pejovich has focused (implicitly) on the sins of the executive and legislative branches of government by pointing to the breaking of the fiscal rule and the monetary rule, I will direct my attention to the contributions of the Supreme Court.

The Supreme Court has played a crucial role in accelerating the evolution toward what I call altruistic despotism by making use of the vague "majestic generalities" of the Fourteenth Amendment, namely, "due process" and "equal protection." As constitutional scholar Raoul Berger has pointed out, the result has been a "truly extraordinary transformation" of the judicial system from the supervision of procedures to "government by decree" in which the "demands

*City College Of The City University of New York.

of social justice" and "humanitarian goals" override the "chains of the Constitution" and "arid legalism" (pp. 249, 288). Berger (p. 408) sees as the underlying premise of this transformation that the "entire Constitution merely has such relevance as the Court chooses to give it, and the Court is truly a 'continuing constitutional convention' constantly engaged in revising the Constitution, a role clearly withheld from the Court." The Justices have become a law unto themselves. This seizure of power, together with the explosion in regulatory activity, has brought us close to the day on which litigation will be the primary method of "solving" social problems.

It is true that in April 1978 the Court in a unanimous decision denounced "judicial activism run riot" and instructed the court of appeals for the District of Columbia to stop blocking the will of Congress by erecting procedural barriers to programs that it politically opposes — in this case, nuclear power plants. It is also true that this theme has been played in several speeches by Chief Justice Burger. In 1976, for example, he said that the problems leading to the Court's school desegregation decision of 1954 and its one-person, one-vote ruling in 1962 could have been resolved by Congress (*New York Times,* April 9, 1978). But he seemed to imply that because the problems were not in fact "resolved," the Court was justified in its activism. If this is a correct reading, we can expect no real U turn in the capital good-destroying behavior of the Supreme Court.

By now it is widely recognized that the welfare state, with its proliferation of open-ended standards and general clauses, has encouraged the dissolution of the rule of law, which is defined by neutrality, uniformity, and predictability. More and more, Unger observes, formalistic legal reasoning is being replaced by commonplace political or economic arguments:

> The decline in the distinctiveness of legal reasoning is connected with the need administrators and judges have of reaching out to the substantive ideals of different groups, or drawing upon a conventional morality or a dominant

> tradition. These changes in the substance and method of law also help undercut the identity of legal institutions and of the legal profession. Courts begin to resemble openly first administrative, then other political institutions. Thus, the difference between lawyers and other bureaucrats or technicians starts to disappear.(p. 200)

Lawyers, like other bureaucrats, must be evaluated in terms of their contributions to "social justice." Thus President Carter's speech to the Los Angeles Bar Association on May 4, 1978, in which he savaged lawyers who "led the fight against civil rights and economic justice," is best viewed not as an example of Carter's (admittedly) idiosyncratic behavior, but as part of the continuing demolition of the rule of law.

Concrete illustrations of the kinds of legal changes that I have in mind are readily available, but in the interest of brevity I will confine myself to a recent case of special interest to economists. In January 1978 the jury in the *Berkey Photo-Eastman Kodak* case ruled that large firms, even in the absence of a demonstrated monopolistic position or intent, must duly warn competitors of their intentions to introduce new products or processes. Berkey had charged that Kodak's introduction of new cameras and film was anticompetitive and that Kodak had the obligation to give competitors information sufficiently early and in sufficient detail so that they would be in a position to market comparable products and services. The jury agreed! Obviously, as one analyst pointed out, the "decision raises far-reaching questions about the nature of antitrust law and about the whole notion of a free enterprise economy." Unfortunately, like Carter's peculiar speech, this decision is not idiosyncratic: It is but one more piece in the pattern of substituting "equality" for other social values.

Why has there been so much counterproductive legal change in the contemporary United States? If the replacement of "smoke-filled rooms" by presidential primaries and of patronage by merit has weakened the party system, why have these changes been allowed to stand? If there is now increased "resort to authority as a method of seeking institutional change," why has this happened? A "responsive" political system is not one that "maintains the existing legal structure," but one that responds to the preferences of those for whom it governs. I submit that the observed changes in the functioning of our legal and political system, — most specifically, the substitution of a social justice outcome for proper procedures, — are consistent with changes in the preferences of the median voter. How does society preserve the "capital-good feature of the law" when the benevolent despot is the public itself? Can one really prevent suicide?

REFERENCES

Raoul Berger, *Government by Judiciary: The Transformation of the Fourteenth Amendment,* Cambridge, Mass.: Harvard University Press, 1977.

Roberto Mangabeira Unger, *Law in Modern Society,* New York: the Free Press, 1976.